The Contemporary Crisis of the European Union

The European Union widened and deepened integration when it introduced the Single Market and the common currency, increasing the number of member countries from 12 to 28. After a quarter of a century, the 2008 financial and economic crisis opened a new chapter in the history of European integration. Prosperity was replaced by economic crisis and then long stagnation, with ramifications far beyond the economic arena.

For the first time, after more than half a century, some countries were almost forced to step out of the Union. History's most frightening migration crisis shocked Europe and led to the strengthening of several anti-integration parties in various countries. This pioneering book discusses the nine crisis elements that could lead to disintegration of the EU. Beginning with the Greek Debt disaster this book delves into the cause of the recent European crisis and then onto the recent immigration influx and its consequences, as well as Britain's exit from the Union. A concluding chapter, based on the facts of positive development during the crises years, gives a cautiously optimistic forecast for the future and asks the question: further integration or disintegration?

This volume is of great importance to academics, students and policy makers who have an interest in European politics, political economy and migration.

Ivan T. Berend is Distinguished Research Professor at the Department of History, University of California, USA. He is a member of the American Academy of Arts and Sciences; the British Academy, the Austrian Academy of Sciences, the Academia Europea, and three other European Academy of Sciences and has published more than 30 books and 200 studies.

Routledge Studies in the European Economy

For a full list of titles in this series, please visit www.routledge.com/series/SE0431

The Contemporary Crisis of the European Union

Prospects for the future

Ivan T. Berend

LONDON AND NEW YORK

First published 2017
by Routledge
2 Park Square, Milton Park, Abingdon, Oxon OX14 4RN

and by Routledge
52 Vanderbilt Avenue, New York, NY 10017

First issued in paperback 2020

Routledge is an imprint of the Taylor & Francis Group, an informa business

British Library Cataloguing in Publication Data
A catalogue record for this book is available from the British Library

Library of Congress Cataloging in Publication Data
Names: Berend, T. Ivan, 1930– author.
Title: The contemporary crisis of the European Union : prospects for the
future / Ivan T. Berend.
Description: 1 Edition. | New York : Routledge, 2017. | Includes index.
Identifiers: LCCN 2016033811| ISBN 9781138244191 (hardback) | ISBN
9781315277066 (ebook)
Subjects: LCSH: European Union countries—Economic conditions—
21st century. | European Union—Membership. | Europe—Economic
integration. | European Union countries—Population—Economic aspects.
| Equality—European Union countries. | National security—European
Union countries. | European Union countries—Economic policy—
21st century.
Classification: LCC HC240 .B39467 2017 | DDC 341.242/2—dc23
LC record available at https://lccn.loc.gov/2016033811

ISBN 13: 978-0-367-66798-6 (pbk)
ISBN 13: 978-1-138-24419-1 (hbk)

Typeset in Times New Roman
by Book Now Ltd, London

Contents

Introduction

I am part of the generation that experienced hatred, discrimination, confrontation, and war in Europe. Our principal personal experience was the most devastating war in history, mass murder and untold suffering, followed by the division of "two Europes" for half a century. The toxic cloud of nuclear confrontation over-shadowed our lives for decades. For me and my generation, the most promising development that ever happened in millennial European history was the integra-tion of Europe. We rejoiced that Europe had learned the lessons of the past and was determined not to repeat it. My generation enthusiastically welcomed European integration. For the first time in our lives, we were proud to be Europeans.

It was never going to be easy to achieve that "ever closer union" of European integration, as the preamble of the Treaty of Rome described the goal of the six founding countries in 1957. For one, integration would not have even happened without the critical contribution of the United States, which pushed, and some-times even forced, Europe to integrate. Its goal was to strengthen an integrated Western European ally, a United States of Europe, to face the Soviet danger in a rancorous Cold War conflict. Soon after the first tentative step, the formation of the European Coal and Steel Community, was made in 1951, it became clear that sectoral integration was not the best way to move toward the end goal. Europe soon found a better way, founding the European Economic Community in 1957. It created a common European market, with common tariffs, common supranational institutions, and common agricultural policy.

Still, European integration was not without its setbacks. Less than a decade after the EEC's founding, its first crisis essentially blocked further progress for twenty years. The "empty chair crisis" of 1965, initiated by French President Charles de Gaulle to stop supranationalization and preserve the sovereignty of nation states, slowed the integration process down and halted further suprana-tionalization. Giving veto rights to each member country effectively thwarted the multi-governmental functioning of the Community for two decades.

However, the integration drive got a second wind beginning in the mid-1980s. In a new age of technological revolution and globalization, Europe found itself dan-gerously behind and unable to compete on the world market, and was thus forced to adjust by expanding integration. Large European corporations felt existentially threatened and saw enhanced integration, and the creation of a genuine common market, as their only hope. Important steps were taken to advance supranationalization. The Single Market of the European Union and the Schengen agreement ended borders within the Union, initiated unrestricted cross-border business activity, and allowed the free movement of goods, capital, and people. This process was significantly strengthened with the introduction of a common currency and a European Central Bank around the turn of the millennium. The corporate world began building up a network of branches, subsidiaries, and value chains across the continent, and essentially Europeanized the European economy.

At the same time, the concept of a truly integrated European Community became more and more appealing, and a continual enlargement process gradually increased the number of member states from the original six to nine in 1973, twelve in the 1980s, to fifteen in 1995, twenty-five in 2004 and twenty-eight by 2013. Five more countries in the Balkans are waiting to join.

Then, a new crisis hit in 2008. The collapse of a leading American mortgage bank led to an international liquidity crisis that shocked the global financial markets, and was then followed by an international debt crisis and the so-called Great Recession, the decline of the real economy. The 2008 crisis was the worst economic catastrophe since the Great Depression. Although it was a relatively fleeting episode in much of the advanced world, it hit Europe particularly hard. Two scholars stated in 2014:

> In the last five years deep cracks have appeared in the European project. The experience of recent years has revealed and exacerbated significant defiance in the European Union's economic and political construction …. And then, the unthinkable became a very thinkable reality: one or more countries could probably leave the euro, the euro zone could implode, or even that the European Union could disintegrate. To make matters worse, Europe faces not just one, but a number of highly complex crises.[1]

Indeed, the international economic crisis in 2008 gradually led to an extended, complicated crisis within the European Union. The hidden weaknesses of an unfinished common currency and a monetary union without fiscal unification (which had never been seen before) soon came to light and pushed the euro to the brink. The euro-crisis was most acute in Greece. The Greek debt crisis culminated in 2009 and remained unresolved until 2015. It strongly undermined European unity and threatened the demise of the common currency. The ideal of a European social market was also undermined by the recession and the austerity that followed. In some member states, welfare institutions nearly collapsed. After years of prosperity, a well-functioning economic system gave way to a deteriorating capitalism with speculative bubbles, massive unemployment, and increasing inequality – all of which endangered the European model of welfare capitalism.

The mostly hidden inner contradictions of the integration process turned out to be open wounds. In 2009, for first time in the Community's history, profound internal conflicts and crises undermined all notions of solidarity, the principal building block of integration. Moreover, the more serious crises in the Union's newer members, the former peripheral countries in the South and East, subverted the idea of a united Europe and reconstructed the "two-Europes" syndrome. One of those countries, Greece, was pushed to the brink and had to be bailed out three times. The Mediterranean countries that were well on their way to catching up with the West now showed surprising weaknesses. The residual repercussions of path dependence were apparent for all to see. The need of some for bailouts, and the insistence of others on austerity to reestablish fiscal balance, that is, the conflicting interests of creditor and debtor nations, gradually created a deep chasm within the Union.

The catching-up process of the less developed, former communist peripheral regions, which had been incorporated into the EU in the early twenty-first century, slowed dramatically. After an arduous process lasting a quarter of a century, it was now apparent that these countries were not even close to meeting their transformation goals. Some were unable to cope with the entrenched corruption, rampant clientelism, and resurgent authoritarianism of their political systems. The whole concept of the European Community now came into question. Had the EU expanded too quickly with countries that were not yet ready for membership? Had this expansion jeopardized the future of further integration?

Although some of the former communist countries of Central and Eastern Europe had quite successfully transformed their systems and adapted to the mores of the European Union, the residual weaknesses and resurgent authoritarianism in several countries underscored the core-periphery conflict within the Union. This problem shed new light on the EU's neighborhood policy, especially toward Eastern Europe. Assisting certain former Soviet republics, and offering associate membership status to them, signaled the EU's intention to expand further and to possibly include certain former Soviet republics such as Moldova, Georgia, Armenia, and Ukraine.

In the 2010s, however, this policy would meet its Waterloo in Ukraine. The Ukrainian crisis, which degenerated into a civil war and a Russian military intervention, led to a heated conflict between Russia and the EU. Suddenly wars and civil wars, the Ukrainian crisis, Russia's involvement and occupation of the Crimea, Russia's military violations of national air-space and waters in Europe, and its provocative military exercises in border regions all endangered European security.

Threatening as well was a revival of Islamic fundamentalism and murderous terrorism, which created an arc of danger around the Union. Europe's security, guaranteed and unquestioned since the end of the Cold War, was suddenly in peril. There were, to be sure, various elements to security, and this required Europe to act in harmony. Europe's dependence on energy imports, partly from Russia, became an important factor in security policy, and it necessitated coordinated arrangements to achieve energy independence. But now, for the first time since the end of the Cold War, security was also once again a military issue. Defense and the integration of armed forces and armament industries – issues that had never been on the EU's agenda before – now attained central importance.

At the same time, the EU's southern neighborhood, the Middle East and North Africa, began blowing up as well with civil wars and Islamic terrorism.

The violence and the misery pushed millions toward Europe. History's most dramatic migration crisis took place in 2014–16, and it led to an even more dangerous divide among EU member states than did the economic crises. The migration crisis pushed to the surface Europe's serious demographic crisis, which has been gradually worsening since the 1980s thanks to rapidly declining birth rates and the speedy aging of the population. Europe has had a dire need for migrant labor ever since the 1950s and especially from the 1980s on. While vital to the economy, immigration invariably created serious social and political difficulties. The EU devised an array of programs and directives to handle the issue, but to no avail. The integration of the several million "old" immigrants since the 1950s–60s had only limited success, while the recent wave of immigration has degenerated into a chaotic flood of refugees from crisis zones as far away as Pakistan and Afghanistan. Human traffickers killed and endangered thousands and created a genuine moral crisis. Europe has been put to the test, and should respond with joint solutions to this humanitarian nightmare. But so far the national interest of individual states has prevailed.

George Soros, the billionaire financier, philanthropist, and integration advocate, bemoaned the deteriorating situation in a recent interview, which was published under the title "The European Union is on the Verge of Collapse," observing:

> The European Union now is confronted with not one but five or six crises at the same time …. The EU was meant to be a voluntary association of equals but the euro crisis turned it into a relationship between debtors and creditors …. That relationship is neither voluntary nor equal. The migration crisis introduced other fissures. Therefore the very survival of the EU is at risk.[2]

Dark clouds began ominously gathering above the European Union in the 2010s. The prognosis on the future of European integration is increasingly dire. The deterioration and even abolition of the common currency, the main symbol of unification, has become an ever-present danger since 2009. After decades of continued expansion, the possibility of the exit of several member countries is now on the horizon. The prospect of "Grexit" and "Brexit," a Greek and British exit, heralds an uncertain new era. Grexit has been avoided but still did not permanently disappear from the horizon. The decision for Brexit, unbelievable for most people, happened in the summer of 2016. Does this mean the end to Europe's commitment to forming an "ever closer union" or the Union itself? Will the European Union be reduced to being a mere free trade zone as some suggest? Actually a majority of Europeans are disappointed with integration and do not want it to continue. They do not believe that the Union is good for them.

Hence, these complicated crises have generated a legitimacy crisis as well. An alarming opposition has emerged within the Union. Parties opposing the EU and the common currency hold nearly a third of the seats in the European parliament and are gaining frightening strength at the national level in quite a few countries.

About this book and acknowledgement

This volume offers description and analysis of the major crisis of European integration at the present time. I will address nine overt or hidden crises in the European Union. Some of these crises, such as the euro-crisis, the Greek debt crisis, the Russian challenge to European security, Britain's exit from the Union, and the migration crisis, are regularly discussed in the political arena and in the media. Others, such as the demographic time bomb, the EU's continuing expansion and its controversial neighborhood policy, as well as the reversals in Eastern Europe's transformation and the negative attributes of contemporary capitalism, are more hidden and rarely mentioned in contemporary discourse. The chapters on these crises attempt to offer a wide-ranging portrait on the troubles in the EU in the 2010s. Will disintegration commence as some observers predict? Or is continued integration still possible? Will Europe find the right answers to the challenges and move decisively forward? Unfortunately, the European Union is almost always slow to respond, and its leaders' failure to find a solution often leads to hysterical interpretations of the crisis. What *really* happened, and is happening, in the mid-2010s, however, is discussed in the concluding chapter on the puzzle and possibility of further integration or disintegration. Some signs point to continued integration. A united banking system, steps toward quasi-fiscal unification through regulatory means, initiatives for joint energy policy, and military integration all signal potential progress toward a closer union. Other factors such as the Brexit and the strengthening of anti-EU forces in France and some other countries, the unsolved immigration crisis, and the reemergence of nationalism in Poland, Hungary, and other countries signal deadly dangers for the EU. I hope that the volume may provide a better understanding of these complex issues.

Ivan T. Berend

April 8, 2016

Lastly, I am very grateful to my wife, Kati, who contributed to my work in various ways – as usual. Let me also express my thanks to Robert Levy who edited and polished my draft manuscript with the greatest professional skill.

Notes

1 Archive of European Integration, AEI.Pitt.edu (always cited in this book as: *Archive of European Integration*), EPC, *Challenge Europe,* Issue 22, September 2014, Janis A. Emmanouilidis and Paul Ivan, "State of the Union and Key Challenges for Europe's Future."
2 George Soros, "The European Union is on the Verge of Collapse," *The New York Review of Books,* February 11, 2016.

Part I

Inside economic and political factors of the crisis

1 Britain: from outsider to inside-outsider and outsider again

Joining late, stepping out early

Britain and the idea of European addition

A handful of day-dreamers nurtured the vision of a federal United States of Europe already in the nineteenth century – one of them being the famous French writer, Victor Hugo. After the devastating Great War of 1914–18, the Austrian Count Richard von Coudenhove-Kalergi formed the Pan-Europe Movement, and the French Prime Minister Aristide Briand proposed establishing a federal Europe to the League of Nations. These movements and proposals, however, went nowhere.

It was Winston Churchill, the most influential British politician in the twentieth century, who first came up with the idea after World War II, in a speech in Zurich in 1946, of a United States of Europe based on French and German reconciliation. Because of the emerging Cold War confrontation that had motivated Churchill, the Truman administration considered this idea to be the best way to hammer out a strong Western alliance system against the Soviet Union and its allies. America, indeed, had the prestige, the power, the military might, and the economic strength to push the dream towards realization. Assisting as well were a few influential European politicians and governments who had learned the lessons of the "thirty years war of the twentieth century," as the two world wars are often called.

President Truman wanted Britain, the closest ally of the United States, to be the initiator and leader of European integration. His Secretary of State, Dean Acheson, revealed that he

> had made it a personal mission to convince Britain to join the European Coal and Steel Community . . . . Together with President Truman, he was convinced long-term U.S. national interests required that Britain be a founding member of an integrated Europe.[1]

Ten years later, in 1960, the British Embassy in Washington reported: "All [US] administration leaders cherished the vision of a Europe with British leadership."[2] Later, from Presidents John Kennedy to Barack Obama, American administrations have always urged Britain to join or remain within the European Union.

British refusal to join

Consecutive British governments, however, whether Labour or Tory, have mostly rejected such an idea. Churchill expressed his view regarding Britain's standing in Europe, which served as the foundation of the UK's policy for generations, when he remarked in 1946: "we are with Europe, but not of it. We are linked, but not comprised. We are interested and associated, but not absorbed." Britain, he promised, would assist the United States of Europe from the outside, but not as a member from within.[3] "Everyone knows," he added in 1950, "that . . . in all our thoughts [f]irst, there is the Empire and Commonwealth; secondly, the fraternal association of the English-speaking world; and thirdly . . . the revival of united Europe . . ."[4]

Between 1945 and 1951, the Labour government of Clement Attlee shared this view and, despite strong American pressure, declined to join or participate in European integration. The first clear expression of British resistance to integrating with the continent had already occurred during the preparatory period of the American Marshall Plan in 1947–48. The Truman administration had sought the political and military unification of Western Europe, which, it believed, would follow a preliminary stage of economic integration with the establishment of a customs union. The administration of the Marshall Plan pushed this agenda forward by establishing an institutional system, the Organization for European Economic Cooperation (OEEC), which enhanced cooperation and joint decision-making, and set lower tariffs and other trade restrictions, during the plan's four-year lifespan. This was not an easy task after decades of economic nationalism and a myriad of quantitative trade restrictions, tariff wars, and quota systems. Is spite of the "carrot" (abundant economic assistance), the Marshall Plan failed to establish the common customs union; but it did pave the way for future integration, with, among other things, the foundation of a Payment Union. One of the primary reasons for the failure was British resistance. Although Britain became the largest recipient of US assistance, it refused to comply. The former Foreign Minister of Holland, Ernst H. van der Beugel, who had worked on creating the OEEC, concluded in a 1966 book about the Marshall Plan: "No single fact has been so harmful to the possibility of the development of OEEC as an instrument for integration as the British refusal to commit itself to full partnership with the continent of Europe."[5]

British resistance would continue in the years to follow, with its refusal to join the European Coal and Steel Community in 1951 and the European Economic Community in 1957. Not unlike Churchill, the Labour Party would declare in 1950 that Britain is

> the nerve center of a world-wide Commonwealth . . . [and] we in Britain are closer to our kinsmen in Australia and New Zealand . . . than we are in Europe . . . . The economies of the Commonwealth countries are complementary to that of Britain to a degree which those of Western Europe could never equal.[6]

When Churchill became Prime Minister again in 1951, his government retained the policy of the previous Labour government and kept Britain outside the integration process.

After World War II, the British political elite continued to consider Britain to be a great power, the winner of the war, the center of the Commonwealth and a vast colonial Empire, and one of the three major Western powers along with the United States and an integrated Europe. This sense of British self-importance was partly a consequence of the country's "island mentality." As David Cameron put it in 2013, "it is true that our geography has shaped our psychology. We have the character of an island nation – independent, forthright, passionate in defence of our sovereignty."[7]

Another motivating factor was the legacy of the past. For centuries, Britain had built up the world's largest colonial empire. In the first half of the twentieth century, the British Empire comprised more than 458 million inhabitants, a fifth of the world's population, and its land mass entailed nearly 34,000,000 square kilometers, almost a quarter of the earth's. Even after the collapse of its colonial system by 1960, Britain remained the center of a Commonwealth containing nearly seventy countries. Following the Industrial Revolution and during the nineteenth century, Britain became the apical industrial nation and the predominant world economic power. The psychology of global preeminence would survive the collapse of the British Empire and the decline of the country's standing, especially during the second half of the twentieth century.

Changing British attitude

A gradual change began with the loss of the Suez War against Egypt in 1956, the first major failure of Britain's traditionally successful "Gunship diplomacy," and culminated with the collapse of Britain's colonial empire by 1960. The psychology of Empire, however, did not die easily. Generations had been socialized accordingly. As an English friend once explained to me in the 1970s, in every classroom he attended as a child hung a world map, much of which had been colored pink, the color of the British Empire. US Secretary of State Dean Acheson's oft-quoted remark is thus quite understandable: "Great Britain has lost an empire and has not yet found a role."

Britain's ambition was clearly expressed by its attempt to counterbalance the foundation of the European Economic Community with the establishment of a competitive British-led European Free Trade Agreement (EFTA) signed in Stockholm by the "Outer Seven" (Norway, Sweden, Denmark, Austria, Portugal, and Ireland, old trade clients of Britain) in 1960. In contrast to the success of the European integration and skyrocketing European trade and growth, Britain's efforts failed. Although three more countries would later join it, the EFTA had incomparably fewer achievements than did the EEC. Britain remained frighteningly behind the continent in the 1950s and 1960s. Consequently, subsequent British governments would understandably change the UK's position and apply for membership in the European Community twice in the 1960s – only to be rejected thanks to the veto of French President Charles de Gaulle. Britain succeeded in joining only after its third application in 1973.

Britain the inside-outsider within the European Community

Inside the European Community, however, Britain always remained an inside-outsider, reluctant to take part in any further moves toward integration. The British political elite were naturally attracted to Europe's large free market zone, swayed as it was by business interests. But it was not interested in participating in other spheres of cooperation, and it jealously defended its sovereignty by requiring special status within the Community. Margaret Thatcher launched frequent attacks against Brussels during her premiership in the 1980s, demanding and receiving a repayment of part of Britain's contribution to the Community budget, opposing a joint-European helicopter production project, and flatly refusing the European Commission's president Jacques Delors' proposal for a supranational reorganization of the Community. As Thatcher defiantly declared in a famous speech in Bruges in 1988, the British government adamantly opposed a "European super-state exercising a new dominance from Brussels."[8]

In her address, Thatcher acknowledged Britain's European roots, "two thousand years of British involvement in Europe, cooperation with Europe and contribution to Europe." She assured her audience that Britain does not want isolation and affirmed that "our future lies only in Europe." However, she forcefully rejected the "dictate of some abstract intellectual concept" and of "endless regulations." European cooperation must be "among independent sovereign states," she insisted, and not the "power... centralized in Brussels" or "a European superstate exercising a new dominance from Brussels." Instead, she demanded the formation of "a family of nations" that is not "distracted by utopian goals."[9]

To preserve Britain's sovereignty and control of its own borders, the Thatcher government declined to join the Schengen Agreement on the elimination of borders and border control within the member countries. This idea had been floated at the same time that a decision had been made to create a single market in the mid-1980s. In the summer of 1985, on a boat near the Luxembourgian township of Schengen, five member countries (France, Germany, and the three Benelux countries) agreed to a single borderless Community, though they initially did not make it an official EEC law. Quite a few non-members were to join subsequently: Switzerland, Norway, Iceland, and some mini-states such as Liechtenstein. Within ten years, the single-market Schengen Area expanded considerably, and the Amsterdam Treaty of 1997 incorporated the agreement into the Community's legal structure. Besides eliminating border controls within the Area, the participant countries introduced identical asylum laws, allowed unhindered police movement across borders, and established a shared database on wanted fugitives and stolen goods. Out of 28 member countries of the European Union, 22 signed on to the agreement; adding the above-mentioned four non-member countries, a total of 26 European countries erased the borders dividing them. Four member countries (Cyprus, Bulgaria,

Romania, and Croatia) are legally obliged to join, but they are still required to establish safe borders and a strict border control with their non-EU neighbors to be eligible to join. Thatcher's Britain (along with Ireland) opted out of the treaty.

A decade later in the late 1990s, a new test of British Community membership emerged. In the 1970s and 1980s, the continent's corporate leaders pushed ahead for further integration, in reaction to Europe's declining competitiveness and the encroachment of American and Japanese companies in European markets (both in the sales of foreign products and the founding of foreign-owned companies in Europe). In 1985, Europe's leaders reached a major agreement: the creation of the Single European Market to eliminate borders for the free flow of goods, services, and capital, and to remake the domestic market of member countries as a European market by 1992. This time, the Thatcher government was fully on board. Britain was eager to exploit the potential of an all-European free market that had gradually expanded to include some 500 million people. This had been Britain's ultimate goal.

Nevertheless, a number of federalist politicians, first among them Jacques Delors, the newly elected president of the European Commission in 1985, wanted to go even further. A single market required a single currency. This idea was already making the rounds in 1970, when the Warren Report recommended its adoption. After two decades of postponements, the genuine prospect of such a development came in 1989 with the collapse of the Soviet Bloc and with German reunification. Opposing the latter were Margaret Thatcher, French President François Mitterrand, Italian Prime Minister Giulio Andreotti, and Soviet President Mikhail Gorbachev; but it was Mitterrand who first realized that it could not be stopped and who found a way to counterbalance the danger of a unified Germany. He determined that introducing a common currency would bind Germany to Europe. German Chancellor Helmut Kohl was more than happy to pay Mitterrand's price for reunification and demonstrate Germany's readiness to be incorporated more strongly into an integrated Europe. "Germany," Kohl declared in the European Parliament, "will be completely united only if progress is made towards the unification of our old continent. Policy on Germany and policy on Europe are completely inseparable." He emphasized that "we are already making preparations for the further development . . . with political union [of Europe] as our goal."[10]

Commission president Delors fully agreed with Mitterrand and Kohl because he saw German unification as an excellent opportunity, a "catalyst" to move Europe toward monetary and political unity, and thus to deeper integration. He maintained that

> economic and monetary union is the *interface between economic and political integration* . . . . It is time, then, for a new political initiative . . . . The Community is faced with the challenge of making a telling contribution to the next phase of our history.[11]

Alongside monetary unification, the Maastricht Treaty set up a new supranational institution, the European Central Bank (ECB), to administer common monetary policy. With these changes, a major part of national sovereignty was shifted to supranational European control. The introduction of the common currency was thus a major *political* step, as well as a step to meet the requirement of a single European market.

Monetary unification was devised and recommended by a committee headed by Delors, which included the heads of the member states' national banks, such as Robin Leigh-Pemberton, the head of the Bank of England. But, as Leigh-Pemberton later recalled, the committee did not believe in the importance of the recommendation. "Most of us, when we signed the Report in May 1989, thought that we would not hear much about it. It would be rather like the Werner Report of 1970."[12] This would prove to be a misreading of the situation. The most effective advocate of European integration, Delors successfully introduced Europe's common currency, the euro, in three stages between 1999 and 2001.

This extended step toward integration – the introduction of the most important new supranational institution, the euro, as well as the European Central Bank – accorded with corporate interests. When the euro was introduced, the British Prime Minister later revealed, "Many of our political and business leaders urged Britain to join at that time."[13] It was undoubtedly a major interest of the British business world. Joining a common currency would definitely have economic advantages for Britain – especially for "The City," Britain's most powerful financial sector.

Nevertheless, such a step proved too much for the bulk of Britain's political elite; consequently, the Labour Government of Tony Blair decided not to join. Britain was not loathed to give up its economic sovereignty and its own exchange rate policy; nor did it have any intention of subordinating the Bank of England to the European Central Bank. Here too, the legacy of nineteenth-century British dominance on the world economy, and the unquestioned importance of the British pound (equated at the time with gold as a world currency), continued to have a tremendous emotional impact. Not unlike the five o'clock tea and left-side traffic, the pound sterling was emblematic of British tradition and self-identification. Opposing a common European currency as well were the members of the Sterling Bloc – more than sixty countries, some small and indigent, others important and affluent (such as Australia, New Zealand, and South Africa), all remnants of the British Empire – that either used the pound sterling as their own currency or pegged their currency to the British pound. In other words, anything more than a free trade zone on the continent was something that was always too much for the British political elite and a good part of the population to swallow. Britain's government negotiated a way to opt out of the Maastricht Treaty's requirements in order to keep intact its national monetary policy. As a consequence, a two-tier Europe, the euro-zone countries and those who opted out (Britain, Denmark, and Sweden), arose. At the turn of the twenty-first century, Britain positioned herself in the outer circle of the European integration process. But that was not all.

Renegotiating Britain's status or stepping out from the EU?

David Cameron's Conservative government resolved to institutionalize Britain's inside-outsider position by renegotiating the terms of British membership in the

European Union. He disclosed this at his so-called Bloomberg speech on January 23, 2013. When he did so, he imposed a deadline of sorts by calling for the British public to decide on Britain's continued standing in the Union in an in-or-out referendum in December 2017. In other words, Cameron sought to outdo Margaret Thatcher. He not only criticized additional steps of integration and bemoaned European supranationalism and a European superstate, but called for legalizing Britain's determined stance to remain unfettered and autonomous, or at the very least reorganizing the European Union to meet British needs.

Echoing Thatcher, Cameron assured his audience at his Bloomberg speech that "we have always been a European power and we always will be … I don't want a better deal for Britain. I want a better deal for Europe too." He suggested that his proposals were sorely needed to fix a defective EU treaty system and to reorganize the European Union as a free trade zone. "Our participation in the single market … is the principal reason for our membership of the EU." He also called for expanding the EU free trade zone to include North America and Asia. But he made it clear that Britain had no desire either to be part of an "ever-closer union" or to commit to extended integration. "The EU is now heading for a level of political integration that is far outside Britain's comfort zone." The EU, he insisted, must be an alliance of "flexible cooperation" where a one-size-fits-all policy does not rule. Power must flow away from Brussels and toward the national governments, and the national governments must be able to veto any EU legislation. The British justice system must retain the right to protect its citizens from the undue interference of EU institutions, such as the European Court of Human Rights. Although Cameron did not discuss in his Bloomberg speech the guaranteed right of migration across borders and of employment in other member countries within the Union, he later incorporated it by requesting limitations on both rights. He would subsequently modify this demand when he realized the extent of European resistance to it, seeking instead an end of migrants' rights of free benefits in other member countries. Continued enlargement to include more countries that Britain always advocated must be combined with a new mechanism to prevent mass migration within the Union. In addition, Britain pushed for granting non-euro-zone countries a vote in enacting euro-zone legislation when majority votes were required. Besides mandating a single market, the euro-zone had no power to force banking regulations on non-euro-zone countries. Cameron proclaimed that there was no need for fiscal coordination or for a single bank. "Why can't we just have what we voted to join – a common market?"[14] Cameron's vision of reorganizing the EU would have destroyed the Union's supranational character by giving power back to national parliaments and allotting them veto rights on EU legislation, including the adjudication of the European Court of Justice.

David Cameron was intent on exploiting Britain's great power status, its pivotal place in European diplomacy, and most particularly its position (shared with France) as the Union's military and nuclear power. With the enduring Greek crisis in mind, he was well aware of just how serious a threat a "Brexit" (Britain's exit from the Union) would be for European integration. "It is hard to argue that the EU would not be greatly diminished by Britain's departure," he mused in his

Bloomberg speech. In other words, he was bent on blackmailing the Union to force it to accept his terms, rearrange its legal system, and prevent any further steps of integration. In 2014 he began direct negotiations with the heads of state of other member countries on how to reorganize the Union, and then offered up his initial ideas on its transformation as prerequisites for Britain's staying in the Union at a summit in the summer of 2015. An EU summit discussed the terms of renegotiating Britain's status in the EU in December 2015, and another one in February 2016. Several member states share the view of Rafal Trzaskowski, the Polish minister of European Affairs, that "Europe wants the United Kingdom to stay but not at any cost."[15] Would the EU emerge stronger without Britain, given that the latter always acts as a brake on further progress? This last prospect is very doubtful, because the Union is already too large to be able to form a functioning political union. In the case of a British exit, the losers would undoubtedly be both the European Union and Britain.

Brexit definitely hurts important British interests, particularly damaging Britain's trade relations with the continent (its biggest trade partner, constituting 56 percent of its total trade). The EU is far more important for Britain than is the Commonwealth. The latter could claim a 40 percent share of total British exports of goods in 1948, but that fell to 17–18 percent by 1973 and to 10 percent in 1990. In 2012, the UK's services' exports to the Commonwealth constituted only 12 percent of the total.[16] In the late twentieth century, the structure of trade between the advanced and less developed countries dramatically changed. Before then, the advanced countries had exported industrial products to the developing world and had purchased raw materials there. At the turn of the century, however, the demand for raw materials fundamentally decreased in the advanced high-tech and financial services-oriented countries, which proceeded to turn to each other in trade. Characteristic of the new reality was the highly successful European Airbus program, in which six advanced European countries, including Britain, collaborated. It is no accident that even within the Commonwealth, nearly two-thirds of Britain's trade relations is concentrated with four advanced countries (Australia, Canada, South Africa, and India), while trade with more than 50 other Commonwealth countries is of little consequence. Cameron himself stated in his Bloomberg speech that "continued access to the Single Market is vital for British business and British jobs." The Union offers several advantages for both British businesses and British citizens, especially for the younger generation and more educated layers who like studying and working on the continent. This is the reason for the founding of the "Britain Stronger in Europe" movement, which first appeared in the early fall of 2015. Supporting its platform to "stay in" were the leading lights of British big business, among them the powerful Confederation of British Industry, representing 190,000 companies. As the organization's general director, John Cridland, declared, "Political isolationism would make us poorer." Its supporters also included leading British multinational corporations such as BT, the telecommunication giant Easy-Jet, and Innocent Drinks.[17] The most important and influential banking industry also rejected an exit from the EU, since they see it as very harmful for business interests. The *New York Times* reported that most banking executives in London ... see much to lose if Britain were to leave the EU ... [They] don't want to risk going it alone .... Banks won't disappear from London overnight, but they will over time if Britain votes 'no' to the European Union.[18]

It added that a number of bank executives donated six-figure sums to the lobbying group "Britain Stronger in Europe."

They appear to be in full agreement with a warning President Obama issued in an interview to the BBC during the June 2015 G-7 meeting in Germany: "Exiting from the European Union," he maintained, "will corrode Britain's global clout" and diminish Britain's influence. Cameron himself agreed with Obama in his speech to the G-7: "we are more powerful in Washington, in Beijing, in Delhi because we are a powerful player in the European Union." A significant part of the British population shared this view: when polled in the summer of 2015, 59 percent of British citizens supported remaining in the EU; if the referendum were held that day, only 41 percent would vote for leaving the Union.[19] Various polls in February and March 2016 reflected a relatively steady but thin majority of supporters of remaining in the EU.[20]

The presumed "advantages" of Britain's exiting the EU are mostly illusions. A lengthy article in *The Economist* precisely demonstrated why Britain would not be able to free itself from Brussels' regulations if it wanted to continue to enjoy its sorely needed connection with the common European markets. After all, non-member countries such as Switzerland and Norway had to pay their share for the EU's budget and accept Brussels' regulations (including the free movement of people) in order to enjoy the great advantages of the single market. Another important factor is how Scotland may act in the future. The advocates for Scottish independence, though defeated in a recent referendum, may win additional support after Britain's exit from the union, because Scotland is demonstrably pro-European Union. "In Scotland the first minister has again made clear that if Britain leaves the EU she will seek a vote for independence (she would probably win)."[21] In another article the same British journal added: "the longer-term costs would go beyond economics. Brexit might well break up the United Kingdom itself" because Scotland could easily bolt, and the problem of Northern Ireland may reappear.[22] Indeed, the Scottish National Party is strongly against an exit. Nicola Sturgeon, the leader of the Scottish party and Scotland's First Minister "threatens to demand another referendum on Scottish independence should Britain vote to leave the EU."[23] She repeated her statement after the referendum: it was "democratically unacceptable that Scotland faced the prospect of being taken out of the EU against its will ... the Scottish government would begin preparing legislation to enable another independence vote."[24]

Northern Ireland's long-lasting conflict between Catholics and Protestants might easily return as a consequence of Brexit. For the Irish nationalist Catholics, joining the EU promised to go down the road toward Irish unification. This was openly discussed. When Ireland filed its first application for membership in the EU in 1961, Irish Prime Minister Seán Leman argued that this step, in the long run, will lead to unification. The European Union was largely a Catholic program for the Irish people, while Protestant Northern Irish are basically Eurosceptic and pro-Brexit. "In a worst case scenario … British exit from the EU would provoke a return of the type of violence which killed over 3,000 people in 25 years."[25] Brexit is also harmful for long-term North–South Irish business interests. After Britain, the Irish Republic is the second largest trade partner for Northern Ireland, and cross-border shopping, advantageous for the population, would also be endangered. Northern Ireland is furthermore a major beneficiary of EU membership and received a huge EU aid contribution: Since 1995, the region has received €1.3 billion, and during the budgetary period of 2014–20 another €2.3 billion and an additional €227 million agricultural subsidy. The farming community in Northern Ireland is a major beneficiary of EU membership.[26] Gerry Adams, the president of Sinn Fein, declared:

> The referendum had nothing to do with Ireland's economic interest … it was precipitated by a toxic mix of factional fighting and leadership intrigue within the British Conservative Party and the rise of far-right, anti-immigration groups …. As a party of Irish republicans and democrats, Sinn Fein believes in Irish unity. The Good Friday Agreement already allows for concurrent referendums on reunification to be held in the North and South. The British and Irish governments are obliged to legislate for the unity of Ireland if a simple majority in the North supports change …. The British government should respect the popular vote in the North for European Union membership.[27]

Political forces working against Britain's continued membership in the EU, however, were still on the rise in early 2016. In Cameron's own Conservative Party has formed a formidable group advocating exit, the "Conservatives for Britain," comprising nearly one-third of Tory representatives. Less than half a year prior to the referendum a great part of the ruling Conservative Party, including a number of cabinet members and the popular mayor of London, Boris Johnson, were strongly urging an exit. They convinced a majority of less educated British citizens, though not the more educated parts of the population.[28] The anti-EU United Kingdom Independence Party (UKIP), founded in 1993 as a single issue party, is also gaining ground. While mustering only 3–6 percent of the vote in Britain's by-elections between 2011 and 2013, UKIP won 20–30 percent in November 2013 and 40–60 percent a year later. Advocating other populist measures like tax cuts and immigration control, UKIP cemented itself in British politics when it won 12.6 percent of the votes at the 2015 parliamentary elections, nearly 10 percent more than its tally in the previous general elections.[29]

Prime Minister Cameron launched a major campaign to change the European Union according to British taste in 2015 and 2016. He reasoned that EU leaders, grappling with the migration crisis, would be more flexible and ready to compromise to avoid a Brexit. Indeed, on February 2, 2016, the President of the Council of Europe, Donald Tusk, offered a compromise, maintaining that "not to compromise would be compromising our common future."[30] Accordingly, Britain would not have to commit to backing an "ever closer union," and it would not have to provide full benefits to workers from other EU countries for the first few years after their arrival. The Union also gave assurances that British banks would not be discriminated by euro-zone decisions. The British demand to overrule EU resolutions and the laws by member countries' parliaments, however, was only formally recognized: a British veto is only operative if it is sustained by 14 other countries. According to Britain's former defense minister, Liam Fox, what Cameron received was not "even close to the fundamental changes [he] promised to the public." [31]

Nevertheless, David Cameron declared victory. On February 19, the 28 member countries unanimously voted to grant Britain this "special status," prompting Cameron to declare that "this is enough for me to recommend the United Kingdom remain in the European Union." He also argued that an exit from the EU would strongly hurt British economic interests. Britain would be "less in charge of [its] own destiny" if it left the Union, he insisted. "You have an illusion of sovereignty, but you do not have power … you can't get things done." [32] During the spring of 2016, Cameron strongly advocated the "stay in" vote. His impact, however, was limited since previously he mostly criticized the EU and spoke on the negative effects of membership on Britain. David Cameron made several serious mistakes and cannot blame anyone else but himself for the outcome of the referendum.

The referendum in June 2016: Brexit

Britain, always schizophrenic about the EU because it wanted to enjoy the benefits of membership in a single European market, but did not like the EU's rules, including the free movement of people and the contribution to a common budget, the prerequisite for the access to those markets, at last held the referendum, earlier than planned, on June 23, 2016. The outcome was shocking. More than 72 percent of the eligible voters participated and almost 52 percent voted for the exit. This has sent shock-waves throughout Britain, Europe, and even in the world. The vote for Brexit looked unlikely, although the history of Britain's relationship with the EU signaled the danger. Britain's refusal to join in the 1950s, its founding the rival EFTA in 1960, its calling a referendum on remaining in the Community in 1975, two years after joining it, its opting out from various integration moves, and its remaining outside the euro-zone and the Schengen agreement clearly referred to the continued "island self-conciseness" of the political establishment and even a great part of the population. The exit campaign became nasty, cynically spreading untrue information and hatred. One of the lies was the huge savings by not paying British contribution to the EU budget. They announced that all of this money might be invested to the ailing health care system. This worked and influenced several people. After the referendum the main advocates for exit had to accept "some mistakes" in their calculations. They "forgot" to deduct from the British payments to EU the amount of the EU's payments to Britain's less developed areas and agriculture that eliminated the greatest part of the advertised "gain." Most of the tabloid journals, which actually published 82 percent of the articles in

British journals, without serious and true argumentation, propagated Brexit during the campaign. This sentiment culminated in the murder of Jo Cox, the Labour MP who campaigned for staying in.

The referendum opened a Pandora's Box. What will come out of it? This is still an open question. Nevertheless, several elements of the outcome for Britain are already clear. First of all, it is not a "united" kingdom any longer. Britain is passionately distanced and divided in many ways. Indeed, millions of citizens must be asking: Is it fair that hardly more than half of the British population can decide upon the destiny of nearly the other half? Is it fair that 1.3 million people – that was the surplus of the "exit" voters in exact numbers over the "stay in" voters – decided upon the life of 65 million citizens? Is it fair that the parent and grandparent generations (who voted by 57 percent to leave) are defining the future of the young generation against its will (since they voted by 57 percent to stay in)? Is it fair that the less educated rural population define the more educated urban people's life? Cambridge voted by 73 percent to stay in, London by 60 percent; Liverpool, Manchester, Oxford, and other cities wanted to stay. Is it fair that the English voters (of which 53 percent voted for exit) decide upon the Scottish (who voted by 62 percent to remain in the EU) and Northern Irish people (who voted by 56 percent to stay in)? The referendum may lead to the explosion of the United Kingdom. Such a crucial vote should require a two-thirds majority as constitutional changes do in most countries – millions of the British citizens argue. Little surprise that in a few days after the referendum 4 million people signed a petition to the Parliament and Scottish and Irish leaders to reconsider their referendum to remain in the EU.

Britain will pay a high price for the referendum. It may lead to the explosion of the United Kingdom itself and generate a Scottish (probably Northern Irish?) referendum to step out from the Kingdom and remain in the European Union. The huge majority of these regions were voting for "stay in." The harsh negative economic consequences for Britain are already evident. It may be disastrous: economic decline, lower value of the British pound, exit of several foreign companies and a significant decrease of foreign investments, a difficult reorientation of the British foreign trade and a diminished role of the heart of the British economy, the banking industry. Britain's political weight and importance may also significantly decrease. The only way to avoid it would be a "Norwegian solution," a close association with the EU via the European Economic Area. In this case, Britain would remain part of the European Single Market. However, as Norway does, in this case the country has to accept the EU rules, including the contribution to the EU budget and the acceptance of the free movement of people. What was the point in this case of stepping out? One should ask Boris Johnson and Nigel Farage.

In spite of the fact that Britain was never a whole-hearted member of the European Union and the various governments kept always a leg in the door to leave, since the exit was realized in the crucial moment of the complex crisis of the EU, it may also be disastrous. The EU is definitely weaker without Britain. More importantly, the strong populist-nationalist anti-integrationist opposition in France, the Netherlands, Austria, Poland, and Hungary will be significantly strengthened. Some of these forces after the next coming elections in these countries may coquet to follow in the British footsteps. The forces of disintegration are not insignificant and may be much more dangerous after the British referendum. What will come out from the opened Pandora's Box? It strongly depends on the reaction of the population of Britain and the leadership of the European Union.

Notes

1 Sarwar A. Kashmeri, "The Sun Never Sets on Britain's Eternal Question: To Be or Not To Be European," review of David Hannay, *Britain's Quest for a Role. A Diplomatic Memoir from Europe to the UN* (London: I. B. Tauris, 2013); accessed at kashmeri.com/category/european-union/.
2 This Embassy report was written before Prime Minister Wilson visited Washington, DC in the 1960s. See: Helen Parr, *Britain's Policy Towards the European Community. Harold Wilson and Britain's World Role 1964–1967* (London: Routledge, 2006), 76.
3 Winston Churchill, speeches (www.winstonchurchill.org/resources/speeches).
4 Winston Churchill's speech in the House of Commons on 27 June, 1950, in Randolph S. Churchill (ed.), *In the Balance. Speeches 1949 and 1950 by Winston Churchill* (London: Cassell, 1952), 299.
5 Ernst H. van der Beugel, *From Marshall Aid to Atlantic Partnership* (Amsterdam: Elsevier, 1966), 224.
6 Walter Lipgens and Wilfried Loth (eds), *Documents on the History of European Integration.* Vol. 3, *The Struggle for European Union by Political Parties and Pressure Groups in Western European Countries 1945–1950* European University Institute, Series B (Berlin: Walter de Gruyter, 1988), 746–53.
7 David Cameron, EU Speech at Bloomberg, January 23, 2013, Cabinet Office, Prime Minister's Office (www.gov.uk/government/speeches/eu-speech-at-bloomberg).
8 *BBC News,* April 8, 2013. "Thatcher and Her Tussles with Europe."
9 Margaret Thatcher, "Family of Nations," in Brent F. Nelsen and Alexander C-G. Stubb (eds), *The European Union. Readings on the Theory and Practice of European Integration* (Boulder, CO: Lynne Rienner, 1998), 49–54.
10 Kohl speech in the European Parliament, Debates of the European Parliament, DEP 3-383, 156–59, November 22, 1989, quoted in Michael Burgess, *Federalism and the European Union: The Building of Europe, 1950–2000* (Abingdon: Routledge, 2000), 193.
11 Burgess, *Federalism and the European Union,* 86–87 (italics added).
12 Quoted by Harold James, *Making the European Monetary Union* (Cambridge, MA: Belknap/Harvard University Press, 2012), 211.
13 Cameron, Bloomberg Speech (see note 7).
14 Ibid.; *The Guardian,* March 16, 2015; *International Business Times,* April 15, 2015.
15 *Reuters,* June 7, 2015.
16 UK – Commonwealth Trade Statistics, December 2012. Library House of Commons (researchbriefings.parliament.uk/ResearchBriefing/Summary/SND6497).
17 *The New York Times,* October 13, 2015, "Potent Campaigns Square Off Over Britain's EU Membership."
18 *The New York Times,* February 9, 2016, "On the Side of Europe. Bankers in London See Risks in Proposal for Britain to Leave the EU."
19 Ibid.
20 www.theweek.co.uk>EUreferendum
21 *The Economist,* October 17, 2015, "Britain and Europe. The Reluctant European."
22 *The Economist,* February 27, 2016, "The Real Danger of Brexit."
23 *The New York Times,* February 22, 2016.
24 www.bbc.com/news/uk-scotland-scotland-politics-36621030

25 *Archive of European Integration,* College of Europe, Bruges Political Research papers 48/February 2016, Patrick Jacques, "Great Hatred, Little Room. Northern Ireland and the EU: Attitudes, Perspectives and the Role of Religion."
26 *Archive of European Integration,* John Bradley, "Northern Ireland and the Island Economy. An Update," I/EA.
27 *The New York Times,* July 12, 2016, Gerry Adams, "Brexit and Irish Unity."
28 A poll confronting the university city of Cambridge, which has a large number of highly educated people, with another Cambridgeshire city of similar size, Peterborough, but with far fewer highly educated people, clearly reflects that the higher educated want to stay in while the less educated are for exit. In Cambridge only 27 percent were for exit, in Peterborough 62 percent. Altogether, among educated people only 16 percent wanted to vote for exit. (*The Economist,* February 20, 2016, "Britain's Great European Divide is Really About Education and Class.")
29 BBC News, November 14, 2014. "UKIP: The Story of the United Kingdom Independence Party's Rise."
30 *The New York Times,* February 5, 2016, "Everyone Losing if Britain Exits the European Union."
31 *The Economist,* February 6, 2016, "Britain and the EU, Slings and Arrows."
32 *The New York Times,* February 22, 2016, "London Mayor is Latest Calling for EU Exit."

2 The crisis of the common currency, the euro

From liquidity crisis to the Great Recession

After an enormous boom period spanning a quarter of a century beginning in the mid-1980s, Europe began to show the first signs of an economic crisis in 2007–8. In September of 2007, Britain's Northern Rock Bank tottered at the brink of collapse and was saved only by a guarantee of coverage by the Bank of England, with a \$4.4 billion credit line. But a year later, in September 2008, the major American mortgage bank, Lehman Brothers, collapsed, shocking the entire international financial system. Banks stopped extending credit, and a global liquidity crisis paralyzed financial markets worldwide. Financial panic engulfed Europe. The first victim was trust: banks and companies began hoarding their money and neither spent nor lent it. Bank loans were no longer available. The crisis began to feed itself. Euro-zone banks wrote down \$500–800 billion, about 10 percent of the aggregate GDP of the euro-zone. The International Monetary Fund (IMF) estimated that no less than \$1.2 trillion dollars were lost in the euro-zone and Britain. The Union's debt level was around 60 percent of the aggregate GDP, only to rise to more than 82 percent by 2011. Because of panic selling, the value of stocks in the euro-zone was cut in half.

Credit and borrowed money had been holding up the entire mechanism of the capitalist economy; consequently the real economy, trade and manufacturing, indeed the entire economic system, stopped working. As the European Commission reported, "the transmission of the financial distress to the real economy evolved at record speed."[1]

Beginning in the last quarter of 2008, the euro-zone's economy declined into recession. Italy suffered a 6.76 percent decline of GDP over seven quarters, Ireland a 12.24 percent decline over 13 quarters, France 3.87 percent over four quarters, Germany 6.62 percent over four quarters, and Sweden, Denmark, and Finland saw a 8–10 percent decline. Reduced GDP continued over an extended period. Although there were major differences between the northwestern and the southeastern member countries, on average the euro-zone saw a –0.5 percent annual decline of GDP between 2008 and 2013.[2]

Unemployment skyrocketed to 27.5 percent in Greece and 25.6 percent in Spain, and averaged 11.9 percent throughout the euro-zone as late as 2014.

In countries such as Greece, where irresponsible spending led to an accumulation of government debt comprising 160 percent of GDP, bankruptcy was the inevitable outcome by 2012. The EU and the IMF were forced to bail Greece out three times between 2009 and 2015 (see Chapter 3 on the Greek issue).

Simultaneous to the banking crisis, a decades-long housing boom suddenly ended. A housing bubble with its soaring housing prices burst from Ireland to Latvia. This hit the banks particularly hard, because they were unable to recover their mortgage loans. In several countries, governments rushed to rescue and recapitalize the banks to keep their economies going. However, this endeavor inflated their national debt to a dangerous degree. In Ireland, for instance, government debt jumped from 25 percent of GDP in 2007 to 112 percent in 2011. In Spain, public debt rose from 35 to 160 percent of GDP. Government indebtedness assumed dangerously high levels from Italy and Portugal to Hungary and Latvia. It had been high in Italy even before the crisis, comprising 103 percent of GDP in 2007; by 2013, however, it had increased to 133 percent. Several countries in the southern and eastern peripheries of the European Union went through similar crises. The so-called PIIGS countries, as Portugal, Ireland, Italy, Greece and Spain were sarcastically called, accumulated enormous debt. Spain and Italy together had a $3.3 trillion debt burden in 2011, and the cost of their debt service was $426 billion in the first half of 2012, larger than the entire amount ($400 billion) that the IMF had lent that year.[3] Like Greece, Portugal, Spain, and Ireland fell into insolvency. The EU and IMF bailed these countries out, too.

Inflation decreased, and was replaced by deflation in some countries such as Greece and Spain. In Italy, inflation dropped from 3.3 to 0.4 percent. Deflation spread from debtor to creditor countries, and the euro-zone's average inflation rate was only 0.4 percent in 2014, way below the 2 percent planned by the European Central Bank. Deflation is a dangerous anti-growth phenomenon because it leads consumers to hold off on buying, which stalls recovery and undermines the sustainability of public debt because it makes repayment more expensive.[4]

The so-called Great Recession, the most serious economic calamity since the Great Depression of the 1930s, is a global phenomenon. Its primary causes are rooted in the transformations and close interconnectedness of the global economy, as well as the neo-liberal deregulation of financial markets that made irresponsible risk-taking the norm. The safety regulations that had been put in place as a result of the Great Depression were thrown by the wayside from the 1980s on. The ratio between borrowed money and owned assets of banks was lowered, thus eroding the banks' reserves that served as a buffer that could counterbalance sudden losses. Several "shadow banking" institutions were established, such as hedge funds, a genuinely speculative, high-risk, and totally deregulated credit institution. Pension funds, insurance companies and other types of funds also acted as investment banks. Securitization (the selling of loans), i.e., mortgage loans repackaged as bonds (securities), made the financial market less transparent and creditworthiness less important in lending. Toxic subprime mortgages were commonplace. Cheap credit was ubiquitous, feeding what was believed to be a new prosperity. The world of finance became more hazardous, offering huge profits but at the risk of gargantuan losses. The deputy-director of the Bank of Greece proudly declared in 2006 that deregulation "would allow the European financial service sector to gradually realize its full potential."[5] Within two years, Greece's financial system and its entire economy had collapsed. Jürgen Stark, a representative of the European Central Bank, noted in 2009: "The current financial crisis is largely the result of excessive risk taking and faulty risk management ... deficiencies in fiscal regulation and supervision in some advanced countries."[6]

This new high-risk business model in the deregulated financial sector became extremely dangerous in the advanced countries, including the European Union, where rapid de-industrialization lessened the role of manufacturing. In the euro-zone and the Union in general, industrial employment fell from 40–48 percent to 27 percent by 2004; in the Netherlands, Britain, and Sweden, it had fallen to 16–20 percent.[7] Finance was now the most predominant sector in the restructured advanced economies of the EU, but it was also the most volatile. Financial speculation was rampant. Germany's Finance Minister, Peer Steinbrueck, told the Bundestag in September 2008 that "reckless Anglo-Saxon financial engineering ... [and] laissez-faire ideology" were responsible for generating a gambling mentality in the financial sector, a "blind drive for double digit profits ... [and an] irresponsible exaggeration of the principle of a free, unrestricted market."[8]

All this had long been a mainstay of the Anglo-Saxon world, and had been popularized by President Ronald Reagan and Prime Minister Margaret Thatcher. But now the European Union, to keep its competitive edge, was jumping on the bandwagon. This was made all the easier with the introduction of the Single Market between 1985 and 1992 and the common currency at the turn of the millennium.

From financial crisis to the crisis of the common currency

After the severe economic shock of 2008–9, it seemed that Europe had begun to recover in 2010. This, however, was not the case. Following the financial and banking crisis was a sovereign debt crisis in the spring of 2010. Public indebtedness rose to 137 percent of GDP in Greece, 119 percent in Italy, and 85 percent in Portugal – way above the European Union's norm of 60 percent.[9] The total debt of the ten most developed countries of Europe – government, financial institutions and households combined – topped 200 percent of GDP in 1995, only to rise to 300 percent by 2008. It totaled 466 percent of GDP in Britain, 366 percent in Spain, 323 percent in France, 315 percent in Italy, and 285 percent in Germany in 2009. The only euro-zone country not to have a debt increase between 2000 and 2008 was Germany.[10]

The recession-generating financial crisis proved to be a temporary problem in the United States and most of the world, but it intensified into a crisis of the common currency in Europe. The European debt crisis significantly worsened in 2011, and the financial markets reacted to this in a hysterical way. A number of newspapers did not exclude the possibility of the common currency's collapse in a few weeks' time. "Eighteen months into a sovereign debt crisis," wrote *The New York Times* on November 28, 2011, "the endgame appears to be fast approaching for Europe."[11] In the same month, *The Economist,* in an article on the European common currency, alarmingly asked: "Is it the end?"

Why was the euro destabilized? The 16-country euro-zone was an economic superpower in 2008. The bloc of more than 320 million people today has a GDP of $13.6 trillion, 22 percent of the world's total and close to the US's $14.1 trillion. The euro-zone has generated 29 percent of the world's exports and received 23 percent of foreign direct investment.[12] The brief, decade-long history of the euro has been a clear success story. After a very short period of decline after its introduction, its value increased by 50 percent compared to the US dollar. Moreover, the euro emerged as a second international reserve currency, used in a quarter of all international transactions. This had never happened in such a short time with any new currency throughout world history.

Why, then, was the euro endangered after 2008, while the American dollar and other major currencies were not? The answer to this question leads back to the introduction of the euro. The integrated market logically called for monetary integration, which had already been put on the agenda as early as 1970 by the Warner Report. But member countries were reluctant to give up a big part of their sovereignty and introduce a common currency and monetary policy. This question logically reemerged in 1985, after the acceptance of the Single Market Act, a program to closely integrate the markets of the member countries by eliminating several existing impediments to the free flow of goods, services, and capital.

Still, more than a decade would have to go by before real changes were made. In the end, what prompted them was not economic necessity but political need. The introduction of the common currency, three decades after it had been initially proposed, was the result of German re-unification in 1991. The fear of an overwhelmingly strong unified Germany produced a united opposition in Britain, France, and Italy. This opposition had been openly expressed only by Margaret Thatcher; all other leaders were reluctant to do so after half a century of Cold War rhetoric lamenting the division of Germany, for which all blame went to the Soviet Union. Opposing German unification became even more difficult once the United States came on board and welcomed a strengthened and unified German ally. French President François Mitterrand scurried to Moscow hoping to facilitate Soviet leader Mikhail Gorbachev's opposition, to no avail. With the collapse of the Berlin Wall and East German communism, millions of Germans voted with their feet and moved to West Germany. Chancellor Helmut Kohl presented a ten-point gradual unification program to the German Bundestag without consulting his Western allies. President Bush welcomed it with open arms. Re-unification was unavoidable.

Recognizing its inevitability, Mitterrand turned to currency unification to anchor Germany closer to the European Union. Kohl was ready to sacrifice the popular D-Mark, the symbol of German economic success, for unification. Jacques Delors, President of the European Commission, was also happy to go ahead with the project. A genuine federalist, he considered German re-unification as a *sine qua non* for further integration toward a federal Europe.

Because the introduction of the euro was a political decision, Europe's leaders ignored the admonition of several economists that monetary unification *without* fiscal unification had never happened before. Indeed, monetary unification was extremely dangerous if fiscal decisions on spending, budgets, and debt remained in the hands of the member states' national governments. Bad fiscal policy, excessive expenditures, and accumulated indebtedness might easily undermine the common currency. Moreover, the European Central Bank (ECB), established to run monetary policy in the euro-zone and responsible for the common currency, did not become a *real* central bank of last resort. The ECB was not allowed to buy government bonds and control private banks of the member countries. As some economists predicted, introducing the euro without fiscal unification was a ticking bomb that could explode in economic downturns.

Another important aspect of the story is the highly uneven distribution of wealth and living standards among the euro-zone's member countries. This was true even of the initial eleven euro-zone countries, some of whom (Ireland, Spain, and Portugal) were part of former peripheral regions of the continent, and it was even more true of the countries that joined afterwards: Greece, Slovenia, Cyprus, Malta, Latvia, Lithuania, Estonia, and Slovakia. With different cultural and economic backgrounds, these former peripheral countries had much lower income levels and much weaker economies, and they reacted quite differently to the common currency.

It is by no means accidental that the original core countries of northwestern Europe were not hit hard and long by the 2008 crisis, while most of the peripheral countries suffered the most and the longest. In times of economic turmoil, the euro did not serve the interests of the weaker euro-zone countries. During the boom years, the euro offered them great advantages. Cheap credit was to be had in all the euro-zone countries, who could sell their government bonds at very low interest rates, barely higher than that of German bonds. The economist Paul Krugman noted that there was general confidence in European Union countries regardless of their real economic strength. "Fiscal fears vanished" in the middle of the 2000s,

> Greek bonds, Irish bonds, Spanish bonds, Portugal bonds – they all traded as if they were as safe as German bonds. The aura of confidence extended even to countries that weren't on the euro yet but were expected to join in the near future.[13]

This situation actually blinded the former peripheral countries, because they were able to spend freely and cover repayment of old debt with cheap new credit. More and more people bought into the myth of pervasive affluence because they could easily purchase homes with seemingly unlimited credit. Home ownership in formerly impoverished Mediterranean countries such as Spain and Portugal skyrocketed to 80 percent, higher than in the United States (67 percent). These advantages turned into a huge disadvantage when the crisis hit those countries hard and their citizens could no longer get credit. Households and countries alike could not pay back their loans and fell into bankruptcy. The euro-zone countries were also paralyzed in the recession because they were unable to use the traditional means of currency devaluation to cope with economic troubles by lowering the amount of debt repayment and increasing their exports.

The common currency strengthened the strong and weakened the weak; hence not all member states were served equally. The structural economic divisions among member countries thus created additional burdens for the weaker economies. Several experts urged the peripheral countries to leave the euro-zone and restore their national currencies.

These two characteristics, monetary unification without a fiscal one, and a common currency for economically unequal member countries, are the severe *birth defects* of the common currency. They did not cause trouble as long as prosperity continued, but they undermined the euro when the Great Recession began. In a December 2011 article entitled "A comedy of euros," *The Economist* observed that "once again Europe's leaders have failed to solve the euro crisis ... Sooner or later, the euro will be beyond saving."[14] Not surprisingly, dangerous political reaction rose up in several member states. Mass demonstrations were seen in Athens, Madrid, Rome, and other major cities. "Italy," warned Prime Minister Mario Monti, will be pushed "into the hands of anti-EU populists."[15] Paul Krugman also warned of the political dangers: "Nobody familiar with Europe's history can look at this resurgence of hostility without feeling a shiver .... Right-wing populists are on the rise."[16] In a speech at the World Economic Forum in Davos in early 2012, the billionaire philanthropist George Soros spoke of "the dangerous political dynamic .... There is a real danger that the euro will undermine the political cohesion of the European Union."[17] The Deputy Governor of the Bank of England, Charlie Bean, saw the euro-crisis as an opportunity: "What about the opportunity to leave the EU altogether?" The euro-crisis offers Britain "huge benefits," even though it has not joined the common currency.[18] Indeed, in several former peripheral countries, the economic crisis was exceedingly severe: investments declined by 12 percent in Spain and 34 percent in Ireland during the last quarter of 2008, and private consumption decreased by 21 percent in Spain and 34 percent in Ireland.[19] Both trends slowed recovery down and, in some countries, caused a double-dip crisis. Cutting the deficit and the debt, though unavoidable, was retarding economic growth and the income of both citizens and the state. This situation intensified the indebtedness crisis and the eroded trust in debt repayment. The financial markets lacked confidence in the solvency of some euro-zone countries, and began turning away from the euro.

Uncertainty in the international financial markets over some countries' ability to pay back their loans rapidly mounted, and creditors considered defaulting on several peripheral member states. Buying government bonds, once one of the safest forms of investment, now lost its attraction, and the bond market metamorphosed from a buyer's market to a seller's market. Investors hurried to rid themselves of risky European bonds. Consequently, the interest rates of government bonds sharply increased: by 200 basis points from 5 to 7 percent in Italy in the second half of 2011. At a certain point, the interest rate of Greek bonds rose to an unsustainable 37 percent. Indeed, in early 2012, investors were willing to sustain some losses in order to keep their money safe: for the first time ever, Germany was able to sell government bonds with negative interest rates.

The debt crisis, and the massive accumulation of government and private indebtedness, in mostly peripheral countries at that point generated a bank crisis in the core of Europe as well, since the leading banks of Germany, France, Britain, and other core countries had been the buyers of bonds and lenders of credit. German and particularly French banks owned vast amounts of Greek, Italian, and Spanish debts, and they were forced to write off significant parts of them. Between the second quarter of 2007 and the third quarter of 2009, Greek, Irish, Italian, Portuguese, and Spanish bond purchases by European banks increased by roughly one-quarter. By December 2010, French banks owned about €650 billion in debts of the PIIGS countries, German banks more than €500 billion, Britain's €350 billion, and the Netherlands' and Belgium's a combined €250 billion. Very few banks were not involved. This nearly €1.8 trillion of poisonous bonds in the portfolios of banks of Europe's stable core countries are the contagion that potentially endangers the EU's healthy economies.

Europe's banks quickly had to be recapitalized, and the European Central Bank pumped €489 billion in cheap, long-term credits into the system on December 21, 2011. In return, the European Banking Authorities required banks to increase their core reserve capital to 9 percent of their assets. Financial institutions were mandated to raise a combined $145 billion by June 2012. This measure definitely reduced risk in banking, but it caused substantial problems for several banks. For instance, UniCredit, Italy's largest bank, made major stock offerings in January, planning to sell stocks for €1.943/share, but it went into a "freefall" when investors demurred. Not much later, shares sold for 47 euro-cents. The bank's shares lost nearly a quarter of their value. It was a tremendous problem for the euro-zone banks and governments to raise the roughly €1.9 trillion ($2.43 trillion) that were needed for financing in 2012.[20]

Extended crisis of the euro

Domestic economic strength in Europe continued to prove elusive. This, along with Europe's failure to find an effective solution to the Greek crisis, and its inability to secure a safety net for highly indebted euro-zone countries (e.g., a "firewall" around Italy and Spain), was greeted in the financial markets with hysteria. Panic began to be manifested in typical ways: demand in the real economy plummeted, and renewed jitters in the financial markets made the selling of government bonds – the primary means to finance government spending, including the repayment of old debts – increasingly difficult. The irresponsible pecuniary practices of several peripheral countries, not staying within the limits of their budgetary constraints – going into debt and then servicing that debt by issuing new bonds to cover the repayment of the principal and interest – led to an endless vicious circle. Such practices and difficulties in repayment pushed interest rates to dangerous heights, making loans extremely expensive for debtor countries. The declining bond market, the higher cost of credit, and the growing prospect of default engendered a frightening downward spiral among highly indebted governments. Added to the mess was the attempt of endangered governments to cut their expenditures further, which ended up eroding demand within the euro-zone.

This downward spiral of debt became particularly precarious in the last quarter of 2011. The crisis worsened considerably in Italy in November, when the Italian crisis significantly intensified, leading to growing fears in France because of the $100 billion worth of Italian bonds in French banks. Consequently, France hiked the rate of its ten-year government bonds to 140 basis points.[21] Because French banks had purchased vast amounts of bonds from peripheral countries, both the French government and the opposition, and indeed a great part of the French public, favored assisting the troubled peripheral countries.[22] France's AAA credit rating began to be questioned. Any downgrading of France's credit rating would have severely endangered the euro-zone as a whole and led to a complete and urgent overhaul of the entire rescue operation. But that is precisely what happened in January 2012. *The New York Times* reported in November 2011:

> The borrowing costs of nations at the heart of Europe jumped sharply … and continued to increase in France, Spain and Belgium. The latter countries' credit rating was already downgraded. Borrowing cost also moved upward in Finland, Austria, and the Netherlands, which have relatively strong underlying financial positions and until recently had mostly been spared the full effect of the financial crisis …. The ubiquitous nature of the increase of the yields suggests that the problem is spreading well beyond the troubled peripheral countries.[23]

This development was no longer just a danger to some national economies; it could have potentially led to the collapse of the common currency. "The euro is endangered!" – decried a number of experts and the international media.[24] Some pundits had already questioned the entire "artificial" edifice of the European Union, the attempt "to build an economic and legal superstructure without linguistic, cultural, historic and civic base …. But now the inherent flaws are undermining the project …"[25]

The "inherent flaws" were partly errors in policy. At the heart of the matter were the unsolved Greek debt crisis and the considerable delay in stabilizing Italy and Spain, two solvent but troubled large countries that were also imperiled by their debt and bank crises. The prospect of default in two or three euro-zone countries endangered the common European currency, the euro. Several of the crisis-ridden countries, in particular Greece, Ireland, Italy, Portugal, and Spain, used the euro. Their enormous debt crises and their possible defaulting have undermined the market value of the common currency, and have negatively impacted all the countries of the currency group. The crisis of the euro has opened a new chapter in the entire European financial system.

The European Union was reluctant to act. No doubt, support for the banking sector helped curb the spread of the crisis: nine countries supported the banks with upfront payments and guarantee measures of $4,979 billion. Sums allotted for bank rescues comprised 82 percent of GDP in Britain, 70 percent in Sweden, 40 percent in the Netherlands, 35 percent in Austria, and 31 percent in Belgium.[26] Except for these liquidity-creating maneuvers, hardly any other significant steps were taken to save the euro for nearly two years after the crisis began. Instead of bailing out the banks and guaranteeing repayment of debts through radical structural changes of the euro-zone's financial mechanisms, the EU limited itself to providing the funds needed at the moment when some government bonds matured and required repayment. Such a small step did nothing to solve the debt problem and, at the end of the day, assured its continuation and the deepening of the financial crisis.

"At every stage of this crisis Europe's leaders have reacted late and inadequately," *The Economist* observed.[27] Experts and the media blamed Germany and Chancellor Angela Merkel personally for the paucity of corrective action:

> At the center of it all sits Germany, leading the bloc of Northern European countries .... Any proposals to share the burden with the heavily indebted countries by collectivizing European debts ... are rejected out of hand, largely for fear of a political backlash .... When Germany's council of independent economic advisers proposed to Chancellor Angela Merkel last week a way to share European debt to protect Italy and Spain, she dismissed the idea ...[28]

The powerful leaders did not recognize in time that the "north Europeans (and Mrs. Merkel's thrifty Germans in particular) will end up footing a good part of the bill, either by transferring money to the south or by bailing out their own banks."[29] Pundits have complained about a lack of political leadership. "The European Union has a particularly acute version of leaders-who-will-not-lead .... Today, across the globe ... leaders are in dangerously short supply."[30]

However, Angela Merkel and the German government had a definite strategy that they consistently followed. Instead of solving the problems by offering immediate financial help, they actually forced the troubled countries to introduce *austerity* measures and accept new rules to the game at the EU's Brussels meeting in December 2011, a major step towards fiscal unification. In the long run, this was crucial for achieving closer integration and correcting the mistaken paradigm of monetary unification without a fiscal one. Without their refusal to immediately transfer money to the insolvent or near-insolvent countries, this agreement would probably have never been accepted. This was the case even though the short-term problems were by no means solved and still required several additional measures to ward off the collapse that was always just an arm's length away for a few countries.

However, in the parliamentary system, with the EU's complicated and measured decision-making process, decisive action often hit the hard wall of political resistance and labyrinthine institutional mechanisms.

For months, France and other euro-zone countries had urged Germany to accept the issuing of euro-bonds that would save Italy, Spain, and others from overpaying on their new debts. Germany consistently refused to do so. It is easy to understand why. Germany's bonds were sold on the financial market at the lowest rates, and the comparative strength of, and the demand for, German bonds only increased as the crisis took hold. Their interest rates consequently dropped from 4.7 percent in the summer of 2008 to 2 percent in late 2011, and even fell to negative interest rates in early 2012, a two-century low. As a Brussels' research institute calculated, Germany saved $26.7 billion in borrowing costs between 2009 and 2011. At the same time, Holland saved close to $10 billion during those years. Both Germany and the Netherlands profited from the debt crisis because investors began preferring their bonds to those of the peripheral countries.[31] The euro-bond, representing as it did the entire euro-zone, would have had higher rates than did the German ones; thus Germany would have had to pay more for their "Europeanized" bonds than for their own bonds. The populace of the Union's core countries did not feel the crisis and even gained from it. Chancellor Merkel, however, insisted that issuing Eurobonds would be possible only when the finances of the entire euro-zone are in order.

The refusal to take effective action to save euro-zone countries from approaching bankruptcy, and the preference to take relatively small steps to ward off an immediate crash when interest payments were due, led to increasing financial panic. In the last months of 2011, the financial markets began pondering the collapse of the euro. "The Eurozone," as analysts maintained, "was never as close to 'doomsday' as in the summer of 2012."[32] The possibility that some euro-zone countries would financially collapse spawned an attempt to escape from the euro. The panic was fueled by frantic predictions. "The euro-zone financial crisis has entered a far more dangerous phase," analysts stated, "a euro breakup now appears probable rather than possible."[33] Regulators in other countries, including the United States, began pushing their banks to reduce their exposure to European banks. The market was increasingly hesitant to buy European bonds at all. In the last week of November, and for the first time, even a third of German bonds offered for sale were left unsold. If only one euro-zone country had defaulted, its impact on the financial markets would have endangered the entire bloc.

The euro-crisis solved

Nevertheless, after an expanded euro-crisis, the common currency survived. Jörg Asmussen, a member of the Executive Board of the European Central Bank, proclaimed in April 2013: "The euro is already saved. It will survive this crisis, it will emerge from it stronger and more countries will join the euro in the future."[34]

Indeed, the European Central Bank saved the situation when its president, Mario Draghi, declared that the Bank "will do whatever it takes" to save the euro during the common currency's worst crisis in July 2012. In truth, the Bank's rescue was nothing short of heroic. An important element of its intervention was the funding it provided banks at fixed rates and in huge volumes. In early August 2012, the Bank announced a massive purchasing program of government bonds that began in the summer of that year with the buying of bonds worth €60 billion in value. Following in the footsteps of the American Federal Reserve, the European Central Bank turned to so-called "quantitative easing," injecting €1.1 trillion of new money into the euro-zone. This was a long-lasting program. In January 2015, the Bank announced that it would continue this policy until September 2016.[35] Printing and pumping money into the euro-zone's economy and buying endangered government bonds on the secondary market (i.e. from various private bonds' owners), had significant positive consequences. Bond rates dropped precipitously, easing the financial burden on indebted countries. The value of the euro also decreased from $1.5 to $1.1 compared to the US dollar, resulting in the much needed "devaluation" of the euro.

The European Central Bank, the IMF, and the European Commission (the so-called "Troika") bailed out all of the endangered countries: Ireland, Spain, Portugal, Cyprus, and Greece, as well as some non-euro-zone countries such as Latvia, Hungary, Bulgaria, and Romania. The bankrupt peripheral countries were soon able to repay their debts. Most countries needed only one bailout, but some, like Greece, needed more. The Troika conditioned the bailout money with an austerity policy that forced the insolvent peripheral countries to cut government expenditures and increase state revenues to attain a balanced budget. Although the austerity regime was bitterly attacked and deemed to be counterproductive, in reality it worked in Ireland, Spain, Portugal, and the Baltic States. Those countries eliminated their budget deficits and returned to economic growth by 2014–15. Actually in the midst of the most severe euro-crisis, some of those countries hastened to join the euro-zone and increased the number of member countries to nineteen.

In its typically slow pace, the European Union also took decisive new steps to build a robust institutional framework for the euro. The Single Resolution Mechanism, the founding the "European IMF," the banking union with the centralized supervision of the European Central Bank instead of the member states' governments, and the taking of significant new steps to create a quasi-fiscal union with regulatory measures and legal-constitutional amendments (the so-called "fiscal compact") all served as a foundation for a solid supranational institutional framework for a stable common currency. Warding off the collapse of the euro and the disintegration of the euro-zone, the European Union took a significant step toward economic integration (discussed in the Conclusion). Most of all, it has effectively modified its pattern of repeated budget deficits. In the early fall of 2015, the average budgetary deficit in the euro-zone was only –2.1 percent of the GDP. Even in the most troubled countries such as Italy, Spain, and Greece, deficits have not exceeded –4.0 percent. Current accounts mostly balanced or exhibited positive numbers. Greece had a 2.5 percent surplus, Italy 2.0, Spain 0.5, and the euro-zone as a whole, 2.8 percent. Economic growth resumed. Greece, Italy, and Spain had 1.7, 0.7, and 3.1 percent growth compared to the previous year. The euro-zone had an average 1.5 percent growth in both 2014 and 2015. Industrial production increased by 5.1 percent between August of 2014 and 2015, and the euro-zone's industrial growth was nearly 2 percent during that period.[36] By 2015, no one was speaking of a collapse of the euro any longer. As *The Economist* rightly noted already in the spring of 2013: "the pessimists did not overestimate the euro's problems, so much as underestimate the political will to do enough to stop a euro break-up."[37]

Notes

1 European Commission, *Interim EPC-SPC Joint Report on Pensions,* May 31, 2010 (europa.eu/epc/pdf/interim_epc-spc_joint_report_on_pensions_final_en.pdf), 42. In this chapter I broadly used my book, *Europe in Crisis. Bolt from the Blue?* (London: Routledge, 2013).
2 *The Economist, Pocket World in Figures,* 2016 edition (London: Profile Books, 2015), 244.
3 European Commission. "European Economic Forecast, Spring 2011," *European Economy,* 1/2011, 121 (ec.european/economy_finance/publications/european_econ omy/2011/pdf/ee-2011-1_en.pdf); *The New York Times,* December 4, 2011, "European Landers Look to IMF for Assistance, Again, as Euro Crisis Lingers."
4 Annamaria Simonazzi, "Beyond Austerity. Scenarios for a New Growth Model in Italy," in *From Crisis to Development: In Quest of a New Development Model for Greece and the European South* (Athens: Friedrich Ebert Stiftung, 2014), 99.
5 Panagiatos Thomopoulos, "Banking Regulation in Europe: A Brief Overview of Current Development," Athens, May 4, 2006 (www.bis.org/review/r06062f.pdf).
6 Jürgen Stark, speech at the finance ministers and governors of the G-20 countries in Sao Paulo, November 9, 2009 (www.ecb.int>press>speechesandinterviews>bydate>2011).
7 Ivan T. Berend, *An Economic History of Twentieth Century Europe. Economic Regimes from Laissez-Faire to Globalization* (Cambridge: Cambridge University Press, 2006), 287.
8 www.dw-world.de/dn/article/0113669958,00.html
9 European Commission, General Government Data: General Government Revenue, Expenditure, Balance and Gross Debts, December 2010 (ec.europa.eu/economy_finance/db_indicators/gen_gov_data/ documents/2010/ autumn2010_country_eu.pdf).
10 Global Finance (www.gfmag.com>Archives>Spetember2010).
11 *The New York Times,* November 28, 2011, "Time Runs Short for Europe to Find a Solution to Its Debt Crisis."
12 Hannah J. Farkas and Daniel C. Murphy (eds), *The Eurozone. Testing the Monetary Union* (New York: Nova Science Publishers, 2011), 6–7.
13 Paul Krugman, "Can Europe Be Saved?" *The New York Times Magazine,* January 16, 2011, 31.
14 *The Economist,* December 17, 2011, "A Comedy of Euros."
15 *Daily Telegraph,* January 16, 2012, "Italy's Monti Warns Debt Crisis Risk Rise of Anti-EU Populists."
16 Paul Krugman, "Depression and Democracy." *The New York Times,* December 11, 2011.
17 George Soros, "How to Save the Euro," speech at the opening session of the World Economic Forum in Davos, *The New York Review of Books* (http://www.nybooks.com/articles/archives/2012/febr/23/how-save-euro).
18 *Sunday Telegraph,* May 15, 2011, "Why Europe is on the Brink."
19 Paola Subacchi, "Europe from One Crisis to the Other," in Paolo Savona, John J. Kirton, Chiara Oldani (eds), *Global Financial Crisis. Global Impact and Solution* (Farnham: Ashgate, 2011, 65).
20 *The New York Times,* January 10, 2012, "UniCredit's Weak Issue a Poor Omen for Other Banks."
21 *The New York Times,* November 10, 2011.
22 *The Economist,* July 23, 2011, "France and the Euro. Bail-outs? Bof ..." The same article quotes Madam Aubry, head of the opposition Socialist Party, who stated in her article in *Libération*: "Greece must be saved in order to save Europe." In contrast to Germany, "in France there has been almost no public debate over whether to help Greece or other troubled peripheral countries."

23 *The New York Times,* November 16, 2011, "Signs of Broad Contagion in Europe as Growth Slows."

24 Bankers of faraway Mauritius are convinced that some of the euro-zone countries "will dump the euro … to free itself from the shackles of the monetary union … it will get rid of the single currency" (*The African Executive,* August 23, 2010, "The Euro Endangered," africanexecutive.com/article.php?section_id=18 && article_id=5398).

25 David Brooks, "The Technocratic Nightmare," *The New York Times,* November 18, 2011.

26 Paola Subacchi, "Europe from One Crisis to the Other," in Paolo Savona, John J. Kirton, and Chiara Oldani (eds), *Global Financial Crisis: Global Impact and Solution* (Farnham: Ashgate, 2011), 71. Between 2007 and 2009, more than $2 trillion was spent in Europe and the United States to support failing financial institutions.

27 *The Economist,* August 6, 2011, "The Euro Crisis. Rearranging the Deckchairs."

28 *The New York Times,* November 13, 2011, "Even as Governments Act to Stem Debts Crisis, Euro's Time Runs Short."

29 *The Economist,* July 30, 2011. "Turning Japanese. The Absence of Leadership in the West is Frightening – and Also Rather Familiar."

30 *The New York Times,* November 16, 2011, Thomas L. Friedman, "Who's the Decider?"

31 *The New York Times,* November 25, 2011, "In Debt Crisis, a Silver Lining for Germany."

32 "How Did the ECB Save the Eurozone Without Spending a Single Euro?" (http://voxeu.org/article/how-did-ecb-save-eurozone-without-spending-single-euro).

33 Ibid.

34 European Central Bank, "Saving the Euro," April 25, 2013 (www.ecb.europa.eu/press/key/date/2013/html/sp130425.en.html).

35 *The New York Times,* January 22, 2015, "European Central Bank Bets Big on Curing the Economy."

36 *The Economist,* October 10, 2015, "Economic and Financial Indicators."

37 *The Economist*, April 25, 2013, "Charlemagne."

3   The tragicomedy of the Greek debt crisis

Referring to the Greek crisis as a "tragicomedy" seems sarcastic and inappropriate. It has been a genuine tragedy for millions of Greeks who have suffered tremendously from wage and pension cuts and seen their standard of living decline precipitously. A quarter of the labor force is jobless, and only 15 percent of them receive unemployment benefits. The old retiree slouched on the walkway and bereft because he is unable to take out his weekly 55 euros from an ATM does not deserve what is happening to him. It's impossible not to sympathize with him and hundreds of thousands like him.

But the continued incompetence and mismanagement of the country by consecutive Greek governments during the entire post-junta period of the last 40 years and during its European Community membership for a third of a century, and their steadfast resistance to enacting badly needed reforms, could definitely be called a dark comedy of governance. The Greek governments since 1975 have lost control of state revenue, irresponsibly squandered the country's assets, and continually falsified statistics to feign solvency. This dark parody of governance created a series of crises between 2009 and 2015 that represent a unique chapter in the history of default repayment and the European Union.

Tradition

Greece had an important strategic position in Europe because of its crucial location bordering east and west, and because of the west's preparations for military confrontation with the east. Consequently, an economically strong, stable and militarily powerful Greece has been in the interest of Europe as a whole. West European credits flowed into the country, but Greece did not use the money for productive investments and was unable to repay the debt. A few years after the first insolvency, however, foreign credit again became readily available, only to be misused by the Greeks a second time. The pattern of Western credit injections and Greek mismanagement would repeat itself again and again. Predictably, the country would fall into insolvency four times.

Did I forget to mention when all this happened? No, this was *not* the story of the 2009–15 Greek crises, but had instead occurred in the early and late nineteenth century, at the time of the birth of independent Greece. Greece was the very first

Balkan country that had received Western credits already in the first half of the nineteenth century. These loans were supposed to help the country prepare for war against Ottoman Turkey. The first bankruptcy actually took place in 1826, before the declaration of Greek independence; the second, in 1843, soon after independence in 1832. The third followed in 1860, and the fourth in 1893. By the 1890s, Greece had received credits totaling 750 million francs, but it had used all but 6 percent of that amount for military expenditures and non-productive investments. The country's inability to repay, therefore, seemed a foregone conclusion.

Of course, repayment defaults were not a specifically Greek malady in the history of finance. Throughout the nineteenth and twentieth centuries, 25 Latin American, 22 African, 15 Asian, and 22 European countries failed to repay their debts. The most extreme case is probably Argentina, with eight bankruptcies by the early twenty-first century. Spain's seven nineteenth-century insolvencies and Ecuador's six since 1830 are close behind, and slightly beat Greece's five bankruptcies prior to 1932. But Greece proved to be the most egregious with three insolvencies between 2009 and 2015. In June 2015, it became the very first "advanced" country unable to repay IMF loans – joining developing countries such as Zimbabwe, Tunisia, and Somalia.

Financial defaults around the turn of the twenty-first century became a typical "peripheral" phenomenon: in the late 1980s and during the 1990s, a number of communist and post-communist countries (first Poland and Yugoslavia, and then Albania, Croatia, Bulgaria, Russia, and Ukraine) became insolvent. They were followed by others after the 2008 financial-economic crisis, including Romania, Bulgaria, Hungary, Latvia, Ireland, Spain, Cyprus, and Portugal.

Who is responsible?

One Greek government after another proved incapable of pursuing a responsible and orderly fiscal policy and racked up uncontrollably massive debt for decades. Later Greek leaders failed to stabilize the situation in an orderly way with millions of dollars of bailout money. Several Greek governments flagrantly lied about their predicament and falsified statistics, and then tried to blackmail the European Union to get it to write off their debt and pump more money into their bankrupt state coffers and banking system. "In the years between 1981, the year of Greece's admission into the EU, and 2009, when the present crisis began, Greece," Yannis Palaiologos observes, "was always the problem child of the European family – from its repeated fiscal crises and its misuse of structural funds to its inability to shut down illegal rubbish dumps."[1]

Several conflicting interpretations collide head on regarding the causes of the Greek crisis. At the top of the list is the austerity policy that was forced on the country. Austerity may be harmful and counterproductive because it decreases the country's income; and with a diminished GDP, the relative debt burden can increase even with a balanced budget, as indeed occurred in the Greek case. As a Bruegel Brussels Think Tank analysis concluded: "Between 2011 and 2013, fiscal tightening caused a severe drag on the euro area's economic growth and thus nullified the intended goal of reducing public debt burdens." In other words, in the situation in which sound fiscal policy was needed to dig an economy out of the mire, fiscal austerity led to quite the opposite. Austerity can be a trap. By slowing growth and keeping inflation low, the result can be an increase in the debt ratio; then further austerity is called for, and the country finds itself in a vicious circle.[2] While this is certainly true, it is not the whole story. Austerity policy can also play an extremely important educational role. Without it there would be little hope that certain countries would ever pursue healthy fiscal policies. It is a bitter pill to swallow, but it definitely mitigates uncontrolled state and household spending. It teaches governments to get their country's fiscal affairs in order. In cases of notorious financial disorder such as Greece, an austerity policy could have historical significance and lead to a long-term positive outcome even if it produces immediate negative consequences.

Not everybody agrees with this, of course. To quote Joschka Fischer, the former foreign minister of Germany: "The belief that the euro can be used to bring about the economic 're-education' of Europe's south will prove a dangerous fallacy – and not just in Greece."[3] Quite the contrary – the Spanish, Portuguese, and Irish cases speak volumes against this argument. As another EU archival document correctly emphasized:

> Over the last two years, the euro-zone's other peripheral countries have proven their capacity for adjustment, by reducing their fiscal deficit, expanding exports, and moving to current account surpluses, thereby negating the need for financing … [Greece] is the only one that has consistently dragged its feet on reforms and sustained abysmal export performance.[4]

Indeed, the other struggling Mediterranean countries and Ireland made tremendous progress and cut their budgetary deficits: Italy by 4.7 percent of the GDP, the others by 8 percent. These are significantly high numbers, since governments spend an average of 8 percent of their GDP on pensions in the EU. "Austerity has not been adopted at random. Those governments that have cut back the most were also those that spent most recklessly before."[5]

Since the Greek collapse, a heated international debate has ensued on the true causes of the calamity. In the Greek Parliament, the newly elected Prime Minister Alexis Tsipras angrily blamed the creditors and maintained that the IMF "bears criminal responsibility for the situation in the country." Undoubtedly, the IMF made serious mistakes. One of its principal tasks is to assess whether a country is able to pay back its loans or not. After the Argentine fiasco in 2001, the Fund as a rule would loan money only if there was a high probability that it would be put to good use. However, the IMF made a "systemic exception" in the Greek case to avoid a broad financial panic. It presented a rosy forecast about Greece's prospects and contributed to the first Greek bailout as member of the creditor "troika." It was major mistake not to burden part of the losses to the creditors. True, at the second bailout, it could convince the European creditors to burden a great part of the losses to the bond investors. Only in the last phase of the third bailout in 2015 did the IMF make it clear that the Greek debt is not sustainable and shift "from being Greece's most persistent scold to its main advocate for a break on its debt."[6]

Both the Greek populace and its political class were more than willing to make the creditors the culprits.[7] Adam Davidson wholeheartedly agreed in *The New York Times Magazine*[8] "Greece is not solely or even primarily responsible for its own financial crisis." The author's "proof" of this in a November 2009 Greek auction in which the government sold bonds valued at €7 billion. The interest rate of 5.3 per-cent was hardly higher than that of the best German government bonds. The lenders were totally irresponsible because the auction was held three weeks after Greece's new prime minister had admitted that the government's official statistics had been falsified and that the country's debt burden was actually much higher, exceeding the value of the GDP. In less than half a year, Greece asked for a bailout. Instead of part of the debt, now the entire debt had to be burdened to reckless creditors during the 2012 second bailout that "effectively transferred billions of euros … to unwise bond investors." Once again, "wealthy German bondholding institutions" will be the beneficiaries of the funds of the third bailout. The author argues that the logic of the market requires that "if you make a bad investment, you are supposed to pay the full price." This is true. It has become axiomatic that financial institutions are so powerful and pivotal in today's economy that their collapse would bring eve-rything down; they are simply "too big to fail." Consequently, while bank profits are always private, bank losses have become socialized.[9] Nevertheless, this does not mean that "the original sin … did not happen in Athens." If you take out loans you are responsible for paying them back. You are responsible for running your financial affairs in reasonable order.

Joining the debate on the Greek crisis is Joseph Stiglitz, the Nobel laureate and former chief economist of the World Bank. Stiglitz blames the creditors for the crisis, but does so in a different way:

> The economics behind the program that the 'Troika' (the European Commission, the European Central Bank, and the International Monetary Fund) foisted on Greece five years ago has been abysmal, resulting in a 25% decline in the country's GDP. I can think of no depression ever that has been so deliberate and had such catastrophic consequences …. It is startling that the troika has refused to accept responsibility for any of this or admit how bad its forecasts and models have been.[10]

In another article, Stiglitz speaks of Greece as the "Sacrificial Lamb" in a "19th-century debtors' prison."[11]

Another Nobel laureate, Paul Krugman, points to the EU's common currency as an important factor:

> It has been obvious for some time that the creation of the euro was a terrible mistake …. Most – not all, but most – of what you have heard about Greek profligacy and irresponsibility is false …. Yes the Greek government was spending beyond its means in the late 2000s. But since then it has repeatedly

slashed spending and raised taxes .... If you add up all austerity measures, they have been more than enough to eliminate the original deficit and turn it into a large surplus. So why didn't this happen?

Krugman attributes the crisis to irresponsible lending by Western banks, the "straitjacket" of the euro that disallows devaluation as a natural solution, and the austerity policy forced upon Greece and that destroyed the country's economy.[12] In the Greek case, the euro currency had indeed become a special burden, but that was mostly because Greece was not yet economically advanced enough to join the euro-zone, and had won admission through sheer deception.

A *New York Times* editorial also blamed the austerity policy forced upon Greece for the crisis. The euro-zone "has made the Greek crisis worse since the first loan was made in 2010, by demanding senseless austerity policies that have inflicted suffering on individuals, contracted the economy and pushed the unemployment rate ... to 25 percent."[13]

Prime Minister Tsipras attributed the Greek crisis to a basic clash of two conflicting ideologies and strategies:

> My conclusion, therefore, is that the issue of Greece does not only concern Greece; rather, it is the very epicenter of conflict between two diametrically opposing strategies concerning the future of European unification. The first strategy aims to deepen European unification in the context of equality and solidarity between its people and citizens .... The second strategy seeks ... the split and the division of the Eurozone, and consequently of the EU. The first step to accomplishing this is to create a two-speed Eurozone where the "core" will set tough rules regarding austerity and adaptation and will appoint a "super" Finance Minister of the EZ with unlimited power, and with the ability to even reject budgets of sovereign states that are not aligned with the doctrines of extreme neoliberalism.[14]

On the other hand, Nikos Konstandaras, editor of the Greek journal *Kathimerini* maintains that the Syriza party's government

> blames the creditors for Greece's woes, claiming they turned the country into a 'debt colony' .... The effort to restore Greece to normalcy has been a failure, because of poor policies, fundamental problems in Greece's dysfunctional state and a pitiful lack of leadership in Greece and among policy makers in Europe .... The collapse of the parties that had mismanaged Greece for decades created a vacuum that Syriza ... filled with promises .... Domestically, the government has overseen the unraveling of many reforms, done little to crack down on tax evasion and corruption, and repeated the cronyism of the past in the public sector.[15]

On the critical day of a possible last-minute agreement, Greece's ousted finance minister, Yanis Varoufakis, published an article in *The Guardian* under the title, "Germany won't spare Greek pain – it has an interest in breaking us." He writes that Germany's Finance Minister, Wolfgang Schäuble,

> is convinced that as things stand, he needs a Grexit [Greece exit from the euro-zone] to clear the air, one way or another. Suddenly, a permanently unsustainable Greek public debt, without which the risk of Grexit would fade, has acquired a new usefulness for Schäuble. What do I mean by that? Based on months of negotiation, my conviction is that the German finance minister wants Greece to be pushed out of the single currency to put the fear of God into the French and have them accept his model of a disciplinarian eurozone.[16]

The blame-game is running amok.

Clearly, Greece was hardly the only country that had behaved irrationally, and clearly, creditors have also acted irresponsibly. Actually, the 2012 second bailout agreement had funneled €107 million – 70 percent of the losses – to the creditors. In 2015, the creditors didn't wish to repeat this and resisted the pressure coming from Greece and the IMF.

When the EU discovered that the Greek government had cooked the books to enter the euro-zone, they did not punish Greece but accepted the Greek government's promises that it would fulfill its requirements in the future. That, too, was irresponsible.

The European Union leaders, especially the Germans, who consider *Ordnung* (order) as normal behavior, maintain that the euro-zone and the EU cannot work without the member countries following the same rules and regulations. The fact that the common currency is not backed by a federal state makes compliance with the rules that much more critical. But the EU was horrible at enforcement and had never successfully sanctioned noncompliant members. This was irresponsible as well.

Without doubt, several parties are to blame. The main responsibility, however, lies with Greece's governments. This simple fact is often forgotten in the debates and the economic and political analyses of the crisis. "Self-defeating austerity," Daniel Gros emphasizes, "does not make sense for Greece." But austerity, he insists, is not Greece's biggest problem, for it would have had an even larger trade deficit and would have needed an even larger bailout without it. "Export performance is thus the key to explaining the austerity trap." Portugal eliminated its external deficit by increasing its exports by one-third. "Portugal, Ireland, Spain and even Cyprus are recovering visibly. They no longer need official financing and unemployment is coming down."[17]

So, why Greece? Were there specific causes of its perpetual financial crisis and its unparalleled three bailouts in the early twenty-first century? Although the deal between Greece and the euro-zone in the summer of 2015 was very instructive, it does not provide an adequate explanation for the crisis, an explanation that is much more complex and historically based. In the following sections I will discuss principal and often neglected factors of Greece's peculiar crisis: the unique structure and weakness of the Greek economy and educational system; the failure of governance embodied in uncontrolled public spending, the inability to raise state revenue, and a reliance on bogus, often falsified statistics.

Economic weakness

The debates and analyses of the Greek crisis rarely touch on the basic economic problem, the unique weakness of the Greek economy. In the best case, some elements are mentioned; but a clear and complex evaluation of the country's economic background is usually lacking. Without this background, understanding the crisis is hardly possible.

Greece was a backward Balkan country until the mid-twentieth century. Its per capita income level lingered behind the East European average, and was only 40 percent of Western Europe's. Throughout the Cold War, however, Greece was considered to be a "Western" country in alliance with the United States, and was a member of the NATO and (beginning in 1981) the European Economic Community, thanks to a number of politically motivated decisions. The Greek economy grew fast, and the country's GDP increased about five times between 1950 and 1990 – surpassing that of Eastern Europe and constituting 60 percent of Western Europe's GDP. This latter figure remained unchanged until 2012. After the European Union's dramatic expansion with the inclusion of more than ten relatively backward countries in the early 2000s, Greece got very close to the EU-28 average income level.[18] In 2014, Greece was virtually at the same income level, measured in per capita GDP, as the three Baltic countries (and former Soviet republics), but behind the Czech Republic, Slovakia, and Slovenia – countries that were quite backward when their communist systems collapsed but had modernized their economies relatively successfully.

From the First Industrial Revolution until the 1970s, economic advancement in the world was based on the strength of modern manufacturing. Greece was not an industrialized country until it joined the European Community's common market in 1981. In the competitive European common market, Greece failed to fill any economic niche and thus began to lose even the little industry it already had. One of the main reasons for this was a dearth of foreign investment in Greece.

Since 1970, the amount of foreign direct investment (FDI) in Greece has varied markedly from a paltry $24 million in 1975 to a hefty $5.7 billion in 2008 – totaling only $35 billion over the past 43 years. In most of those years, it amounted to less than 1 percent of Greece's GDP, and it exceeded 1 percent in only 11 of those years. Capital inflow to Greece declined by 27 percent per year between 1985 and 1988, and it continued to fall in the early 1990s. Greece received only $9.3 billion in FDI between 1993 and 2002, while the Netherlands got $273 billion and Spain $153 billion. Greece's $9.3 billion was insignificant compared to the massive amounts pouring into the post-communist states: Poland received $49.4 billion in Western FDI, Hungary $22.7 billion, and Slovakia $9.6 billion. On a per capita basis, FDI in Greece was half that of Slovakia and slightly more than a third of Hungary's. Among the 29 advanced OECD countries, Greece ranked 28th in capital inflow. Between 1999 and 2002, capital inflow to the European Union countries was equal to 23–42 percent of their GDP, and globally FDI constituted 15–20 percent of the world's aggregate GDP. In contrast, the inflow to Greece remained small.[19] Joining the European Community in 1981 "did not influence as positively as expected the FDI attractiveness" of the country; "[T]he weak economic environment kept the country away from the international developments with direct result to the attraction of FDI inflows."[20]

The lack of adequate industrialization, followed by actual de-industrialization, created an imbalance of trade with continual large deficits. Manufactured goods constituted a measly 13 percent of exports, almost the same as food and live animal exports (12 percent). By far, mineral fuels, including oil that had been imported and processed domestically, made up the biggest share of total exports (38 percent). Before the 2008 crisis, income from Greek exports was less than a third of what was spent on imports. In 2014, the country's exports totaled €27,188 million, but its imports cost €47,734 million. Indicative of this trade imbalance was the fact that the value of Greek exports was equal to 15 percent of GDP, which was far behind the EU's 48 percent. While the volume of Greece's exports is 65th in the world, the volume of its imports is 37th. The country's trade deficit has been mostly offset by services like tourism and shipping. But trade surpluses had never improved the country's financial situation.

What distinguishes Greece from other EU countries is its extreme deficiency in manufacturing. In the early twenty-first century, mining and manufacturing constituted less than 10 percent of the country's GDP. Altogether, industry made up only 17 percent, while two sectors, tourism and shipping, constituted (along with other services) 79 percent of the GDP. However, the most important shipping industry is not really integral part of the Greek economy. This sector does not pay taxes and employs very few Greeks, for most of its employees are from low-wage countries. Such a one-sided economic structure, in which the largest sector has few connections with the country's economy, is quite unique and has made the Greek economy exceptionally fragile.

Education

Another important factor is the backwardness of Greece's educational system. At the end of the twentieth century, no less than 56 percent of Greeks between the ages of 25 and 64 did not complete an upper secondary school education, while only 29 and 13 percent had completed upper secondary and tertiary levels, respectively. The structure of the Greek economy, with its predominant tourism and shipping industries, did not create the need for an educated populace. The figures did improve somewhat in the early twenty-first century, with 38 percent completing upper secondary school in 2009, and 24 percent receiving a tertiary education. Enrollment at colleges and universities increased from 32 to 47 percent at that time. But that had no impact on Greece's economic performance before the crisis. The paucity of well-educated citizens precluded the development of modern high-tech sectors. Greece continues to lag behind the OECD and EU in education, spending 3.5 percent of its GDP on education, while the EU-27's average is

5 percent. In 2007, its educational expenditures per student were only 71 percent those of the EU. In 2009, 47 percent of Greek 15-year-olds did not attain level 3 proficiency (out of 7 levels) in reading – one of the worst records in Europe.[21]

Failure of governance: uncontrolled spending

Joining the European Community and adopting the common currency led to a massive inflow of cheap credit to every euro-zone member state. The governments of countries with weak economies in the peripheries of Europe were able to sell government bonds at very low interest rates, only slightly higher than that of German government bonds, because the euro was considered an absolute guarantor for investors. The enormous inflow of cheap credit created a *mirage of affluence* in Greece, Ireland, Spain, and Portugal. Delusion abounded among untold numbers who "thought they were rich"[22] and started spending way beyond their means – precipitously buying real estate with deceptively inexpensive mortgages. In the span of one generation, a number of previously poor countries attained a higher proportion of home-ownership – around 70–80 percent – than that found in the United States (67 percent), or Western Europe (around 50 percent) or even wealthy Switzerland (44 percent). The spending spree was covered with credit, and old loans were paid off with new ones. The credit then dried up with the collapse of Lehman Brothers in 2008 and the world-wide liquidity crisis that followed. Seemingly overnight, indebtedness led to the collapse of creditor banks. Governments scrambled to bail out their banks, and consequently suffered their own indebtedness crises. A whole series of bailouts was needed to rescue bankrupt states such as Ireland, Spain, Portugal, and several others.

The Greek story, however, was much more complicated than that of the other peripheral countries. At around the turn of the millennium, private consumption in Greece accounted for 67 percent of GDP, while the euro-zone average was only 57 percent. By 2004, this relatively impoverished Balkan country had rapidly attained the same car-density (at 368 cars per 1,000) as found in Western Europe with nearly twice the income. Home-ownership rose to 76 percent. *The Economist,* recalling the previous decade in 2010, reported an "exuberant [Greek] consumer market, complete with smart cars, foreign travel and personal trainers." It referred to an "unprecedented consumer prosperity" based on cheap credit.[23]

This irresponsible profligacy, however, was not limited to household spending in Greece, as it was in Ireland and Spain. Partaking in this credit-based spending spree was the Greek government, leading to massive state indebtedness, and quite uniquely so in Europe. One of the main areas of public spending was *military outlays*.

Greece embarked on a mini arms race with Turkey,[24] a much larger country with a formidable army. During the 1960s and until the Cyprus crisis in 1974, several conflicts and near-war situations prompted the Greeks to gradually increase their military budget. The numbers show to what extent they did so: until 1966, Greece spent $200–300 million per year for its military; that number rose to $500–700 million per year between 1968 and 1974, to $1–1.5 billion per year between 1974 and 1977, and to $2.5 billion per year between 1978 and 1987.

In 2003, Greece's military budget was $8.5 billion; in 2008, $9.7 billion. Greece's relative military spending is larger than Turkey's: in 2002, Turkey's per capita military expenditure was $164; Greece's was $709. Between 1953 and 1974, military outlays consumed 4–5 percent of the country's GDP; after that date, it would rise to 6–7 percent. Greece's governments are among the world's largest arms purchasers: fifth in the world, acquiring 4 percent of the arms sold on the world market between 2005 and 2010. Top of their shopping list were various military aircraft including the Eurofighter Typhoon, one of the world's most advanced combat planes, the Mirage 2000, and the F-16C/D Fighting Falcons. Purchased as well were SA-15 Gauntlet systems, AH-64 gunships, and Hawk and SA-8 Gecko missiles. During the 1970s and 1980s, Greece's military expenditures made up 6.6 percent of its GDP, while the NATO countries' constituted 4.7 percent, Turkey's about 5 percent, and the United States' 5.9 percent.[25] According to experts, the country's major spending on arms purchases between 1980 and 2000 in an attempt to outdo Turkey played a major role in the dire straits the country fell into as the global financial crisis settled in.

Another principal area of government spending was the creation of an overly generous *welfare system* in post-1975 Greece. During the rule of the military junta, only members of the army and the police were eligible to receive welfare benefits, which were obviously problematic and needed to change. After democratization, and especially after Greece's membership in the European Community, societal demands definitely required expanding benefits. At the time when cutting welfare expenditures was central to welfare reform throughout Europe during the 1980s–90s, Greece – in a completely different historical situation – began to build up its welfare system. In 1980, Greece spent only 10.2 percent of its GDP on social expenditures, compared to the EU-15 countries' 24 percent. The country established a National Health Service, building new hospitals and health centers as part of a new institutional network. Healthcare expenditures increased from €4 billion in 1990 to €14.377 billion in 2006, constituting 23 percent of the GDP– almost the EU-15 average.

And yet, healthcare expenditures were only the second largest item in public spending. The country went beyond its means to develop its healthcare service; its new pension system bordered on the delusional. It was completely unsustainable for Greece's economy. The retirement age was *lowered* to 58 (!) for public employees, and was as low as 45 for certain occupations – nearly twenty years lower than most EU-15 countries. Allowing people early retirement in their forties was a common practice, especially for women and those employed in so-called "hazardous working conditions." Included among the latter were radio and television broadcasters, musicians playing wind-instruments, and hairdressers. As a result, 75 percent of Greek pensioners retired before the age of 61, and all could retire with full pensions after 35 years on the workforce. The average Greek pension contained 80 percent of the previous wage (compared to 46 percent in Germany). A generous two-month bonus was added to each pension every year. In the early 2000s, the government increased pension payments by 3 and 4 percent almost annually. Lacking any controls, it often continued paying pensions for people who had died. Administration of the pension system was chaotic and inefficient. Before the crisis, 133 separately administered sectoral pension funds operated in the country with 15,000 employees, which, according to some estimates, was twice the number needed. Because the pension system was so chaotic, the government lacked accurate statistics on how much it was actually spending. After the system's reorganization as one of the prerequisites of the bailout, 120 pension funds were shut down and pension payments began being managed in a transparent way. It was then that the government realized that much more was being spent than had been officially reported. In 2012, in compliance with the terms of the second bailout, the government imposed stronger controls and discontinued welfare and pension payments for 200,000 people, most of whom were not alive.

When Greece established its pension system, most of Europe was undertaking major pension reform. The one-pillar pension system (paid by the state) was transformed into a three-pillar regime, in which the first pillar (state-covered pensions) was reduced in significance, and the second (compulsory personal contributions) and third pillars (voluntary contributions) assumed the bulk of financing. Nevertheless, Greece maintained the one-pillar system when it inaugurated its pension plan, which predictably became a heavy burden on the state budget. No less than 66 percent of social spending went to public pensions – nearly 18 percent of the country's GDP, by far the highest in Europe.[26] As Manos Metsaganis noted, "social expenditures were allowed to spiral out of control."[27]

Greece's handling of the 2004 Olympic Games is a typical example of out-of-control government spending. Athens had been desperately eager to be awarded the centennial 1996 games to commemorate the anniversary of its hosting the first Olympic Games, and had somewhat arrogantly suggested in its application that it "had the right" to host them. But it lost out to Atlanta, GA. In 1997, Greece submitted a better-worded application and was selected to host the 2004 Olympics. But it did not begin planning for the games until 2000. The three-year delay forced Greece to undergo an exceedingly expensive rush job. Construction quickly commenced, and was not completed until two or three weeks before the opening ceremony in August 2004. Much of the work was commendable, and it led to a major modernization of Athens. The Greeks built stadiums and sports complexes close to the capital and in the towns of Faliro and Hellinico, and erected a massive Olympic Village and "Nerve Center" with 11,000 computers and 23,000 telephone lines. They modernized Athens' entire transportation system, constructing a new modern airport, new metro lines, new tram and light rail lines, and new toll motorways. Streets in the old parts of the city were transformed into attractive pedestrian walkways. The original budget for the project, €2.5 billion, quickly ballooned to €4.6 billion, with an additional €1.9 billion appended for transportation and other investments. But the government could not control spending, and real expenses neared €10 billion, 4 percent of the GDP. Most of the costs were covered by foreign loans. The modernization of Athens was useful but definitely not a profitable investment that could assist the country in financing debt repayment. The massive overspending served, to use John Kenneth Galbraith's term, as "symbolic modernization" so typical in some Third World countries.[28] Indeed, the country's public debt rapidly rose from €168 billion in 2004 to €262 billion.[29]

Inability to raise state income

Uncontrolled debt-financing of the government's expenditures led to an ever-increasing budgetary deficit and an accumulated mountain of debt. Budget deficits constituted nearly 14 percent of the GDP at the end of the first decade of the twenty-first century, while the accumulated public debt burden of €300 billion totaled 110 percent of GDP. By the mid-2010s, it had risen to 170–180 percent, the largest in Europe and second largest in the world. All these figures were several times above the compulsory EU norm of a maximum 3 percent budgetary deficit and a 60 percent debt burden compared to GDP.

As a consequence, the standard means of debt financing – issuing and selling government bonds – failed. Greece's credit rating by Standard & Poor was downgraded to A– in January 2009 and to BBB– that December, and Greek bonds were given a junk-rating the following spring. The government was thus forced to pay ever-rising interest rates. By the summer of 2011, the interest rate reached 27 percent, which assured that its debts would spiral out of control. The IMF, the European Central Bank, and the EU launched two major bailouts, similar to several others that had been offered in Europe, to save Greece from collapse. They issued €110 billion in bailout money in May 2010 to cover due repayments. In return, Greece was required to introduce major reforms to eliminate budget deficits and gradually consolidate the country's finances. Several other European countries had been able to turn things around with similar reforms. But the bailout did not have the desired effect in Greece because it government could not control and stabilize its finances. In May 2012, Greece was allotted a second bailout, a "first aid" of €130 billion. In addition to the austerity requirements to manage the financial situation, this time the creditors, mostly foreign banks, were mandated to accept a €107 billion loss (70 percent) on their bond investments.

Still, the bailout money did not end Greece's indebtedness crisis. One third of the bailout money was spent to bail out private creditors; another third financed Greece's current account deficit in the budget that had been mainly caused by trade imbalances; and the final third was used to offset the capital flight from the country.

By the summer of 2015, it became clear that the country had fallen into a new crisis and could not repay €1.5 billion to the IMF and €3.5 billion to the European Central Bank. After a series of unproductive talks with the new Syriza government, the creditor "Troika" were not reassured that Greece would, this time around, make financial order. The Greek government rejected the austerity prerequisites of the loan, and asked to write off a great part of the old debt as well as another €50 billion (or more) bailout. Thereupon the creditors opted not to throw good money after the bad and refused to issue the last €7.2 billion payment of the bailout.

One of the primary sources of state income in modern economies is tax collecting. Greece's taxation system, also unique in Europe, failed to produce the expected revenue. For one, the so-called *black economy,* which is a limited sector in advanced European countries, forms an unusually large part of the Greek economy. According to some assessments, it constitutes no less than a third of all economic activity in Greece. It goes without saying that revenues from the illegal black economy are not taxable. Another factor, partly related to this, is Greece's unique employment structure, which is almost never found in advanced econo-mies: one-third of employed Greeks are *self-employed,* compared to an average of 15 percent in the European Union. The self-employed are required to report their income and pay taxes accordingly. A recent study found that self-employed middle-class Greeks, such as medical doctors, restaurant owners, small-business entrepreneurs, and people renting out houses or rooms to tourists, reported an aver-age of €1,289 in monthly income and €1,057 in monthly debt payments. At times debt payments even exceeded monthly income in tax filings.[30] The Greeks' exceed-ingly low tax morale is probably the principal factor behind Greece's insolvency.

Tax evasion is considered to be a virtue and is ubiquitous throughout the country. This is hardly surprising, for it characterizes most of the Mediterranean and European peripheral countries, even the much more advanced Italy. In the Balkans, a lack of tax morale is certainly deeply rooted in history. The Ottomans' occupation of the region for half a millennium made tax evasion a patriotic act, a rebellion against foreign rule. It is well known that not a few Balkan farmers had fled agricultural lowlands and settled in the mountains (turning to animal husbandry) in order to escape from Ottoman tax collectors. Greece's govern-ments proved incapable of altering this situation. It is commonplace that shops in Greece offer lower prices if their customers agree not to ask for receipts. The state apparatus was totally ineffective in cracking down on tax evasion. Such ineffec-tiveness is a main characteristic of the Greek state bureaucracy in general. It pays to mention the case of land registration as a typical example. Only 7 percent of the country is adequately mapped. The only part of Greece with substantial land reg-istration is the Dodecanese Islands, an area that was under Italian administration between 1912 and 1945 and is still guided by Italian law. In the 1990s, the govern-ment asked for $100 million from the EU to complete land registration, but it has still not done so. Dimitris Kalondiotos, the newly appointed head of the National Land Registration Authority, remarked: "If you calculated the total deeds that are registered, the country would be twice as big as it is."[31]

Aside from chaotic and inefficient administration, *corruption* is another major factor in tax evasion. Government officials are usually bribed. Bureaucratic over-regulation uniquely characterizes Greece's regulatory system and is the hotbed of corruption. It typically takes more than four years to implement a commercial contract and establish a new company because it requires the per-mission of multiple ministries. According to the World Bank's "Easy to do business" rankings, Greece ranks 61st in the world, behind Rwanda and nearly all the European countries, except some successor states of the former Soviet Union. The way to "oil" the bureaucratic machinery is by bribing officials. As is usually the case in countries with widespread corruption, the price of bribes is virtually stable: about €1,400, for instance, "for services ranging from a tax

audit to a driver's license."[32] Corruption and cronyism penetrate the higher echelons of the public administration as well. George Papaconstantinou, Greece's
Finance Minister from 2009 to 2011, personally removed the names of three of
his relatives from the list of suspected tax evaders. According to the international
corruption perception index, Greece ranks 80th out of 185 countries – among the
worst in Europe. Former Prime Minister Papandreu acknowledged that "Greece
was riddled with corruption, which he claimed was the main reason for its economic woes." His Finance Minister added: "tax collection ... collapsed almost
totally" because of corruption.[33]

Two-thirds of the population, mostly employees with low income, pay their
taxes because they are deducted from their paychecks. But the third of the
population with higher income, the middle class and the very rich, does not.
Direct and indirect taxes would bring in an average of €50 billion a year, but
the state loses between €10 and 20 billion of that amount through tax evasion
and corruption. As Tryfon Alexiadis, the newly appointed deputy chief of the
tax collection office put it in 2015: "Even with a low estimate of the amount
lost – say €5 billion [instead of €10–20] a year . . . over the last 12 years, that
would make €60 billion." If tax collection worked, he concluded, "there would
be no debt problem."[34] The IMF fully agreed: "the country's debt crisis could be
largely resolved if the government just cracked down on tax evasion. Tax debts
in Greece are equal with about 90 percent of annual tax revenue, the highest
shortfall among industrialized nations, according to the OECD."[35]

The official tax rates, at least during the crisis years, were basically normal.
Those with low income pay 22 percent, and those in the highest category pay 42
percent. The corporate tax rate is 26 percent of revenues, and the capital gains tax
for individuals is 15 percent. The tax burden is 31 percent of the GDP, higher than
Ireland (28 percent), but much lower than the Netherlands (39 percent), Finland
(43 percent), France (44 percent), or Italy (43 percent). The real problem, however, is tax collection: while Germany collects an estimated 98 percent of taxable
income, and Spain the United States collect 85 percent, Greece managed to collect
only 62 percent in 2008 and 57 percent in 2010.

The huge deficits in tax collection are closely connected to the inefficiency,
corruption, and clientelism in the Greek government. Public offices regularly
employ more people than they need, many of whom are friends and relatives. In
Greece, 3.3 percent of the population is employed in the public sector. Although it
is not the highest in Europe, it is at least one-third higher than the EU-27 average
of 2.47 percent.

Statistics or fairy tales?

Indicative of the inefficiency and immorality of Greece's governments is the
unique fact that its statistical reports were often doctored to serve political interests. The most notorious case was the falsification of budgetary figures when
the country joined the euro-zone. Greece did not fulfill the EU's requirements
on budgetary deficits and indebtedness in order to join the common currency.

Prime Minister Costas Simitis lied to the EU and to his countrymen in a televised 2001 New Year's message, when he declared that Greece did in fact fulfill the prerequisites and could now join the euro to ensure "greater stability and open up new horizons."[36] A few years later, in November 2004, the international media reported the stunning news that the Greek government had admitted that "it has not actually met the qualifying standard to join the euro zone at all. Revised budget data show that the Greek budget deficit has never been below 3% since 1999 as European Union rules demanded."[37] A second major falsification came to light after the October 2009 elections, when Prime Minister George Papandreu announced that his predecessor had falsified the statistics about the Greek budget deficit, and that it was actually more than twice as much than what was reported, 13.6 percent of the GDP, and more than four times larger than what the EU rules allowed.[38] Another telling example was the government's report to the EU in 2000 about its military expenditures. The statistics indicated that they had spent 0.7 percent of the GDP on the military, but, in reality, it turned out to be 4.34 percent. A series of false declarations led the EU to demand in July 2015, as one of the requirements of the third bailout, that Greece create an agency independent of the government that would put out accurate and truthful statistics.

The third bailout: end game in the summer of 2015

All in all, because of its inability to govern, consecutive Greek governments were unable to cope with the crisis of 2008 and its consequences. The country needed an unprecedented third bailout in 2015. Will they, at last, put their financial affairs in order? Will they crush tax evasion and significantly increase state revenues? Will they end the expansion of the state bureaucracy and make it more efficient? Will they decrease military expenditures, reform the pension system and significantly cut government spending? Will the behavioral patterns and cultural norms of the government and the populace radically change? Only time will tell. These questions were clearly on the minds of the European Union's leaders when they imposed the harsh terms for their third bailout in the summer of 2015. Those terms were mostly drawn from the OECD's assessments of what needed to be done. As Spyros Xanthis, the owner of a Greek marine export company, aptly put it: "We've been asking for these changes for years, but they've never happened. It's a pity the creditors are now dictating something that we should have done ourselves."[39]

The six months leading to the final agreement were painful, bumpy, ugly, and disappointing for both sides. The process started in January 2015, when a deeply disappointed and desperate Greek population, fed up, impoverished, and exhausted from five years of stringent austerity measures, unemployment, and wage and pension cuts, voted for a newly formed left-wing party, Syriza, that promised an end of the austerity regime. The new Prime Minister, Alexis Tsipras, and his Finance Minister, Yanis Varoufakis, launched a frontal offensive against the EU and especially Germany, accusing them of trying to destroy Greece, enslave its population, and push millions of Greeks into poverty by forcing a counterproductive austerity regime on the country, which was only serving the capitalist interests of the creditors. They persistently demanded that Greece be allowed to write off a major part of its debt and that the creditors be burdened with the losses.

In his first speech to Parliament after forming his government, Prime Minister Tsipras announced that his government was demanding €278.7 billion in compensation from Germany for Nazi atrocities in Greece during World War II. This figure was somewhat larger than Greece's debt to Germany and the other creditors. Tsipras stressed several times that German war crimes were "open wounds" in his country, and that Germany had the "moral obligation" to pay. Nikos Paraskevopoulos, the Greek Minister of Justice, even prepared a legal brief asking the courts to seize German property in Greece and 8,500 Greek archeological treasures in Germany if the Germans did not comply.[40] These demands hardly fazed the Germans, however, because they had no legal basis.[41] The Syriza government issued one diatribe after another blaming Germany and the EU for Greece's plight. The Greek media published cartoons of Chancellor Angela Merkel in Nazi uniform and donning a Hitler mustache, and of Germany's Finance Minister Wolfgang Schäuble, also in Nazi uniform, shouting: "We will make soap from your fat." The Greek leaders were convinced that the Eurozone countries would pay handily to prevent Greece's exit and to protect the common currency. They misunderstood Angela Merkel's remark that the failure of the euro is the failure of the EU. They were brashly confident that they were playing a winning card. At several meetings with his European colleagues, Finance Minister Yanis Varoufakis lectured his colleagues about what they ought to do but said nothing about what his government would do. Prime Minister Tsipras visited President Putin of Russia, conveying to the EU that he would reorient toward the Russians if the EU turned its back on Greece. He also travelled to Italy and began hammering out an anti-austerity bloc with bailed-out euro-zone countries that were also bristling from austerity requirements. This attempt to counterbalance the EU leadership with a bloc of anti-austerity countries, however, also failed. Nevertheless, the recent elections in Portugal and Spain led to the collapse of governments that had obediently followed the EU's austerity requirements. Membership in mainstream political parties is sharply decreasing throughout Europe. According to a research team of Leiden University in the Netherlands, the "mainstream parties in France, Italy and Britain have lost about two-thirds of their members since the 1990s."[42] If this trend continues, it may spell the end to the prevailing European policy on the debt crisis.

However, Greece remained isolated in the spring and summer of 2015 and continued to act out in desperation. In June 2015, several weeks before its failure to repay the IMF in July, the Greek leaders refused to cut pensions and government spending any further, as required by the euro-zone leaders, and declared that it would cover expenditures only by increasing taxes. They rejected the EU's new bailout offer and halted negotiations. Tsipras called for a referendum on the bailout's terms, asking Greeks to say *oxi* ("no") to the EU. *Oxi* had clear historical connotations of Greece's past rejections of its adversaries' ultimatums.

Indeed, Syriza won a decisive victory with more than 60 percent of "no" votes. They believed, and they assured their supporters, that the vote would strengthen the government's position in talks with the euro-zone leaders.

These were serious miscalculations. Greece's strategy alienated most of the creditors and euro-zone officials. It also destroyed all *trust* that the Greek government would honor any agreement. Instead of forming an anti-austerity block, all of the former bailed-out countries turned against Greece's call for special treatment and stressed that they, unlike Greece, did not need Brussels to solve their problems but could do so themselves. Impoverished neighbors and post-communist countries, such as Bulgaria, Slovakia, and the Baltic states, grew hostile towards Greece, decrying that their average pensions were only a third the size of the Greeks', but that they still managed to abide by the EU's rules, carry out the required austerity measures, and avoid additional bailouts.

When the Greek government realized how badly it had miscalculated, it reversed course, capitulated, and agreed to bailout terms that were more stringent and humiliating than the ones the referendum had rejected a week before. The Greek Parliament voted 229 to 64 to accept an initial package of new terms and agreed to a second and third package as well. One of the most humiliating requirements of the new offer was the creation of a new trust fund, probably in Luxembourg, managed by Greece, with €50 billion of Greek assets that would serve as an asset-based mechanism for paying off parts of the loan. At the same time, the Greek parliament was forced to adopt laws to reform key parts of its economy, including the streamlining of the pension system and the boosting of tax revenue (especially with a VAT), before the EU money would begin flowing into Greece. A clear indication of the lack of trust was the stipulation that the European Central Bank, the euro-zone finance ministers, and the IMF would closely monitor Greek compliance with the bailout's conditions. This was a new European ultimatum. The creditors also used the weapon of delaying (or rejecting if needed) parts of the bailout payment if their conditions were not met, as had indeed occurred in November 2015.

The Greek government's main request was to write off parts of its debt. They pointed to the London Agreement, signed by 26 countries in 1953, writing off half of Germany's debts. In the midst of the Cold War, the United States and its allies were in need of Germany's fast economic recovery, and thus wrote off German debt not as a humanitarian gesture but an out of cold political calculation. The Debt Agreement led to the rapid development of the German economy. Unfortunately for Greece, this was not the situation in 2015; nor was there any belief that Greece could create the necessary economic conditions for successful development. Hence, Greece's request was flatly refused, mainly by Germany, which had contributed some €50 billion to the second bailout. Acceding to the Greeks, they argued, would be a slap in the face for bailed-out countries such as Ireland, Spain, Portugal, and others. Furthermore, the second bailout required the approval of various parliaments, including the German, because this time it was mostly governments, and not private banks, that were providing 60 percent of the credit from their taxpayers' money. The parliaments were in no mood for munificence.

The Greek government's main request, a significant decrease in Greece's debt burden, was, during the last phase of the "end game," supported by the IMF in a 1,184-word memorandum. Greek indebtedness of €310 billion, the IMF concluded, was simply not sustainable. In fact, the IMF argued that a debt generally above 110 percent of the GDP is not sustainable. All the experts were aware of this. Latvia' president, Andris Berzins, concurred: "Greece's debt is so great," he declared, "that everyone understands – it will not pay."[43] The IMF had proffered this "Emperor Has No Clothes" moment when it proposed to extend to Greece major debt relief or a three-decade repayment holiday.[44] Actually, the IMF had made it clear that keeping the euro-zone intact meant that the wealthy countries had to subsidize the poorer ones, and that Europe had to move toward a fiscal union. But the Greek crisis quashed any appetite for such an outcome.

Europe did not accept the IMF's argument. One can only guess whether, in late 2015, Europe's leaders had fully agreed about the unsustainability of Greece's debt burdens, but had wanted nonetheless to force the Greeks to carry out the required reforms, cut spending, increase state revenue, and abide by the rules of the European game. In other words, the EU is seeking to forcibly change Greece. Other options, like rescheduling repayments with low interest rates, had already been accepted. If one can be so bold as to predict the EU's future actions, when the dust of the controversies has finally settled, and when Greece has finally complied and put its financial affairs in order, the unavoidable debt forgiveness would probably follow. Until that time, the "European IMF," the fund that assists the Union's crisis-ridden countries, will provide an umbrella of €86 billion for three years to keep Greece solvent and assure its ability to repay. No doubt, the third bailout has not solved the crisis. About €25 billion will go to rescue the Greek banks that had lost most of their deposits. No less than €40 billion had been withdrawn from those banks between December 2014 and July 2015. The rest of the bailout money will serve debt and interest payments. This is fairly similar to the previous bailouts, when 90 percent of the bailout money served the same goals.

Greece's government had lied about its financial situation in order to join the euro-zone. It has never been able to abide by the rules and requirements for members of the monetary union. Would it have been better for Greece to have left the euro-zone as Germany's finance minister Schäuble and several economists implied? A majority of Greek citizens and politicians rejected such a solution, and political considerations precluded it as well. Of course, the fundamental changes that the terms of the third bailout require provide Greece the opportunity to reorganize itself into a functioning modern state with an efficient economy. This depends on the political will and ability of Alexis Tsipras' old-new government, reelected in September of 2015, to eradicate corruption, clientelism, tax evasion, and other major impediments, and to create an efficient state administration, a functioning pension system, and a sensible economic policy that will develop industry and increase exports. The new Tsipras government has promised all of this. The EU can help determine the outcome by continuing to condition future bailout funds to Greek compliance. Will the Greek government deliver? This is an open question. Mr. Tsipras and much of his party have turned away from leftism.

A testament to this is his spending the summer of 2015 at a Greek ship-owner's seaside villa and his commuting to work each day by helicopter[45] – still without a tie. He has had to endure rampant disappointment, mass demonstrations, and even a general strike in late 2015. Will he deliver? One cannot exclude the possibility of a continuing debt crisis and economic collapse in the coming years. The IMF,

> ever skeptical of Greece's capacity to keep a lid on spending and to increase taxes over the years … project that the debt will approach 300 percent of GDP by 2060 … Greece would never be able to pay back such a tremendous amount of debt.[46]

The Greek crisis threw sharp light on the exaggerated enlargement process of the European Union, which led to its accepting countries with weak economies and cultural-behavioral backgrounds rather different from the Western cores. Greece and several other bailed-out states were all peripheral countries that had been accepted between the 1980s and 2000s for political reasons and in line with corporate economic interests. This expansion, of course, had a compelling rationale, in that it was seen to stabilize peace and economic cooperation, and enhance competitiveness, in Europe. However, in light of the 2008 crisis and its enduring impact, and particularly in light of the unique Greek crisis, one might also see the EU's and euro-zone's over-enlargement as a suicidal misstep that endangers the future of European integration (discussed in Chapter 5).

Notes

1 *Financial Times*, June 30, 2015. Yannis Palaiologos, "Syriza is not Greece."
2 *Archive of European Integration,* aei.pitt.edu, Bruegel Working Paper 2015/03, Ashoka Mody, "Living (Dangerously) Without a Fiscal Union."
3 *The New York Times,* July 30, 2015, "How the German Approach Prevailed in the Greek Bailout."
4 *Archive of European Integration*, aei.pitt.edu, CEPS Commentary, Daniel Gros, The Greek austerity myth, February 10, 2015.
5 *The Economist,* September 12, 2015, "Prudence and Profligacy, Austerity is Hard to Measure but, by Any Reckoning, Europe's Periphery Has Purged."
6 *The New York Times,* August 16, 2015, "The Greek Debt Deal's Missing Piece."
7 *The New York Times,* July 24, 2015. "Personalities Clashing over New Greek Bailout."
8 Adam Davidson, *The New York Times Magazine,* August 2, 2015, "Rather than Condemn Greece for its Unwise Borrowing, We Should Worry About Why Our Economic System Refuses to Punish Unwise Landing," 14–17.
9 An exceptional case was Iceland where the entire tragic crisis was caused by three major gambling banks. The new government let them collapse, burdened the bad investors, and created state-owned banks to recover from the crisis. They even imprisoned responsible bankers and politicians. Iceland, a very small and rich island country had successfully coped with the crisis in its unique way. Could the Icelandic way be used as a general solution? The capitalist system should be reformed for that.
10 *Project Syndicate,* June 29, 2015, Joseph Stiglitz, "Europe's Attack on Greek Democracy."
11 Joseph Stiglitz, "Greece, the Sacrificial Lamb. The conditions imposed on the country make it a kind of debtors' prison," *The New York Times,* July 26, 2015.

12 *The New York Times*, June 29, 2015, Paul Krugman, "Greece Over the Brink."
13 *The New York Times*, June 12, 2015, "Greece, a Financial Zombie State."
14 *Le Monde,* May 31, 2015, "Europe at a Crossroads."
15 *The New York Times,* July 4, 2015, Nikos Konstandaras, "Greece's Sorry reckoning."
16 *The Guardian,* July 10, 2015, Yanis Varoufakis, "Germany Won't Spare Greek Pain – It Has an Interest in Breaking Us."
17 *Archive of European Integration*, aei.pitt.edu, CEPS Commentary, Daniel Gros, "Why Greece is Different," May 22, 2015.
18 Based on Angus Maddison, *Monitoring the World Economy 1820–1992,* Paris: OECD, 1995; The Economist, *Pocket World in Figures,* London: Profile Books; *Eurostat Yearbooks, Europe in Figures,* Luxembourg: European Union. Important to note that the official statistics of the European Union, the Eurostat, marks an 83 percent level in 1999, and 93 percent by 2008 compared to the EU-27 countries average in purchasing parity prices.
19 IMF Index Mundi, International Financial Statistics and Balance of Payment Database (www.indexmundi.com>countries>Greece)
20 Aikaterini Kokkinou and Ioannis Psycharis, *Foreign Direct Investment, Regional Incentives and Regional Attractiveness in Greece,* Discussion Paper Series, 10(11), 283–316 (www.prd.uth.gr/uploads/discussion_papers/2004/uth-prd-dp-2004-11_en.pdf).
21 *Eurostat 2011,* 211, 218; Education at a Glance, 2011. *OECD Indicators Country Note –Greece* (http://www.oecd.org/edu/skills-beyond-school/48657344.pdf).
22 *World Property Journal,* September 29, 2010 (www.worldpropertyjournal.com/real-estate-listings/)
23 *The Economist,* May 8–14, 2010, 51–52.
24 See: Christos G. Kollias, "Greece and Turkey: The case study of an arms race from the Greek perspective," *Spoudai,* University of Pireus, Vol. 41, No.1, 69, 75, 76; Nadir Öcal and Jüldine Yildirim, "Arms Race Between Turkey and Greece: A threshold cointegration analysis," *Defence and Peace Economies,* Vol. 20, No. 2, April 2009, 123–129.
25 https:www.defensetalk.com/forums/air-force-aviation/arms-race-greece-turkey-4225
26 World Bank 6th Global Pension and Savings conference, April 2–3, 2014, George Symeonidis, Hellenic Actuarial Authority. The Greek Pension System, (siteresources.worldbank.org/FINANCIALSECTOR/Resources/GreekPublicPensionSystem_GeorgeSymeonidis_Pension2014.pdf); *The Guardian,* June 15, 2015, "Unsustainable Futures?" *Wall Street Journal,* February 27, 2015, "Greece's Pension System isn't that Generous Afterall"; (www.businessinsider.com/greece-germany-pensions-2010-4); John Nic Yfantopoulos, "The Welfare State in Greece" (www.minpress.gr/minpress/__outgreece_welfare_state.pdf).
27 Manos Matsaganis, "The Welfare State and the Crisis: The case of Greece," *Journal of European Social Policy,* Vol. 21, No. 5, 2011, 501–512.
28 John Kenneth Galbraith comments:

> In the less developed lands the simple goal of an expanding production … is not satisfactory guide …. Leaders have always known the importance of the concrete and visible expression of national being …. These include a decently glittering airport … impressive buildings … multi-lane highways.

("Economics, Peace, and Laughter," in *The Essential Galbraith* (New York: Houghton Mifflin, 2001), 111–112.)
29 Simon Nixon, "Will Greece be an Olympic Winner? October 31, 2005 (moneyweek.com/will-greece-be-an-olympic-winner/).
30 Business-insider, February 15, 2015 (www.businessinsider.com/this-is-the-real-reason-greece-has-a-massive-tax-evasion-problem-2015-2?r=US&IR=T).

31 *The New York Times,* May 13, 2013, "Who Owns This Land? In Greece, Who Knows?"
32 *The New York Times,* July 20, 2015. "Critics Fear Greek Pact's Overhaul."
33 *The Economist,* November 21–27, 2009, 53, 89.
34 *The Guardian,* February 24, 2015, "Greece Struggles to Address its Tax Evasion Problem."
35 *The Wall Street Journal,* February 25, 2015, "Greece Struggles to Get Citizens to Pay Their Taxes."
36 BBC News, January 1, 2001, (news.bbc.co.uk/business/1095783.stm)
37 *The Guardian,* June 21, 2011.
38 *The New York Times,* October 24, 2011.
39 *The New York Times,* July 20, 2015. "Critics Fear Greek Pact's Overhaul."
40 *The Guardian,* March 12 and April 8, 2015.
41 In 1960, Germany paid, and Greece accepted, 115 million D-marks as war crime compensation. When Greece signed the "Treaty on the Final Settlement with Respect to Germany" (also known as the 2+4 Treaty) in 1990, it did not require further compensation, and the case was closed.
42 *The New York Times,* December 23, 2015, "Election Results in Spain Cap a Bitter Year for Leaders in Europe."
43 *The New York Times,* July 24, 2015, "Personalities Clashing Over New Greek Bailout."
44 *The New York Times,* July 16, 2015. "What the I.M.F. is Telling Europe: The Eurozone Won't Work Like This."
45 *The Economist,* September 26, 2015, "Greece's Elections. The Prime Minister Pivots Away from Leftism, and His Party Follows."
46 *The New York Times,* April 18, 2016, "Rising Signs of Strife as Parties Quarrel Over Greek Debt Restructuring."

4 Dangerous demography
Lack of reproduction

Although there had been indications of this earlier, Europe underwent dramatic changes in demographic development beginning in the last third of the twentieth century. For the first time in two thousand years, Europe's population stopped growing. Its populace was not reproducing itself, had started aging, and was decreasing in numbers. Of course, population growth always underwent lengthy cycles and multifarious stages throughout European history. Let's take a bird's-eye view of it.

Demographic background – until the late eighteenth century

Demographic trends exhibited consistent characteristics in the first millennium in Europe. Very high birth rates (about 30–40/1,000 people) were counterbalanced by almost similarly high death rates (35–36/1,000). The latter was partly caused by very high infant mortality: one-half of the newborn children died in the first year of life. Life expectancy at birth was very low. The population of Europe stagnated during the first millennium at around 32–38 million. Population growth remained very slow in the second millennium as well until the mid-eighteenth century, when it slowly increased by 0.5 percent per year. Life expectancy at birth remained stagnant at about 25–26 years from Roman times until the late eighteenth century in Europe.

The famous British clergyman and scholar, Thomas Malthus, presented the first scholarly analysis of population growth in his 1798 book, *An Essay of the Principle of Population.*[1] His main thesis, often called the "Malthusian check," explained population stagnation as a consequence of the different growth trends of populations compared to food production. While the potential of population growth, Malthus explained, had a geometric increase (1–2–4–8), food production grew at only an arithmetic rate (1–2–3–4). The only way to increase food production was to expand the amount of cultivated land, but that, too, had strict limitations. This could only happen by including less fertile, more marginal lands that decreased productivity. Consequently, the lack of adequate food production resulted in repeated famines that decimated whole populations and, in the long run, slowed down population growth. Indeed, famines reappeared in medieval and early modern Europe with regular frequency. Annals recorded no fewer than

89 famines in France between the tenth and eighteenth centuries. This was also the case in less developed peripheral regions during the eighteenth and nineteenth centuries. Ireland experienced repeated failures of its most important food staple, the potato crop, in 1740–41, 1799–1800, 1816–17, 1819, 1836, most tragically in 1845–48, and continuing as late as 1851 and 1879. The mid-century Irish food crisis killed more than one million people, and it pushed another million to emigrate. Before the food crisis, Ireland could claim 8.2 million inhabitants; in 1911, however, there was only half the population than there was in 1841.[2] Spain and Russia suffered similar fates during the nineteenth century. One of the last great famines in Finland in 1866–68 killed 8 percent of the population.

In addition to famine, there were frequent wars (half of the last 400 years, altogether 200 years were devastated by catastrophic warfare until the twentieth century in Europe). In addition, the so-called medieval diseases (cholera, typhus, plague, and smallpox) basically killed half of all people infected, and thus contributed as well to the check of population growth.

Demographic revolution in the nineteenth century

Nevertheless, when Malthus published his book at the end of the eighteenth century, dramatic changes were already underway that led to new patterns of population growth. This had first started in two countries, the Netherlands and Britain. For the first time in history, these two countries more than doubled their population (rising by 225 percent) between 1700 and 1820. This trend accelerated during the nineteenth century up through 1913, with Britain quadrupling and the Netherlands roughly trebling their populations. This development was duplicated throughout Europe during the nineteenth century. Hence, Europe inaugurated a genuine "demographic revolution," to use the term the French demographer Adolphe Landry coined in his influential *La revolution démographique* in 1934.[3] Europe's population increased by 360 percent between 1800 and 1910.

The principal factor behind this change was the tremendous advance of knowledge and innovation. First among these historical advances was an agricultural revolution that began first in the Netherlands and then quite vigorously in Britain in the eighteenth century, and then mushroomed across Europe during the nineteenth. One of its core elements was the invention of the three-rotation system, which increased cultivated land by at least a third and as much as one-half by replacing the one- or two-rotation regimes and thus enabling a half or a third of the uncultivated land to recover.[4] Within a short time, more modern, scientifically based rotation systems (such as the British Norfolk rotation of 14 kinds of crops) decisively contributed to the growth of output. The use of manure and then artificial fertilizers raised productivity to an impressive degree, as did the mechanization of cultivation. Horse-driven sowing, harvesting machinery, the steam thresher, and, in the early twentieth century, the tractor all signaled an ongoing agricultural revolution. Stall-feed animal husbandry became possible thanks to the modern rotation system and the production of fodder, and it quickly replaced traditional grazing. This led to a dramatic change: in several regions, farmers were now able to keep their animals alive during the winter and early spring when grazing was impossible, whereas before they regularly had to slaughter sometimes half their stock. This innovation led to the rapid increase of cattle and other animal populations. These revolutionary changes eliminated the Malthusian check by increasing the productivity and output of land cultivation by several times.

A miraculous scientific development, a series of discoveries and inventions, vaccinations, and modern hygiene, all eliminated medieval diseases and dramatically decreased infant mortality. Death rates dropped to half (14–16/1,000 people). True, birth rates also fell (to 25–26 births/1,000 people) in the modern industrialized and more urbanized Western Europe, where families lived in small and overcrowded apartments and women worked long hours outside the home. But the net result was rapid population growth.

Once it had begun in Europe's advanced core countries, rapid population growth would quickly follow in the continent's less developed peripheries as well. But the reasons for rapid population growth in the industrializing-urbanizing core were quite different from those in the still rural-agricultural peripheries. In the latter, "medieval" birth rates continued to soar while death rates declined thanks to medical advances, though they fell not nearly as sharply as they had in the West. Life expectancy increased significantly and roughly doubled to 46–50 years in the West by World War I.

Europe continued to advance demographically in the twentieth century, albeit at a slower rate. Thanks to the "therapeutic revolution," improved health care, and the rise of welfare states, death rates dropped to 10 deaths/1,000 inhabitants, infant mortality fell to 8–10/1,000, and life expectancy rose to about 75 years by the 1970s. Although its yearly growth decreased to 0.6–0.8 percent per year in Western and Eastern Europe, respectively, Europe's population continued to increase: from 226 million in 1820, to 432 million in 1900, and then to 604 million by 1960.[5]

U-turn in population development in the late twentieth century

Beginning in the last third of the twentieth century, yet another dramatic change transformed Europe's demographic development. Once the cradle of the demographic revolution, the continent now experienced the world's first demographic "counter-revolution." While the world's population continued to increase from 3,023 million in 1960 to 6,909 million by 2010, thus more than doubling (increasing by 229 percent) in half a century, Europe's natural population increase halted. Compared to their more than 2 births per woman in 1960, the EU-27 countries could claim only 1.56 births by 2010; thus their birth rate had dropped to below the reproduction level of 2.1 children per family. The proportion of young people in their population dropped from 20 to 14 percent between 1990 and 2010. Rapid aging began to characterize European society. Life expectancy rose to about 80 years in Western Europe and to 75 years in the less developed European regions. The proportion of Europe's population that was older than 65 jumped from less than 14 to 26–30 percent. This was in a sharp contrast to the world's average of less than 12 percent. The working-age population declined from almost 67 to 56 percent in Europe.

A demographic crisis is in the making. The Austrian Academy of Sciences ominously warned that, if population trends remain unchanged in the coming decades, the proportion of the elderly in the population will attain unsustainable levels. In 2007, the ratio of working-age Europeans (15–64 years old) supporting one person in retirement (65 or older) was 25.2, thus roughly 4 working-age Europeans supporting one elderly person. By 2030, the ratio will be 40.2, and by 2050, 56.3; in the advanced former EU-15 countries, it will climb to 57.3, i.e., less than two supporting one elderly person.[6] According to Europop2013, a Eurostat forecast until 2080, the fertility rate will remain basically unchanged and mortality rate will continue declining. Aging of the population thus will accelerate. While the average age of the population was 30–35 years in 1960, 40–42 years in 2010, it will be 43–48 years by 2060.[7]

This demographic trend prevails across Europe, though certain regions are more endangered than others. This is quite natural. However, it is surprising that the trend is most egregious not in the most developed regions, but in one of Europe's peripheries. According to the United Nations' World Population Prospects, the ten countries in the world that can expect the largest population loss are all Central and East European countries, led by Bulgaria. Between 1990 and 2015, Bulgaria lost 1.8 million people, including nearly 600,000 over the last decade. The country's population plummeted from 9 million to 7.2 million. If the demographic trend does not change, Bulgaria will lose 12 percent of its population by 2030, and 28 percent by 2050. Romania and Ukraine will lose 22 percent of their populations by 2050, Moldova, Latvia and Bosnia nearly 20 percent, and Lithuania, Serbia, Croatia and Hungary 16–17 percent. About two-thirds of these losses are the result of sharply declining birth rates, and one-third by continued emigration.[8] While virtually ending in the West, emigration continues unabated in Central and Eastern Europe, where disappointment in the post-communist transformation and quixotic expectations of a better life generate perpetual migration of the young and particularly the more educated. For instance, Bulgarians "in general are just frustrated with the political situation," one journalist reported.

> They cannot rely on the judicial system. Their leaders lack any sort of political vision. They have been waiting since 1989, and they are tired of waiting for this change to happen .... These days, close to 80 percent of the medical class leaves after graduation. People feel that life is too unpredictable here.[9]

This sentiment is common in the region as a whole. Ever since the Schengen agreement opened the borders with the European Union member countries, large numbers are moving to the West. According to a Gallup Poll, some 36 million East–Central Europeans wish to move to Western Europe (see Chapter 6).

Throughout modern European history, non-democratic regimes (Italian Fascism, German Nazism, and East European communism) banned abortion and other forms of birth control. Benito Mussolini launched a program to increase

Italy's population from 40 million to 60 million. Hitler rewarded mothers who had several children, and communist regimes criminalized abortions and imprisoned doctors who illegally performed them. Even the most draconian measures, however, resulted in only temporary increases in birth-rates that were quickly reversed after a few years. Nothing could change the general demographic trends.

Causes of natural decline of population

What caused this dramatic and seemingly permanent demographic downturn? Among a multitude of factors, the changes in Europe's social structure certainly contributed. After the industrial revolution and Europe's rapid industrialization during the nineteenth and twentieth centuries, the industrial countries on the continent became rapidly urbanized. The social structure of those countries changed dramatically; its rural populations gradually disappeared; and, in the end, three-quarters of Europeans moved to urban centers. This proportion today surpasses 80 percent in the most advanced northwest regions, but totals a good 70 percent in the southern and eastern parts of Europe as well. As is well known, this social structure has an adverse effect on birth rates, for urban residents have fewer children and smaller families.

A byproduct of urbanization, the changing family structure is another factor of Europe's demographic decline. During the nineteenth century, the so-called nuclear family, comprising two parents and their children, predominated. This replaced the stem or extended family, in which three generations, including the siblings' families, often numbering 30 or 40 people, lived together under one roof. The extended family was standard for agricultural-rural societies, but it was supplanted by the nuclear family after the industrial revolution in Europe beginning in the eighteenth century. As most urban adults lived in small apartments and were employed outside the home, it was perhaps inevitable that urban Europeans would wish to have fewer children than did rural ones.

Economic progress should also be mentioned. This was seen already during the last third of the nineteenth century, when income levels began to rise. In the twentieth century, a relatively large well-to-do middle class emerged. Family incomes dramatically increased in the second half of the twentieth century, partly by economic advance, and partly by political motivations, generated by Cold War competition. While Europeans, even in affluent countries like Switzerland, spent nearly 60 percent of their income on basics like food and accommodation until the early twentieth century, they spent only 10–15 percent on them thereafter. Instead, they have spent most of their money on their health and entertainment as well as for goods and services – all previously considered luxuries. Since World War II, the vast majority of Europeans have gradually embraced a fervent consumerism. The bulk of their income has been spent on purchasing homes and automobiles, on paying for their vacations and travel, and on their health and leisure. Vacations lasting more than a month, and overseas travel even to faraway continents, have all generated a more selfish conception of life for most of middle-class European society. Having more than one child is now considered a burden for many.

This was seen in Hungary in the 1960s and 1970s, where there arose a modest consumerism that paled in comparison with that in the West. A debate raged in the Hungarian media over whether it should be "*kicsi vagy kocsi?*" (a child or a car). For most Hungarians, the choice wasn't even close; they naturally chose the car.

Yet another factor in this transformation has been the role of women working outside the home in modern urban, industrial, and post-industrial societies. In the nineteenth century, it was considered a shameful stigma for a man not to be able to be his family's sole breadwinner. But that would soon change. In a number of countries the proportion of women in the working population increased from one-third to nearly one-half, and in some countries the proportion of women workers almost equaled their percentage of the population as a whole. This was the case in Scandinavia, the Baltic countries, and Russia. The Lisbon decision of the European Union in the early twenty-first century proposed attaining 60 percent female employment rates, though this has not yet been achieved in some peripheral countries.

Expanded education, including tertiary education with women participating in equal numbers, prevailed in Europe during the postwar half-century, and it has led women to delay getting married or having more children. Moreover, competing religious influences held less and less sway as Europeans became increasingly secular. Family planning became the norm as abortion was legitimized in most countries, and as modern "single pill" birth control became ubiquitous from the 1960s on.

The declining number of children was also connected with the decline of the family itself as the basic institution of society. The median age for getting married rose from 25–26 to 28–29 for both men and women, which definitely contributed to a decrease in fertility. The number of marriages itself sharply declined around the turn of the millennium, from 7.9/1,000 people to 4.9/1,000 between 1970 and 2010. In some countries such as Slovenia and Bulgaria, the marriage rate dropped to 3.2 and 3.4/1,000 respectively. As an average, single member "families" constituted nearly a third of all households. Births outside the marriage, hardly more than 17 percent in 1990, jumped to more than 37 percent by 2010. Meanwhile, the number of divorces have more than doubled, with between a third and a half of all marriages ending in divorce. These fragile and transitory family units naturally led to fewer child births.

Lack of reproduction – but still increasing population

All these factors have led to a birth rate that is below reproduction levels, and has presumably led to a drop in Europe's population. In reality, however, that did not happen. Population growth slowed down in the half-century between 1960 and 2010, but it still increased by one-fifth from 604 million to 733 million. Why? The answer is simple: massive immigration to Europe. That was an entirely new development, as Europe had always been a continent of emigration at least till the mid-twentieth century. A new age of immigration to Europe began after World War II when several advanced countries required guest workers to keep their economies going. After the collapse of colonialism, millions returned to Europe from Africa and Asia as well. Europe has become a continent of immigration since the second half of the twentieth century. By the second decade of the twenty-first century, 15–16 percent of the populations of several West European countries are immigrants. Mass immigration has created a serious crisis and some chaos during the 2010s (discussed in Chapter 9). The future of immigration in Europe is hardly foreseeable in the longer run. Nevertheless, if the demographic trend basically continues in the coming decades, both controlled immigration and longer working life are needed in Europe. Retirement age only partly changed in recent decades and is still around 65 years. Improved life and health conditions and extended life span make possible the increased involvement of people in the labor force between the ages of 65 and 74. Education may positively influence this trend since more educated people are working longer. Nowadays the average working life is 33–39 years. In the coming decades it may increase by 5–7 years.[10]

Notes

1 Thomas Robert Malthus, *An Essay of the Principle of Population* (London: J. Johnson, 1798).
2 The Vanishing Irish: Ireland's Population from the Great Famine to the Great War (www.historyireland.com/20th-century-contemporary-history/the-vanishing-irish-irelands-population-from-the-great-famine-to-the-great-war/).
3 *La révolution démographique. Études et essais sur les problèmes de la population* (Réédité à Paris, 1934).
4 Traditionally, for thousands of years, the one- or two-rotation system dominated: half, or one-third of the arable land remained fallow to recover and used for grazing animals.
5 Angus Maddison, *Monitoring the World Economy* (Paris: OECD, 1995); *The World Economy. A Millennial Perspective* (Paris: OECD, 2001); Fernand Braudel, *Civilisation matérielle, économie et capitalisme*, XVe–XVIIIe siècle, Vol. I (Paris: Colin, 1979).
6 Marija Mamolo and Sergei Scherbov, Population Projections for Forty-Four European Countries: The Ongoing Population Ageing (www.oeaw.ac.at/vid/download/edrp_2_09.pdf).
7 *Archive of European Integration*, CEPS Working Document, No. 417, February 24, 2016, Mikkel Barslund and Marten von Werder, "Measuring Aging and the Need for Longer Working Lives in the EU."
8 esa.un.org/wpp; *The New York Times,* October 2, 2015, "A Shrinking Eastern Europe Resists Migrants."
9 *The New York Times,* October 2, 2015, "A Shrinking Eastern Europe Resists Migrants."
10 See note 6.

5 Suicidal enlargement of the European Union?

The homogeneity of the "founding six"

The forerunners of the 28-member European Union were the European Coal and Steel Community (1952) and the European Economic Community (1957). Both had been established by six West European countries: France, Germany, Italy, Belgium, the Netherlands, and Luxembourg. These six countries had been on the same playing field economically, for all were highly industrialized and were very close in GDP. Minus the smallest and most affluent member, Luxembourg, the average per capita income level of the founding countries in 1957 was $12,234 (about 10 percent higher than the United States' $10,981); the richest (Germany) was only 7 percent higher, and the poorest (Italy) was 15 percent lower, than the average income. All these countries had somewhat similar cultural-historical backgrounds, hammered out by the Greek-Roman-Judeo-Christian, Renaissance, Enlightenment, and Romantic traditions. Some went through the Protestant revolution as well. All successfully industrialized during the nineteenth century and, after a great deal of political turbulence, emerged as strong pluralistic parliamentary democracies after the Second World War. These founding member countries, therefore, were Western states par excellence.

The postwar political elite of these six countries believed in the need of integration, and some of them strongly adhered to a federalist solution to avoid new wars and to combat isolationist economic nationalism, the means of economic warfare in peacetime that had prevailed between the two world wars. They resolved to bind their countries together because of the outbreak of the Cold War, the danger of a Third World War, and their forming a political-military alliance with the West's unquestioned world leader, the United States. The latter pushed its West European allies into a united community, a United States of Europe, as a condition for receiving American economic and military assistance.

American interest in the enlargement of the European Community

From the beginning of the integration process, the United States urged its European allies to expand the Community. Both the Truman and Eisenhower administrations pushed Britain to take the lead and initiate integration – all to naught because of British resistance and its refusal to join the Community. Britain retained Churchill's policy of focusing instead on nursing a special cross-Atlantic relationship with the "English speaking people" of the United States. Britain not only stayed out of the European Economic Community, but it hastened to establish a competitive free market alliance with European countries that were not members of the Community, forming the European Free Trade Association (EFTA) in 1960.

Until the 1960s, the US continually prodded Britain's governments to join the European Economic Community. Britain would ultimately relent because of the incomparable economic advantages of doing so, as well as the sobering realization that its colonial empire was disintegrating. After the Suez debacle in 1956, Britain grappled with the reality that it was no longer a great world power, but was a relatively small country with a sagging economy.

In the 1960s, Britain finally applied for membership. After being rebuffed on two occasions thanks to President Charles de Gaulle's vetoes, Britain formally joined the Community (together with its two close clients, Ireland and Denmark) only in 1973. Britain and Denmark were on par economically with the original six member states and thus strengthened the Community, but Ireland was the first peripheral country to join. She was not sufficiently industrialized, had an average per capita income level that was hardly more than half that of the Community, and was but a cheap source of labor for England, with whom she shared a troubled history. While Britain was in a much better position to integrate smoothly with the EU, her enduring self-image as a great world power and her detached island consciousness kept her, even after 1973, highly ambivalent about her Community membership (see Chapter 1).[1]

US pressure to incorporate the dictatorial countries of the Mediterranean

Britain's governments continually called for expanding the Community to incorporate other countries from Europe's peripheries and to make federalization more difficult. They were successful in sustaining American appeals for expansion from the inside. Consecutive American governments had called for an expansion of the European Community by incorporating more countries, virtually all of them anti-communist regimes and member states of NATO, the Western military alliance established in 1949. The logic of the Cold War required the largest possible anti-communist alliance inside Europe.

The US established military alliances with anti-communist dictatorships in Spain, Portugal, Greece, and Turkey during the 1950s and 1960s. Both Churchill and President Dwight Eisenhower agreed on the need to accept problematic dictatorships if they were anti-communist. In a speech about the North Atlantic Treaty Organization in May 1949, Churchill praised Franco's Spain for its services during the war and for giving "far greater freedom to the individual" than was accorded in Soviet Russia. Not having Spain in NATO, he suggested, would constitute "a serious gap in the strategic arrangements for Western Europe."[2] In 1960, President Eisenhower asserted that the Salazar dictatorship in Portugal is "something *necessary* in countries whose political institutions are not so far advanced as ours."[3] In the American view, integrating anti-communist countries into the European Community would strengthen NATO and enhance political cohesion among the members of the military alliance. President John F. Kennedy reiterated this traditional American concept: "*It is only a fully cohesive Europe that can protect us all against fragmentation of the alliance.*"[4] The Nixon administration also disregarded the human rights violations and anti-democratic policies of Mediterranean dictatorships.[5] The logic of the Cold War led the US to incorporate these right-wing dictatorships into the "Western world," and to seek to include them in the emerging European Economic Community.

"Cold War fears caused the western allies to support repressive regimes on the southern boundaries of 'free' Europe."[6] The US was determined to prevent "the Soviet Union from controlling Greece, which would deny the United States access to the strategically important Aegean and eastern Mediterranean seas and grant it to the Soviet Union."[7] The US signed the first defense cooperation agreement with Greece in 1953, enabling it to establish military installations in the country. The US pushed the European Community to start its own negotiations with Greece, which actually took place in the fall of 1959 and convened in March 1961. The European Community signed an agreement "based on customs union to be established . . . over a transition period and intended to enable Greece to become at a later day, when its economic progress allows, a full member of the Community."[8] The European Parliament expressed opposition during the period of negotiations, but the Community, "reacted half-heartedly and inconsistently to the political change in Greece" and the agreement was accomplished.[9]

In October 1947, the State Department modified its policy toward Franco's Spain, a political pariah in the Western world since 1939. In December, the National Security Council's "Report on US Policy toward Spain" made this reorientation official. Financial and military aid to Franco soon followed. The regime's isolation effectively ended: with US assistance, Spain was able to join the Organization of European Economic Co-operation (OEEC) in late 1950.[10] A September 1953 agreement between the two governments on establishing American military facilities in Spain included the following preamble:

> Faced with the danger that threatens the western world, the Governments of the United States and Spain, desiring to contribute to the maintenance of international peace and security through foresighted measures which will increase their capability and that of the other nations which dedicate their efforts to the same high purposes, to participate effectively in agreements for self-defense.[11]

The United States also included Turkey in its military defense strategy and prodded Europe to build a close alliance with the country. Although a number of West European democracies initially vetoed the idea, Turkey was allowed to become a NATO member after the Korean War. It joined NATO's Middle East Command in 1951 and the Balkan Pact with Greece and Yugoslavia (against potential Soviet aggression) in 1954. In March 1957, the US Congress formally accepted the "Eisenhower Doctrine" and agreed to the formation of the Central Eastern Treaty Organization (CENTO), with the participation of Turkey, Iran, and Pakistan. From that point on, Turkey served as a bridge between NATO and CENTO and became a major player in the Western Cold War policy in the Near East. This close connection was not adversely affected when the Turkish military staged a coup in May 1960.[12] As it did with Greece and Spain, the US called for the inclusion of Turkey into the European integration process.

Throughout the 1950s and 1960s, the most perilous years of the Cold War, the US maintained close military, political, and economic ties to the Mediterranean dictatorships and never stopped urging the European Economic Community to include those countries. A 2013 Congressional Research Service report noted:

> Successive U.S. Administrations and many members of Congress have long backed EU enlargement, believing that it serves U.S. interests by advancing democracy and economic prosperity throughout the European continent. Over the years, the only significant U.S. criticism of the EU's enlargement process has been that the Union was moving too slowly, especially with respect to Turkey, which Washington believes should be anchored firmly to Europe.[13]

At the core of the argument, another Congressional Research Service report emphasized, was Turkey's NATO membership:

> The United States believes that Turkey's membership in NATO has demonstrated that Turkey can interact constructively with an organization dominated by most of the same European countries that belong to the EU . . . . The US has been disappointed that it has not been able to use its influence to help shape a more constructive EU–Turkey relationship.[14]

American Cold War policy had a powerful influence on a highly dependent Europe. A year after the US–Spanish agreement, Helmut Burckhardt, the vice-president of the Consultative Committee of the European Coal and Steel Community, spoke of an expanded Community with "the eventual inclusion of Scandinavia, Spain, Portugal, and possibly Great Britain and Austria."[15] Turkey and Franco's Spain were encouraged to apply for membership, which they indeed did in 1959 and 1962, respectively. The Community, however, shelved these politically inconvenient applications for some time.

> Without much fanfare, however, the European Community signed a Preferential Commercial Agreement with Spain . . . with highly favorable terms. European tariffs were immediately and substantially reduced by 60 percent . . . . The goal was to establish completely free trade, and all

quantitative restrictions against Spanish exports were removed . . . Spain . . . [became] an 'external' member of the European Community.[16]

In 1963, Turkey and the EEC also signed the Ankara Agreement, an association agreement that initiated a process of building closer economic ties. In 1970 the agreement was supplemented by an Additional Protocol, which led to the creation of a customs union.

The Treaty of Rome (1957) stipulated that the Community "may conclude with one or more third countries . . . agreements establishing an association involving reciprocal rights and obligations."[17] Greece applied for such an association in 1959, and it signed an association partnership agreement with the Community in 1961– as did Turkey in 1963. Here was the enlargement of an integrating Europe that American Cold War policy envisioned, though it was in the *form of informal associations* and semi-concealed partnerships with Spain, Portugal, Greece, and Turkey. Greece, Portugal, and Spain became full members of the EEC in the 1980s. Although it had first applied in 1959, Turkey – not even a European country and ruled by a military dictatorship that kept its distance from European values and democratic arrangements – had to wait until 1999 to be recognized as an official candidate.[18]

With two stages of expansion in 1973 and the 1980s, and with association memberships granted to the above-mentioned countries, the Community lost the coherence that it had with its six founding members. A number of countries of the European peripheries, with less developed economies, now joined the Community. At the time of their acceptance in 1973 and the mid-1980s, these countries could muster per capita GDPs at the level of Ireland, Greece, Spain, and Portugal: no more than $9,000, only 60 percent of that of the Community of Six minus Luxembourg ($15,063). Turkey's GDP of $3,500 was not even a quarter of that of the EEC-6. The new Mediterranean member or associate countries, moreover, had only been recently freed from the yoke of dictatorial regimes, and were just beginning the long road of democratization. The cultural and behavioral patterns of these countries were also starkly different. This was especially the case in Greece, but even more so in Turkey.

1989 and enlargement toward the East

After 1989, the collapse of the Soviet Bloc provided a new opportunity to include additional countries in the Community, and a "big bang enlargement" of the EU soon took place. First to join were a number of neutral countries, such as Sweden, Austria, and Finland, that had historically avoided political affiliations, but who changed their minds after the Cold War ended and entered in 1995. All were advanced countries with an average per capita income of $16,400, virtually on the same level as the founding six. The inclusion of these three formerly neutral countries definitely strengthened the Community.

The collapse of communism cleared the way for further eastward expansion. As early as December 1989, even before those countries had applied, Chancellor

Helmut Kohl informed Secretary of State Baker that in the future "the Czechs as well as the Hungarians and Poles will join the European Community." Baker agreed and immediately underscored the "extraordinary role of the European Community in the entire process [of East European transformation]."[19] Kohl also maintained that they would encourage investment in the Soviet Union, Poland, Hungary, Bulgaria, and Romania.[20]

At the time of the collapse of communism, the six post-communist countries' average per capita income was hardly more than $6,000 – 36 percent of that of the twelve EU members. Nevertheless, a few months after the collapse of communism, the Dublin meeting of the European Council approved the outlines of association agreements with the former communist countries. Political dialogue began on economic, cultural, and financial cooperation, and the Union offered immediate financial assistance.[21] When the European Council met in Maastricht in December 1991, the Union had already signed the so-called Europe Agreement – a new version of earlier association agreements – with Poland, Hungary, and Czechoslovakia. In May 1992, negotiations on similar agreements began with Romania and Bulgaria, and somewhat later with Slovenia and the three Baltic states. At the Copenhagen Community meeting in 1993, the former communist countries were essentially invited to join:

> The associate countries in central and eastern Europe that so desire shall become members of the European Union . . . as soon as . . . [they have fulfilled] the obligations of membership by satisfying the economic and political conditions required.[22]

These countries were economically backward. In most cases, their per capita GDP throughout their modern history had never totaled more than half that of Western Europe. Even in 2004, when eight of these countries were brought into the Union, their average per capita income was just $9,240, which was more than double that of the two joining in 2007 (a mere $4,000) – in stark contrast to the Union's per capita average of $29,000. The former Soviet Bloc countries were also in difficult financial straits and suffered from 250 to 600 percent inflation, and in some cases 1,000 to 1,500 percent hyperinflation, between 1989 and 1993.[23] Almost all these countries were heavily indebted. Their aggregate debt burden increased from $6 billion in 1973 to $100 billion five years later. Poland, Yugoslavia, and Bulgaria were soon unable to repay and had to ask for rescheduling.[24] This sorrowful economic situation was combined with the lack of market economic structures and traditionally non-democratic political regimes. In other words, these countries had classic characteristics of non-Western economic, social, and political backwaters.

To help them along, the Copenhagen European Council drafted specific political and economic conditions for joining the Union in 1993. The following year, *acquis communautaire,* a thirty-one-chapter, nearly ten-thousand-page document specified the tasks to be completed before acceptance. Between 1994 and 1996, Hungary, Poland, Estonia, Latvia, Lithuania, Bulgaria, the Czech Republic, and Slovenia all applied for membership, and they began adjusting their political, economic, and legal systems to meet Union standards. The processes ended in 2004 and 2007, with ten former communist countries becoming members of the European Union.

Why was the European Union so ready to accept economically bankrupt countries that had stagnated with non-market, centrally planned economic systems and one-party, non-parliamentary political regimes? Why was the Union so eager to include countries that had rather different historical experiences and cultural backgrounds? Why was it so willing to risk diluting its relative homogeneity in order to embrace countries that had departed so markedly from the community's norms?[25]

As is well known, path-dependence is an important historical factor. It often resurfaces at later stages of development. Indeed, during the decades of post-communist transformation, authoritarian political tendencies again gained the upper hand in certain countries: with the Mečier government in Slovakia, the two Kaczynski regimes in Poland, the governments of Victor Punta and others in Romania, and Viktor Orbán's "illiberal democracy" in Hungary. These governments stood for limiting democracy and imposing strong state control on political and economic life, including the partial renationalization of previously privatized companies.[26]

As in peripheral countries everywhere in the world, the new Eastern European member nations were heavily burdened with a deeply rooted profusion of clientelism and corruption. Bulgaria, Romania, and even Greece proved unable to free their public sectors from corruption and criminality. Bulgaria, for one, stopped even trying to do so after being accepted into the EU. The Greek crisis exposed the country's profound corruption for all to see. The Corruption Perception Index of 2013 and 2015, which ranks the relative level of corruption of 177 (and 168) countries, clearly illustrates the problem. On a scale of which 100 indicates an absence of corruption, the Western European EU members all ranked above 70, with the Northern European countries deemed the least corrupt, at about 90. The Mediterranean and Central European countries ranked in the 50s – evidence of severe corruption. Several of them, including Italy, Romania, Bulgaria, and Greece, scored in the 40s, suggesting dangerous corruption. But the most egregious cases are the countries of the former Soviet Union, Russia, Belarus, Ukraine Tajikistan, Uzbekistan, and others, all ranking in the 20s. These countries are ranked at the 50th (Hungary and Slovakia), even 58th (Greece and Romania), or 69th (Bulgaria) places in the world. Their level of corruption is definitely not a European level.[27]

The World Bank also developed a corruption indicator. According to its findings, Europe represents two extremes. On one side of the spectrum stands the Nordic countries, which rank among the top twenty least corrupt countries of the world; on the other side are the Balkan countries, Croatia, Bulgaria, Greece, and Romania, ranked 90th, 101th, 103rd, and 104th among the world's most corrupt countries:

> [O]ffering a gift to a public employee … in Germany … is considered bribery, … while in … Bulgaria, it is in the line with long-standing traditions and practices […] [I]n Central-Eastern and South-Eastern Europe, corruption is far more pervasive and intricate because it is strongly rooted in a culture of particularism, where unequal treatment is the norm.[28]

Despite these stark differences, the EU has legitimate reasons for incorporating the region into the fold. First among them is maintaining the peace. The Balkans have traditionally been the "powder keg of Europe," and the civil war in Yugoslavia and the Kosovo crisis in the 1990s serve as ominous reminders of its explosive potential. The dissolution of the multinational states, and the creation of 29 independent countries out of the 8 that existed before 1989, also point to the dangers of conflict. This was soon demonstrated with the outbreak of hostilities in the former Yugoslavia, Moldova, Ukraine, and the Caucasus. Particularly menacing is Russia, a humiliated great power with a nuclear arsenal and an uncertain future. An EU-affiliated Central and Eastern Europe could and did serve as a calming influence, and could guarantee a measure of security for the West.

NATO, the corporate world – and the EU enlargement

Taking advantage of the situation, NATO rushed into the region along with the European Union. Just a few months after the collapse of communism, the countries of the region were invited to participate as associate members in NATO's Parliamentary Assembly. Then in 1997, Poland, Hungary, and the Czech Republic were invited to join NATO. Within a few years, the three former Baltic Soviet republics, now independent countries, along with Bulgaria, Romania, Slovenia, and Slovakia, were also invited to join. By 2004, the former Soviet Bloc became part of the Western military alliance simultaneous to its joining the European Union. Enlarging NATO was closely connected to expanding the EU, and was part of an ongoing process that began decades earlier.

In addition to political and military considerations, the inclusion of the eastern peripheries was definitely a central goal of the Western corporate world.[29] Immediately after the collapse of communism, multinational corporations began building up their affiliate networks in the region. Attracted by the low-wage environment, they established low-tech, medium-high-tech and even high-tech industries and created new export sectors. Leading West European banking institutions also rushed to the area. No less than 25 percent of international investment went to Central and Eastern European, while only 16 percent went to Asia. In 1990, only 10 percent of the region's financial capital was in foreign hands; by 2004, the figure was 87 percent. In the Czech Republic, Slovakia, and Estonia, it was a whopping 96–97 percent.[30] In the first decade and a half of the post-communist transformation, Central and Eastern Europe and the Baltic States received $204 billion FDI, equaling 3–5 percent of their GDP. This was a significantly larger amount in relative terms than the FDI the Mediterranean countries had received in the 1980s. Of that $204 billion, $135 billion went to the Czech Republic, Hungary, and Poland. Foreign multinational companies predominated in the region. In Hungary, foreign multinationals employed 47 percent of industrial employees and made 82 percent of the country's industrial investments, while producing 73 percent of all purchased goods and 89 percent of industrial exports. In Poland, they employed 29 percent of the workforce and produced 59 percent of the country's exports. In the Czech Republic, foreign companies were responsible for 27 percent of industrial employment, 61 percent of exports, and 53 percent of investments.[31] By 2003, the amount of direct foreign investment was equal to 49, 29, and 23 percent of the Croatian, Bulgarian, and Romanian GDPs, respectively.[32] In effect, the transforming countries had become low-wage producers for West European markets, a backwater of the European Union.

West European corporations were eager to exploit the tremendous wage differential between the West and the peripheral regions. Just after the collapse of communism, Central and Eastern European wages (on exchange-rate parity) were only 7 percent of Western wages, and were only 15 percent a decade later. In 1993, 70 percent of foreign investment targeted the labor-intensive consumer goods area in the Czech Republic; in 2002 it dropped to 16 percent. Western companies were beginning to exploit new resources, the well-trained cheap labor force in these relatively more advanced Central European countries. Companies began targeting medium-high-tech sectors, establishing new factories and even research and development (R&D) centers in areas no more than 500 kilometers from their Western headquarters.

The cost-reductions were substantial. With its Slovakian factories, for example, Volkswagen saved $1.8 billion on wages and related expenditures per year. After China, the fastest growing auto-making center in the world was Central Europe, which had received $24 billion in multinational investment; 20 percent of the West European car output was eventually shifted to the former communist countries. Ten leading multinationals owned 82 percent of the Central and East European auto industry. High-tech multinationals also entered the region.[33]

Tapping a population of more than 100 million for its labor and consumption potential brought vast profits to European corporations. Transporting labor-intensive branches of industry to a low-wage backwater, and significantly expanding service branches (including financial services) in that area, enabled the EU to rearrange its overall division of labor and cut its production costs. All this contributed to a restructuring of European corporations that was so urgently needed if they were to stay competitive in the fierce global market. It seemed obvious to the EU that countries offering such economic benefits ought to be incorporated organically into the Community, first by association and ultimately through full membership. Such incorporation offered the most reliable way to secure the EU's investments.

To put it another way, incorporating the post-Soviet countries rid Western Europe of its disadvantages in competing in the global economy. The EU's main rivals in that economy, the United States and Japan, had their own backwaters in Latin America and Asia. Prior to 1989, Western Europe had nothing of the sort. With EU expansion, Europe's disadvantage effectively vanished.

Additional eastern expansion with former Soviet republics?

The European Union plans to culminate its expansion in the west Balkans. Croatia became the EU's twenty-eighth member country in 2013.[34] The region had already received massive direct investment from the core countries of the Union. When the future accession of the West Balkans was put on the agenda, foreign direct investment began to flood the region. In 2002, it totaled $2.1 billion; by 2008, $13.3 billion.[35]

Doubts have been raised, however, over the wisdom of accepting such backward former communist countries into the EU. The most recent experience of expanding into the Balkans was rather sobering. Bulgaria, which joined the EU in 2007, still suffers from poverty, lawlessness, and endemic corruption. In July 2013, enormous demonstrations were held in Sofia, where protesters, quietly supported by EU officials, expressed a lack of trust in their government.[36] Romania has had similar difficulties. In these countries it is reasonable to wonder whether the substantial EU assistance has been properly utilized. Were they really ready for EU membership?

What about the other west Balkan countries? Albania, Kosovo, Serbia, Macedonia, Montenegro, and Bosnia-Herzegovina are either official candidates or are waiting to be designated as such. Albania and Serbia both applied for membership in December 2009. The Serbia–Kosovo agreement in the spring of 2013 paved the way for future membership. Montenegro applied at the end of 2008, earned candidate status in 2010, and could become an official member by 2020.[37] As before, all candidate countries are expected to meet European requirements. The process looks extremely painful and slow. In 2014, the latest progress report presented a rather bleak picture. Political interference in the judiciary, inter-ethnic tensions, corruption, restrictions of the media, and even violent attacks on journalists "have not only not diminished, but in many instances have gotten worse." While a modicum of progress has been achieved in Serbia and Albania, a clear regression has taken place in Macedonia and Bosnia.[38] Future acceptance of these countries would have definite repercussions on security and peace, and represents yet another extension of the EU's backyard with all the requisite economic advantages (with extremely low wages of $1.20–$1.30/hour). Yet acceptance is more than problematic. At the moment, it is clear that in the best case, these candidate countries won't be ready to join for another five years. The new president of the European Commission, Jean-Claud Juncker, announced after his election that there will be no enlargement until the end of the 2010s.

Nevertheless, the European Union has ambitious plans to expand to the east, south, and south-east. At the time of the "Big Bang" enlargement of ten countries in 2004, preparations were also made (in 2003–4) for what was dubbed a "Neighborhood Policy." Javier Solana, High Representative for the Common Foreign Policy and Security Policy of the EU, in his proposal for the EU Council, "A Secure Europe in a Better World" in 2003, spoke about increased security for Europe as the outcome of further enlargement: "Our task is to promote a ring of well-governed countries to the East of the EU and on the borders of the Mediterranean with whom we can enjoy close and cooperative relations."[39] The policy aimed at extending European values, democracy, the rule of law, and respect for human rights, as well as building political and economic ties and expanding free trade. The Neighborhood Policy framework was proposed to the 16 closest neighboring countries: to the former Soviet republics Armenia, Azerbaijan, Belarus, Georgia, Moldova, and Ukraine in the east; and to Algeria,

Egypt, Israel, Jordan, Lebanon, Libya, Morocco, Palestine, Syria, and Tunisia in the south and south-east. Through its Multinational Financial Framework, the EU began distributing €20 billion to these 16 countries between 2004 and 2010.[40]

In April 2007, the European Commission presented the "Black Sea Initiative" to the EU's Council and Parliament. The Commission noted that "the Black Sea region is a distinct geographical area rich in natural resources and strategically located at the junction of Europe, Central Asia and the Middle East," and it argued that the EU's presence in the Black Sea region "opens a window on fresh perspectives and opportunities."[41] There seems to be a permanent hunger for expansion among the Union's business circles, a hunger that is closely connected both to globalization and to security concerns.

While the Mediterranean Partnership (launched in Paris in July 2008) was not linked to future membership in the Union, the Eastern Partnership was ambiguous on that point. Countries in this program might end up with association-status or even full membership. In fact, Moldova, Georgia, and Ukraine signed Association Agreements with the explicit goal of joining the EU. The European Commission in 1996 had already stated quite unequivocally that it wished to add Ukraine to "the European architecture drawn up by the Copenhagen European Council, to develop partnership relations with Ukraine." A few days later, the Union's Council of Ministers envisioned incorporating Ukraine into the EU orbit: the EU, it stated, "wishes to see the Partnership and Cooperation Agreement . . . [to] establish the fundamental basis for a privileged partnership with Ukraine."[42] From the Union's perspective, the integration of Ukraine, a country of 52 million people and a cheap labor force, would not only be beneficial economically but would also create political conditions that would prevent "any possible return to the former ways," and "loosen the grip of dependence upon their powerful neighbor [Russia]."[43]

At play in this eastward expansion was a combination of security and economic interests. The plan was to expand both NATO and the EU with the inclusion of the former Soviet Republics, now independent states. Ukraine, Georgia, Moldova, and possibly others were targeted in NATO enlargement plans soon after the collapse of the Soviet Union. Secretary of State Warren Christopher coined the term "coupling of EU and NATO expansion to the East" already in 1993. President George W. Bush was much more explicit when he told NATO's Secretary General Jaap de Hoop Schaffer in 2006 that he wanted those countries to be members of NATO by the time he left office in 2009.[44] The process was pushed along by the Revolution of Roses in Georgia in 2003 and the Orange Revolution in Ukraine in 2004. The new Ukrainian President, Viktor Yanukovich, declared that he fully intended to join NATO. Before the NATO summit in Bucharest in the spring of 2008, President Bush told him quite openly: "Your country made a bold decision and the United States strongly supports your request." By that time Secretary of State Condoleezza Rice had already signed the not legally binding Charter on Strategic Partnership between the two countries. Germany's Angela Merkel had warned Bush several times that this step would be an "unnecessary offense to Russia." French Prime Minister François Fillon also opposed the plan, arguing that the acceptance of the former Soviet republics is "not the good answer to the balance of power within Europe and between Europe and Russia." This plan to enlarge NATO was rejected because of France and Germany's more cautious approach, which was supported by Italy, the Benelux countries, and Hungary.[45] The same NATO meeting, however, agreed to invite Croatia and Albania by offering them Membership Action Plans.

In contrast to the cautious European attitude regarding NATO expansion toward former Soviet republics, the EU did not follow the same policy regarding a gradual expansion in the region. The partnership policy with the former Soviet republics sought their rapid democratic transformation and a more explicit and permanent separation from Russia. The EU's summit meeting in Vilnius in November 2013 ratified a thousand-page Association Agreement seeking the "further Europeanization" of Armenia, Georgia, Moldova, and Ukraine. Unfortunately the EU did not take into account the fact that those newly independent countries had been historically connected to Russia and had been part of a critically important sphere of Russian security interest. While the EU countries were wise enough in 2008 not to challenge the European balance of power and risk uprooting their relationship with Russia, their Eastern Partnership Policy was oblivious to the political fragility of the region and the dangers that EU expansion posed. It was tremendously naive for them to believe that they could spread so-called European values in countries with no democratic traditions and long-established autocratic practices. Moreover, several of these newly independent countries were ruled by oligarchic mafias. In Georgia, the multi-billionaire Bidzina Ivanishvili, the founder and undisputed leader of the "Georgian Dream" coalition, at times governs as prime minister, and at times through cronies. He has ruthlessly eliminated all opposition – launching police investigations against some 10,000 members of "enemy parties" and imposing long prison terms for about a hundred of them, including former prime ministers. Ivanishvili has corrupted his clientele by raising state pensions by 50 percent.[46]

Ukraine is quite simply the epitome of corruption. According to the Ukrainian Ministry of Economic Development and Trade, nearly 30 percent of the country's GDP was produced in the "black economy" in 2007, and almost 50 percent in 2015. Ukraine is also acutely divided between the Catholic, Western-oriented regions to the west, and the Orthodox, Russian-oriented and heavily Russian populated regions to the east. The 25 million Russians living in the neighboring independent former Soviet republics constitute a natural fifth column for Russia. *The Economist,* however, went so far as to state in late September 2015 that

> the biggest threat to Ukraine is not the Russian invasion, but corruption so pervasive that it long ago ceased to be a disease of the post-Soviet system and became the system itself. [The] privatized state is divided between several oligarchic groups… corruption is decentralized …. The new government [of President Poroshenko] appointed several oligarchs as governors of the country's most vulnerable regions. Ihor Kolomoisky, a billionaire with interest in banking, oil, television and an airline, took charge of Dnepropetrovsk.

He financed a private army... Prime Minister Arseniy Yatsenyuk... [was accused] of being in the pocket of the oligarchs.[47]

Further:

The Ukrainian state ... still resembles a giant mafia ... Oligarchs and their political cronies still dominate Ukrainian life. Should the government do too much to fight corruption, the oligarchs may use their private armies to stage a coup.[48]

Moldova is ruled by two oligarchic families, of whom Vlad Filat and Vladimir Plahotniuk control the country's two political parties through their cronies and their state and business empires. They persistently resist introducing any substantive political reforms. Beyond that, the country is almost equally divided by Western- and Eastern-oriented halves. Transnistria, Moldova's eastern Slavic-populated region bordering Ukraine, tried to secede from the country in 1990, fought a civil war on the issue in 1992, and held a referendum on joining Russia in 2006. Another region of Moldova, Gagauzia, has also declared its determination to secede. In a referendum that had 70 percent participation in February 2014, only 2 percent voted for joining the EU, and a majority voted for Gagauiza's secession should Moldova choose to do so.[49] The country was rocked by an immense bank fraud with clear political connotations in the fall of 2014, when $1 billion – one-eighth of the country's entire annual output – was stolen from three Moldovan banks. Former Prime Minister Vlad Filat was arrested. In less than a year, a third prime minister was appointed in early 2016, but continual mass demonstrations throughout the country demand that he resign as well. It seems not to matter which gang is ruling the country at any particular time, as the situation remains the same.[50]

The Ukrainian crisis in 2014 plainly reveals the serious repercussions of the EU's miscalculation. As a special subcommittee of the British Parliament concluded when investigating the failure of the country's Ukrainian policy,

Britain and the European Union made a catastrophic misreading of Russia ... and sleepwalked into the Ukrainian crisis, treating it as a trade issue rather than as a delicate foreign-policy challenge .... Member nations [were] insensitive [to the political consequences when they chose] to negotiate a closer political and economic relationship, known as an 'association agreement' with Ukraine.[51]

As a 2014 analysis of the neighborhood policy self-critically noted, the program "was simply not political enough."

Pushing on [with the Ukraine policy against all warnings,] we set in motion a chain of events that led to an (itself unpredictable) Russian overreaction. Thus we learned about the geopolitical implications of technical cooperation, export of norms and trade relations the hard way… Activities under the flag of the Eastern Partnership went on without it being clear which relationship the EU eventually aspired to with the six countries concerned … activity is not substitute for strategy.[52]

On April 6, 2016, a Dutch referendum with the participation of one-third of the voters rejected he association agreement with Ukraine by 61 percent majority. Although the referendum officially is not binding, it certainly will block the road for Dutch ratification of the agreement. This was a clear expression of rejection further overenlargement.[53]

Turkey?

Turkey plays a special role in the European Union's expansion plans. The NATO country, whose acceptance was originally promoted by the United States, joined the EU's customs union in 1996, and was an official candidate for EU membership at the end of 1999.[54] Open-ended negotiations, however, were stopped in 2005 then renewed in 2012, only to be delayed again in the summer of 2013. According to the European Commission, the negotiations now won't be completed for another ten to fifteen years. Nevertheless, the migration crisis in 2015 magnified Turkey's importance for the EU. Negotiations to keep Syrian refugees in Turkish camps began, and the Erdoğan regime tried to exploit the crisis and to win an earlier acceptance. The regime's authoritarian attributes, however, were a major stumbling block. Considering the EU's enlargement program as a whole, we find Turkey's candidacy considerably more problematic than that of the previous candidates. Turkey represents an area of great economic potential, roughly 80 million inhabitants with a very high reproduction rate, thus constituting a limitless low-wage labor force. (The minimum hourly wage is only $3.14.) Turkey's population has increased eight-times faster than the EU's since 1990. The country's GDP per capita level is only 30 percent of the EU average, and its rate of economic development is even lower than Central Europe's. It is a huge backward market with more than a third of its labor force working in agriculture. Hence there are considerable economic advantages for extending the EU across the Bosporus.

But Turkey's inclusion is more than controversial. In the end, the EU was forced to retract chapters 23 and 24 of the adjustment charter, the chapters on justice, freedom, and fundamental rights, because of Turkey's flagrant violations. Since the Justice and Development Party (AKP) of Recep Tayyip Erdoğan took over the country in 2002, the country has been "drifting away from the West … [and has been] increasingly alienated on the international stage … Turkish foreign policy [is] incompatible with its partners' expectations."[55] Erdoğan's Turkey is gradually Islamizing, is putting limits on the legacy of Kemal Atatürk, and is ending the army's role as the safeguard of secularism. The crushing of the alleged "Sledgehammer" coup in 2003, and the arrest of 500 members of the "Ergenekon" secret organization in 2011, effectively halted the military's influence over politics. The government violently suppressed protests in 2013, and banned YouTube in the country. Turkey dropped to 154th place in the World Press Freedom Index, and became "the world's largest prison for journalists."[56] "Turkey's leadership," concluded a 2014 EU analysis, "has become increasingly belligerent." Throughout, the government has sent contradictory signals. On the one hand, Deputy Prime Minister Bülent Arinç has unveiled a three-stage action plan to accelerate the accession process to meet a 2023 target date.[57] On the other, the government has embraced anti-Western Millî Görüş (national vision) Islamist ideology, has established relations with the Muslim Brotherhood, and has endeavored to become a regional power with an independent foreign policy.[58] Despite this, there are powerful political and corporate forces that continue to press for Turkey's quick inclusion in the EU. They point to security considerations of Turkey's geopolitical situation, its bordering Russia and the Middle East, and its potential to serve as an effective bridge to the Muslim world. The economic advantages of including Turkey also cannot be denied. When Turkey joined the European common market, multinational car manufacturers clamored to establish new production facilities, and today sell 68 percent of all cars made in Turkey on the European market. Nevertheless, if it ever did become a member of the Union, Turkey by then could very well have 100 million inhabitants – the largest in the EU – with only about 5 percent living in the small European part of the country. Incorporating Turkey would transform the Union in ways beyond imagination and would certainly lead others to walk away and ultimately reduce the EU to being a simple free trade zone.

Turkey's acceptance would have been a deadly blow to the European Union from the very day of its application and candidacy. After the summer of 2016, however, when President Erdoğan exploited a failed military coup, Turkey practically disqualified itself for future membership. Retaliation became the introduction of a brutal dictatorship. Erdogan started eliminating his political opposition, regardless of participation in the coup – beside thousands of soldiers and officers, everybody who ever criticized him and advocated secular democracy, or even potentially may be dangerous for him such as 21,000 teachers, 15,000 educational ministry employees, 1,500 university deans, and a huge number of journalists. Altogether about 60,000 people were dismissed or arrested, and a great many tortured in a country where the government wants to reintroduce the death penalty.

The Mediterranean challenge

The so-called *Mediterranean challenge*, the linking of the EU with the southern, North African and Middle Eastern Mediterranean regions, also poses some attraction for the EU. In November 1995, the foreign ministers of fifteen EU member states and twelve southern Mediterranean countries met in Barcelona and initiated the "Barcelona Process," a Euro Mediterranean partnership with Morocco, Algeria, Tunisia, Egypt, Jordan, Palestine, Lebanon, and Syria, to establish a common Euro–Mediterranean Area. Péter Balázs, the former EU Commissioner, speaks of "exactly thirty-six countries . . . as potential EU members."[59] As with the

East, however, the southern neighborhood has become highly destabilized since the so-called Arab Spring, and has suffered extremely negative consequences.

As a 2015 analysis concluded, the neighborhood has become an "arc of instability stretching across the EU's borders from the south West to the North East [and] highlights Europe's own fragility at a time when ... [the EU is] less able to address external challenges and foster stability beyond its borders."[60] This analysis came to the grim conclusion that the EU's neighborhood policy had failed because the entire neighborhood, both in the east and the south, has severely deteriorated in the decade since the policy's launching. The failure had also been due to the EU's inability to differentiate between countries and to come up with a clear set of goals. The Union must consider the huge diversity in the neighborhood that does not allow a one-size-fits-all policy; and it must clarify what its end goals are. In 2014, the European Union continued pursuing the central goals of its neighborhood policy, "avoiding the emergence of new dividing lines between the enlarged EU and our neighbors and instead strengthening the prosperity, stability and security of all."[61] By that time, however, the entire neighborhood was burning – both east and south alike. In other words, the EU must rethink its objectives and make a *tabula rasa.* "The EU should not shy away from more direct interventions and mediations in emerging conflicts." A new neighborhood policy is badly needed.[62]

Dark prophecies, prospect of disintegration?

As indicated earlier, the 2004–7 enlargement had more than its share of detractors. The ongoing Greek crisis created certain fissures among the member countries. Anti-integration forces are gaining strength in several countries. Expansion is but one of a number of issues under contention, but it could be a contributing factor leading to a breakup of the EU.

In the 1990s, an alternative eastern enlargement strategy was suggested to integrate the post-communist countries in "an outer free trade area," but not as full members of the Community.[63] This solution would have been advantageous in many respects. The candidate countries would have been included in the common market, but the EU would have maintained control on the pace of democratization and economic reform. Evidently, the former peripheral countries need more time to adjust their societies to meet West European standards. Unfortunately, however, this proposal was dropped and replaced by a full membership approach. Some experts speak of a "vicious spiral" of continuous enlargements that might overstretch the Union . . . increased heterogeneity may cause spill-back and a loose Union . . . further enlargement will cause disintegration and deconstruction of the Union we see today."[64] Accepting additional Balkan countries and the increasingly remote integration of Turkey "may overburden the capacities of the Union and stretch the integration process to breaking point."[65]

Former French President Giscard d'Estaing, speaking on the 2004 eastward expansion, proclaimed: "That this enlargement will water down the community is not a risk but a certainty."[66] Are these predictions of doom the direct result of the ongoing Greek economic crisis and the immigration crisis? Should the European

Union settle with association and free trade agreements in the place of additional enlargements? Such arrangements with those countries now seeking membership could well serve trade and economic interests without exposing the Union to the risks entailed in further enlargement. All these issues remain open to debate. In response to growing criticism, the newly appointed president of the European Commission, Jean-Claud Juncker, affirmed that "negotiations would continue, but no further enlargement will take place over the next five years."[67]

The enlargement drive has indeed endangered the entire Union as we know it. It has already undermined EU homogeneity, and has made the process of true integration much more difficult. Progress toward an "ever closer union" seems more and more a pipe dream. As we saw during the economic crisis of the 2010s, the common market and the common currency in the euro-zone worked far better for the stronger economies than it did for the weaker peripheral countries. The federal organization would counterbalance these outcomes of diverse economic level, but there is little chance for federalization any longer.

When the 2008 crisis hit Europe, the countries that were in most trouble and required bailouts were all former peripheral countries that had been brought in during the past thirty years. Several had joined the Community decades ago, such as Ireland, Greece, Spain, and Portugal; others had become members only recently, such of Cyprus, Bulgaria, Romania, Latvia, and Hungary. The difficulties of the peripheral countries shocked the entire Union during the 2010s. While the North-Western core of Europe had only a short, rapidly recovered crisis after 2008, the weakness of the peripheries generated the long-lasting and still not recovered economic and social troubles for the EU. The GDP of the Mediterranean countries declined by 6–8 and even 19 percent between 2009 and 2013, and healthcare spending dropped by 16 and 20 percent in Greece and Spain. According to Eurostat figures, the percentage of the population below poverty and social exclusion lines is 16–20 percent in Sweden and Germany, 23.1 percent in the EU-15 countries, but 27 and 35 percent in Spain and Greece respectively. These latter two countries had 25–26 percent unemployment, in contrast to the 10.7 percent in the EU-15 countries in 2013. According to the World Economic Forum's competitiveness index in 2014, Finland stands at 4th place, Germany at 5th, and the Netherlands at 8th among 140 countries. Spain is 33rd, Portugal is 38th, Greece is 81st, and, reflecting the level of some of the Central and Eastern European countries, Hungary – compared to its 33rd place in 2003 – declined to 63rd place. The main reasons for this decline of Hungary are the low quality of institutions, which occupy 97th place, business ethics at 116th place, and the quality of higher education, at 99th place among 140 countries.[68] Not a single core country required a bailout. The austerity measures that accompanied the bailouts hit the peripheral countries hard. The Greek crisis particularly heightened the difference between lenders and borrowers, between efficient Western core countries and those in the southern and eastern peripheries.

There is very little hope for establishing a common cultural-behavioral pattern throughout the Union for generations to come. The cultural legacy of being part of the periphery continues to have a strong impact even in countries like Ireland

and Spain that have successfully caught up economically. Any additional enlargement deepens all of these contradictions and creates new obstacles for further integration. The recommendation of the Dutch government to establish a small-euro-zone and a small-Schengen area only with West European countries clearly expresses the need to rethink EU expansion. We have recently seen the emergence of several new plans for rearranging the Union as "à la-carte" ad hoc groupings of various countries for different kinds of cooperation, or for simply a free trade association. In other words, most of the experts do not see any possibility for further supranationalization or for moving towards federalization.

The historian Walter Laqueur gloomily predicted the future in his 2011 study, *After the Fall. The End of the European Dream and the Decline of the Continent.*[69] In late 2011, Larry Elliot, the economic editor of *The Guardian*, was but one of a number of informed observers who entertained the possibility of a break-up of the euro-zone.[70] Robert Bideleux argued more specifically that the euro-zone was not serving the interests of the peripheries, in particular Ireland and the southern countries, and he speculated that a smaller unified monetary zone might be a better configuration for Europe. He, too, feared that the euro-zone was in danger of breaking up because of the problems in the peripheries.[71] One possible scenario of a euro-zone break-up is offered by the economist Roger Bootle in London's *Daily Telegraph*:

> The euro could be reduced to something like the Northern core . . . through the process of the Southern countries leaving, either individually or *en bloc*. But it would be possible for the euro-zone to break up via the departure of the strong core economies to establish their own union.

He added that "it would be in the interest of the 'stronger' countries that remain in the smaller euro-zone to support the exit of their weaker partners."[72] The Harvard economist Martin Feldstein was even blunter in 2012: "The euro should now be recognized as an experiment that failed."[73] François Heisbourg, in *La Fin du Rêve Européen* (The End of the European Dream), concluded in the fall of 2013 that the only really positive solution would be a federal Europe; but since such a Europe is politically impossible, the only realistic solution is to cut out the "euro-cancer" and end the common currency in an orderly manner.[74] Paul Krugman, already on record with concerns about a possible collapse of the common currency, worried in May 2014 that the union itself might not be able to survive the latest troubles:

> The euro is still holding together, surprising many analysts–myself included– who thought it might well fell apart . . . the [European] elite has been able to hold things together. But we don't know how long this can last, and there are some very scary people waiting in the wings.[75]

The Economist expressed a somewhat similar view: "returning [more] power to the states and institutions that voters trust . . . [i.e. with] the national parliaments given more say in EU legislation."[76] In an early 2016 interview entitled "The European

Union is on the Verge of collapse," George Soros warns of the danger of five or six crises combining and ultimately destroying the EU.[77] On the surface, a number of developments since the end of 2013 would seem to support such pessimism about the future of a unified Europe. According to a December 2013 Euro-barometer poll, trust in the EU among EU citizens, shared by 57 percent in the spring of 2007, had dropped to less than a third. A January 2014 *New York Times* article entitled "Europeans United in Hating Europe" warned of a growing alliance among right-wing parties opposing the EU. It went on to note that these parties promise to give power back to various nations "by dismantling the technocratic decision-making power amassed in Brussels and returning powers back to individual member states. They would pause, if not quite reverse, six decades of growing integration."[78] Bernhard Clemm has a similar prediction:

> The future of an 'ever closer' Europe is increasingly uncertain . . . . Old animosities between Europeans are reappearing with alarming seriousness . . . . All this makes questions about a possible European disintegration plausible . . . . Europe will disintegrate when people are fed up with the EU.[79]

These forecasts are ominous indeed in the light of Eurobarometer's poll results in 2012 and 2013: "fewer and fewer people still think that the EU serves them well . . . . Only 33 percent of Europeans trust their common institutions and only 30 percent have a good image of the European Union."[80] The May 2014 European parliamentary elections produced shocking electoral results along these lines. In four countries the outcome could be called tragic. Anti-euro and even anti-EU parties gained significant ground. In Greece, the extreme left and extreme right both grew by 40 percent. The openly neo-fascist Jobbik Party came in second place in Hungary, the anti-EU United Kingdom Independence Party won 27 percent of the vote, and Marine Le Pen's French National Front won 25 percent of the French electorate. The situation deteriorated further during the "end game" of the Greek crisis in July 2015. In mid-2015, no less than 30 percent of the seats in the European Parliament were filled by anti-integration and even anti-EU representatives. All these trends were crowned by the British referendum to leave the EU in the summer of 2016. There can be no doubt that the recent trends and troubles in the EU have nurtured a resurgent nationalism among certain strata of the population and among politicians in some countries. Opposition to immigration and to the recent plans for EU expansion is the primary stimuli, but nationalist, anti-EU sentiment is also being fed by the economic hardship of the past several years.

One of the most interesting analyses on the present and possible future of the EU came from Giandomenico Majone, a preeminent expert on the topic, who concluded that the EU is "over-integrated," and "over-enlarged."[81] "The depth of the current crisis," he said, "justifies the widespread opinion that integration has gone too far." The euro was a political concept, inspired by the goal of political union, "to make the integration process irreversible" regardless of the economic realities. It failed and its collapse in unavoidable. "The end of the monetary union appears to be only a question of time . . . ."

It pays to summarize Majone's argument and recommendations: "By the latest enlargement of the EU," he suggests, there was "produced . . . [a] high level of socioeconomic heterogeneity . . . Income inequality is today much greater in the socially minded EU than in the supposedly arch-capitalist US." Furthermore, even in the integrationist countries such as Germany, Italy, Spain, and Belgium, "there is no agreement about how far integration should go, with the majority of the countries favouring economic, rather than political, integration." However, "the political benefits of monetary union are even more doubtful than the economic ones." The crisis de-legitimized the EU because economic development and prosperity had been the main legitimizing factor. "Popular distrust in the European institutions and widespread disenchantment with the very idea of European integration [emerged]." A survey of five euro-zone countries shows that only a median of 37 percent believe that the euro is a good thing.

Europe, Majone also argues, must again be ruled by the nation-state. "The search for alternative integration methods . . . must start from the realization that despite globalization and regional integration the nation is still vitally important." "Reducing the autonomy of democratically elected national governments is likely to be self-defeating." And he goes on to say:

> Some form of differentiated integration is no longer an option but . . . a necessity . . . [Federalists and scholars] greatly underestimated the effectiveness of the nation state and of its institutions . . . . Neither globalization nor European integration have reduced the central role of the nation states in economic development and innovation . . . and hence must avoid too rigid limits on their freedom of action . . . . The long century of nationalism . . . was an aberration in European history . . . . European history suggests that there is something unnatural in this [federalist] approach.

As Majone sees it, the EU must step back and look for a less ambitious system of cooperation that is restricted to the countries' economies, since no one wants political integration and federalization any longer. *A looser cooperation of otherwise competing countries would be the solution.*[82]

"In a speech to the European Parliament," reported the *New York Times*, the newly elected president of the European Commission, the federalist Jean-Claude Juncker "acknowledged that the next five years . . . would be the '*last chance*' to get citizens of the bloc's member countries to fully support the concept of European unity."[83] Will it succeed? Or will a slow and gradual disintegration take its place?

Notes

1 During the 1980s and again in the 2010s, British governments of Margaret Thatcher and then David Cameron clearly expressed their concept to degrade the Community into a free trade zone in Europe and not an "ever closer union" with more and more supranational institutions, inching toward a federal solution. They opted out from the introduction of the common currency and distanced Britain from the core of the Union as

much as possible. The Cameron government renegotiated the terms of British membership and, at last, in the summer of 2016 came the referendum decision to leave the Union.

2 Winston Churchill's speech in the House of Commons about the North Atlantic Treaty on 12 May, 1949, in *In the Balance. Speeches 1949 and 1950 by Winston Churchill*, ed. Randolph S. Churchill (London: Cassel, 1951), 61–62.

3 Quoted in Kenneth Maxwell, *The Making of Portuguese Democracy* (Cambridge: Cambridge University Press, 1995), 96. Italics added.

4 Ernst H. Van der Breugel, *From Marshall Aid to Atlantic Partnership. European Integration as a Concern of American Foreign Policy* (Amsterdam: Elsevier, 1966), 369. Italics added.

5 Argyris G. Andrianopoulos, *Western Europe in Kissinger's Global Strategy* (New York: St. Martin's Press, 1988), 17.

6 Helen Graham and Alejandro Quiroga, "After the Fear Was Over? What Came After the Dictatorships in Spain, Greece, and Portugal," in Dan Stone (ed.), The *Oxford Handbook of Postwar European History* (Oxford: Oxford University Press, 2012), 502.

7 William D. Harris, *Installing Aggressiveness. US Advisors and Greek Combat Leadership in the Greek Civil War, 1947–1949,* (Fort Leavenworth, KS: Combat Studies Institute Press, 2012).

8 *Archive of European Integration,* Athens ceremony for EEC-Greek associations. Bulletin from the European Community, No. 48, July 1961.

9 Thomas Mehlhausen, *European Union Enlargement. Material Interests, Community Norms and Anomie* (London: Routledge, 2016), 84–85.

10 Oscar Calvo-Gonzales, "Neither Carrot nor Stick: American Foreign Aid and Economic Policy Making in Spain during the 1950s," *Diplomatic History,* Vol. 30, Issue 3, June 2006, 409–38; here 410–11, 412, 416.

11 The text of the agreement can be found in the Law Library of Yale University, accessible at Avalon.law.yale.edu/20th_century/sp1953.asp

12 Nasuh Uslu, *The Turkish-American Relationship Between 1947 and 2003. The History of Distinctive Alliance* (New York: Nova, 2003), 23.

13 Kristin Archick, "European Union Enlargement," Congressional Research Service, February 4, 2013, 1, 10; accessed at www.fas.org/sgp/crs/row/RS21344.pdf.

14 Congressional Research Service. "European Union Enlargement: Status Report on Turkey's Accession Negotiations"; accessed at fas.org/sgp/crs/row/RS22517.pdf.

15 *Archive of European Integration,* Speech [on European unity] by Mr. Helmut Burckhardt, Vice- President of the Consultative Committee of the European Community for Coal and Steel, at the Duquesne Club, Pittsburgh, October 22, 1954.

16 Ivan T. Berend, *An Economic History of Nineteenth-Century Europe* (Cambridge: Cambridge University Press, 2006), 259.

17 Article 217, Treaty of Rome (1959).

18 Turkey was unable to accomplish the required reforms regarding the rule of law, human rights, gender equality, a new, democratic constitution, and other issues. Several countries are strongly against its acceptance, arguing that historical, cultural and religious differences separate Turkey from Europe.

19 Ibid., 640; Additionally, see Gespräch des Bundeskanzlers Kohl mit Aussenminister Baker, Berlin (West), 12 December, 1989, in *Dokumente zur Deutschlandpolitik, 1998*.

20 Schreiben des Bundeskanzlers Kohl an Generalsekräter Gorbatschow, Bonn 14 Dezember 1989, in *Dokumente zur Deutschlandpolitik, 1998, 649*.

21 Including the debt-burden relief to Poland, the only country whose debt burden was severely reduced, the aid package provided to the transforming countries was $19.1 billion. On this see Krzysztof J. Ners and Ingrid Buxell, *Assistance to Transition Survey* (Warsaw: PECAT, 1995), 34.

22 *The European Councils, 1993: Conclusions of the Presidency 1992–1994*, Report of the European Council in Copenhagen 21–23 June 1993 (Brussels: European Commission, 1995).

23 Based on *The Economist Intelligence Unit, Quarterly Country Reports in Estonia, Latvia and Lithuania,* 1st quarter, 1996; *European Bank of Reconstruction and Development, Transition Report* (London: EBRD, 1996); *European Bank of Reconstruction and Development, Transition Report 2000, Employment, Skills and Transition* (London: EBRD, 2000).
24 *The Economist, World in Figures* (London: Profile Books, 2006), 42–43.
25 Neill Nugent, *The Government and Politics of the European Union*, 7th ed. (London: Palgrave Macmillan, 2010), 47, 48.
26 About re-nationalization in Hungary see Péter Mihályi, "A privatizált vagyon visszaállamosítása Magyarországon 2010–2014," Discussion Papers, MTA Közgazdasági- és Regionális Tudományi Kutatóközpont, Közgazdaság-Tudományi Intézet, Budapest, 2015, MT-DP – 2015/7. The author presents the story of renationalization of more than 200, previously nationalized banking, energy, manufacturing and other companies by the Orbán government that look to Putin's Russia as a model.
27 World Corruption Perception Index: 2013:www.transparency.org/research/cpi/overview; 2015: http://www.transparency.org/cpi2015.
28 *Archive of European Integration,* Background Report on international and European law against corruption, December 15, 2014; World Bank's Worldwide Governance Indicator (WGI) Control of Corruption in 2012.
29 See Andrew Moravcsik and Milada A. Vachudova, "National Interest, State Power, and EU Enlargement," *East European Politics and Society,* Vol. 17, No. 1, February 2003, 42–57.
30 András Bethlendi, "Foreign Direct Investment in the Banking Sector," *Development and Finance,* no.1 (2007); *Wall Street Journal* (June 2 and November 7, 1995; March 30 and April 5, 1998); Österreichische Nationalbank, *June Report* (Vienna: ÖN, 2006).
31 *Revue Régional. Revue Elargissement* (April 12, 2003); rsa.tandfonlive om/doi/pdf/10.1080/714042091).
32 UNCTAD, *World Investment Report* 2004, 371 (unctad.org/en/ Docs/ wir2004_en.pdf).
33 Ivan T. Berend, *From the Soviet Bloc to the European Union. The Economic and Social Transformation of Central and Eastern Europe Since 1973* (Cambridge: Cambridge University Press, 2009), 123–31.
34 Ivo Sanader "was jailed for ten years for taking bribes." See "As Croatia Struggles, Some Wonder if It Won Entry to European Union too Soon," *The New York Times,* July 24, 2013.
35 Based on UNCTAD World Investment Report (http://unctad.org/en/pages/DIAE/World%20Investment%20Report/WIR-Series.aspx).
36 On the protest in Sofia, see "Bulgarian Police Break Up Protest Outside Parliament," *The New York Times,* July 25, 2013.
37 "EU Enlargement: The Next Seven," BBC News Europe, July 1, 2013, (www.bbc.co.uk/news/world-europe-11283616).
38 *Archive of European Integration,* CEPS Policy Brief, Erwan Founéré, "The EU's Enlargement Agenda – Credibility at Stake?" No. 324, October 31, 2014.
39 Council of the EU, European Security Strategy, A Secure Europe in a Better World, Brussels, December 12, 2003, 8 (https://www.consilium.europa.eu/uedoc/cmsllpload/78367.pdf)
40 http://eeas.europa.eu/enp/about-us/index_en.htm; http://europa.eu/rapid/press-release_MEMO-11-878_en.htm/local-en
41 *Archive of European Integration,* "Black Sea Synergy – A New Regional Cooperation Initiative," Communication from the Commission to the Council and the European Parliament COM (2007) 150 final, 11 April, 2007.
42 *Archive of European Integration,* "Action Plan for EU Relation with Ukraine, Extract from the Council of Ministers," press release, 6 December 1996. The statement dates back to the time of preparations for the admittance of the original ten former communist countries.

43 *Archive of European Integration* "Action Plan for Ukraine. Communication from the Commission to the Council," COM (96) 593 final, 20 November, 1996.
44 *Archive of European Integration,* Zentrum für Europäische Integrationsforschung, Discussion Paper 226/2014, Lothar Rühl, "European Foreign and Security Policy Since the Lisbon Treaty – From Common to Single."
45 *The Guardian*, April 1, 2008, "Bush Backs Ukraine and Georgia for NATO Membership"; *The Washington Post*, September 4, 2014, "That Time Ukraine Tried to Join NATO – and NATO Said No"; *The New York Times*, April 3, 2008, "NATO Allies Opposes Bush on Georgia and Ukraine."
46 *Archive of European Integration,* OSW Commentary, No. 133, April 15, 2014, Marek Matusiak, "Georgia – Between a Dream and Reality." Former prime minister Vano Merabishvili is imprisoned. Ivanishvili "appointed" the 32-year-old Irakli Garibashvili as "his" prime minister.
47 *The Economist,* September 26, 2015, "Rule of Law in Ukraine."
48 Ibid., "Progress in Ukraine."
49 *Archive of European Integration,* OSW Commentary, No. 129, March 10, 2014, Kamil Calus, "Gagauzia: Growing Separatism in Moldova."
50 *The New York Times,* January 26, 2016, "Opponents Unite to Protest New Moldova Government."
51 "Britain and Europe 'Sleepwalked' Into the Ukrainian Crisis, Report Says," *The New York Times,* February 20, 2015. The journal's article was based on the report of European Union External Affairs Subcommittee of the British House of Lords.
52 *Archive of European Integration,* Egmont Paper 67, Sven Biscop, "Game of Zones: The Quest for Influence in Europe's Neighbourhood," June 2014.
53 *The New York Times,* April 7, 2016, "Dutch Voters Reject Deal Between EU and Ukraine." The journal misinterpret the Dutch "no" vote as a "new blow to supporters of European integration."
54 *Archive of European Integration,* Annabelle Littoz-Monnet and Beatriz Villanueva Penas, "Turkey and the European Union. The Implications of a Specific Enlargement," Egmont European Affairs Papers, April 2006.
55 *Archive of European Integration, Warsaw Centre for Eastern Studies, Szymon Ananicz,* "Alone is virtue. The 'new Turkish' ideology in Turkey's foreign policy."
56 *Archive of European Integration,* CEPS Policy Brief, No. 317, March 26, 2014, Steven Blockmans, "EU – Turkey relations: Turning vicious circles into virtuous ones"; *Reporters without Borders* (https://rsf.org/index2014/eu-index2014.php#).
57 *Archive of European Integration,* EPC Commentary, September 29, 2014, Armand Paul, "Why the EU must reengage with Turkey."
58 Necmettin Erbakan established the movement in 1969 and warned against rapprochement toward Europe.
59 "History Beyond Nations, Interview with Péter Balázs," *Visegrad Insight* 1, no. 3, 2013, 44.
60 *Archive of European Integration,* Bertelsman Stiftung, "The EU neighborhood in shambles. Some recommendations on a new European neighborhood strategy."
61 See: http://ecas.europa.eu/org/about us/index_en.htm; http://europa.eu/rapid/press-release_MEMO-11-878_en.htm/local-en
62 Ibid.
63 Jürgen Elvert, "The Institutional Paradox: How Crises Have Reinforced European Integration," in Ludger Kühnhardt (ed.), *Crises in European Integration. Challenges and Responses, 1945–2005* (New York: Oxford University Press, 2009), 54, 56.
64 Wolfgang Wessels and Thomas Traught, "Opportunity or Overstretch? The Unexpected Dynamics of Deepening and Widening," in Kühnhardt (ed.), *Crises in European Integration,* 81.
65 Michael Gehler, "Challenges and Opportunities: Surmounting Integration Crises in Historical Context," in Kühnhardt (ed.), *Crises in European Integration,* 109.

66 *Frankfurter Allgemeine Zeitung,* October 12, 2005.
67 "The Western Balkans and the EU. In the Queue," *The Economist,* September 27, 2014.
68 reports.weforum.org/global-competitiveness-report-2014-2015/
69 Walter Laqueur, *The Last Days of Europe: Epitaph for an Old Continent* (London: Thomas Dunne, 2007); *After the Fall. The End of the European Dream and the Decline of the Continent* (New York: St. Martin's Press, 2011).
70 Larry Elliott, "We've been Warned: The System is Ready to Blow," *The Guardian,* August 14, 2011.
71 Robert Bideleux, "European Integration: The Rescue of the Nation State?" in Dan Stone (ed.), *The Oxford Handbook of Postwar European History* (Oxford: Oxford University Press, 2012), 402, 404, 405.
72 Roger Bootle, "Leaving the Euro: A Practical Guide" (www.policyexchange. org.uk/ images/WolfsonPrize/wep%20shortlist%20essay%20-%20roger%20bootle.pdf).
73 Martin Feldstein, "The Failure of the Euro," *The Foreign Affairs,* January/February 2012.
74 François Heisbourg, *La Fin du Rêve Européen* (Paris: Stock, 2013).
75 For Krugman's earlier concerns, see Paul Krugman, "Eurodämmerung," *The New York Times,* May 13, 2012. Here Krugman forecast "the endgame" of the euro, ending with a sentence: "and we are talking about months, not years, for this play out." For his mid-2014 views, quoted here, see Paul Krugman, "Crisis of the Eurocrats," *The New York Times,* May 23, 2014.
76 "Europe's Angry Voters Bucked Off," *The Economist,* May 31–June 6, 2014, 12.
77 George Soros, op. cit., February 11, 2016.
78 "Europeans United in Hating Europe," *The New York Times,* January 3, 2014.
79 Bernhard Clemm, "Integration on Trial: EU Disintegration is Still Possible," in *European Politics and Society,* January 7, 2013.
80 *Standard Eurobarometer* 78, Autumn 2012; Stefan Collignon, "Italy and the Disintegration of the European Union," *Social Europe,* February 28, 2013.
81 My quotes in this paragraph and the next three are taken from Giandomenico Majone, *Rethinking the Union of Europe Post-Crisis. Has Integration Gone Too Far?* (Cambridge: Cambridge University Press, 2014), 19, 38–40, 110, 210, 228, 265, 279, 297, 322.
82 Giandomenico Majone, *"European Integration: From Collective Good to Club Good,"* paper presented at the Hertie School of Governance in Berlin on May 15, 2013, 6, 8, 15.
83 "European Union's Executive Branch Approves Slate of Commissioners," *The New York Times,* October 23, 2014.

6   The state of transforming Eastern Europe

Backward starting position

One of the most important events in the more than fifty-year history of the European Union was the incorporation of eleven Central and Eastern European former communist countries between 2004 and 2013. Some in the Western Balkans, Serbia, Montenegro, Albania, Bosnia-Herzegovina, and Kosovo, are on the waiting list, several already enjoying associate member status. All these countries were in terrible shape when their communist regimes collapsed in 1989 (see Chapter 5). They emerged from one-party dictatorial regimes and state-owned, centrally planned economies. They were frozen in an obsolete economic structure and a hopeless dearth of technology, and they suffered from high, in some cases hyper-, inflation and heavy indebtedness. Their economic standing, based on per capita income, was about a third of the EU-15 countries' average.

The future prospects of the European Union depend to a significant degree on whether this region, now incorporated into the Union, will be able to gradually close the huge gaps and catch up with the West. The past record of European integration leaves room for optimism. When the first economically backward peripheral countries – Ireland (1973), Greece (1981), Spain and Portugal (1986) – joined the European Community, they, too, had emerged from dictatorial, non-parliamentary regimes and obsolete economic structures. In the 1970s, the average per capita GDP of these countries was less than 60 percent of that of the West. However, after their acceptance as new members of the Community, most of them experienced rapid political transformation, economic modernization, and development. When Ireland joined the EU, its GDP was only 57 percent of the EU's average; by 2000, in less than thirty years, it had exceeded it. The Mediterranean member countries' income level rose from two-thirds of that of the West to three-quarters after 15 years of membership. Integration was indeed helping these countries catch up. Was the same thing happening with the former communist states of Central and Eastern Europe, after twenty-five years of transformation and a decade-long association with the EU?

The heavy burden of the past

The region's transformation began almost immediately after the collapse of communism in 1989. This process was an unbeaten path, a complete historical novelty. Still, these former communist countries were hardly improvising, but rather following a clear-cut blueprint provided in part by the International Monetary Fund (IMF), whose financial assistance they sorely needed to stabilize their economies. IMF assistance was combined with a compulsory transformation road-map, called the Washington Consensus,[1] a neo-liberal economic program requiring them to open their closed economies and end the protectionist economic nationalism they had followed since World War I.

Joining the EU was also conditioned on a comprehensive transformation program, as the EU's Copenhagen Council Summit in 1993 made clear. The European Commission closely monitored candidate members' compliance. All candidates were handed the *acquis communautaire,* a 31-chapter, 80,000–100,000-page collection of political and economic requirements, including a long list of laws to be incorporated in each country's legal system. The introduction of pluralistic parliamentary democracy that guaranteed human rights, and the establishment of a functioning market system based on private ownership and free trade were mandatory. The EU left no room for doubt that candidate countries could join up only when they had met the economic and political conditions that they required.[2] The first group of former communist countries – Hungary, Poland, Latvia, Lithuania, and Estonia – applied for membership in March and April 1994, followed by Bulgaria in late 1995, and the Czech Republic, Slovakia, and Slovenia in 1996. The first eight countries became members of the Union in 2004; Bulgaria and Romania did so in 2007, and Croatia in 2013.

The countries of Central and Eastern Europe have embarked on a steady path toward Europe – both economically and politically – since the fall of communism. The 1989 slogan "Back to Europe!" expressed an understandable dream. But, what had to change in the region were not merely the former communist regimes, but also centuries-long cultural, social, political, and economic patterns and behaviors. The region had not been industrialized, but had remained rural and agricultural backwaters until the mid-twentieth century. It had never fostered pluralistic democracy. Emerging from nineteenth-century autocracy, it remained basically authoritarian during the twentieth century. It could not claim to be part of a Europe that was characterized by industrialized democracy. In other words, the region was burdened not only by the 40–50 years of communist rule, but by its entire modern history. The deformities of the past now poisoned the present. Path-dependence is a mystical but significant historical force. History matters. Central and Eastern Europe could not just "return to Europe" after a half-century detour.

Moreover, the history of Central and Eastern Europe has been considerably different from that of Western Europe since medieval times. Christianization, feudalism, and settled agriculture began in Central and Eastern Europe a half a millennium later than it did in the West. The Renaissance, the Enlightenment, the Protestant

Reformation and the Industrial Revolution had passed the area by. Nation-building was not a completed process even at the end of the twentieth century, as the disintegration of a number of multi-ethnic states demonstrates. Hence the region lacked not only democracy, but consolidated nation states as well. Extreme nationalism was therefore the rule. Although there were attempts to emulate Western European democratic institutions in these countries during the late nineteenth century, most of the results were devoid of any real substance. A second attempt after World War I also proved futile. Central and Eastern Europe traditionally exhibited a continuing pattern of "forms without substance," a land in between Russia and the West – *Zwischen-Europa*, as some interwar German writers called it. As Oscar Jaszi described it, the region was the "unfinished part of Europe."[3] Social development in these non-industrialized peasant countries paled in comparison to that of the West. Until the middle of the twentieth century, most Central European countries were dominated by a deeply entrenched aristocratic anti-capitalist tradition that glorified profligacy and sneered at work and frugality. The peasant societies of the Balkans upheld a strong collectivist, anti-capitalist legacy. The middle class was weak and consisted mostly of minorities, Germans and Jews. Both were eliminated during World War II (in the Holocaust) and soon afterwards (the Germans' expulsion). The region had to radically transform itself to reach West European standards. As in poor, inefficient countries generally, corruption and clientelism was endemic to all its regimes. Much the same remains today.

Post-communist transformation and its weaknesses

The region embarked on a democratic transformation[4] after 1989, with many countries holding free, multi-party elections – a nascent democratic system that has continued to endure. According to a 2104 Freedom House report, *Nations in Transit*,[5] eight of the region's countries remain "consolidated democracies" after a quarter of a century. Only three of the eleven EU member countries (Bulgaria, Romania, and Croatia) lag behind, for they along with Serbia and Montenegro, have been deemed to be "semi-consolidated democracies." But the report's analysis seems to be an overly optimistic reading of the situation.

The transformation of most of the region has been plagued by extreme nationalism. Civil wars have erupted in former Yugoslavia, Moldova, and the Ukraine. In 1989, Eastern Europe was made up of eight countries east from the River Elbe; today, there are twenty-nine, many with explosive border problems and conflicts with their neighbors. Right-wing nationalist governments with authoritarian leanings have predominated in some countries since the 1990s. The Mečiars in Slovakia, the Kaczynskis in Poland, Tuđmans in Croatia, Milosevič in Serbia, Ponta in Romania, and Orbán in Hungary are telling examples. The countries of the region had to make the necessary adjustments to meet the EU's political requirements. Constitutional treaties and rules of the European Union clearly declared that "the EU is founded on a set of values, one of which is the rule of law" as Article 2 of the Treaty on the European Union contains. The Preamble of the EU Charter of Fundamental Rights states that the rule of law is a founding principle of the EU and "serious and persistent breeches may lead to suspension of rights of member countries." In other words, member states are bound to respect EU values. In 2014, the European Commission initiated a new framework to strengthen the rule of law in the Union. But some of the countries that already have been accepted made a sharp U-turn and resumed previous practices neglecting the rule of law. Unfortunately, the EU, in spite of the available devices, has not enforced its rules and requirements.[6]

Irena Grudzinska-Gross speaks of a "backsliding" of the democratic transformation. She argues that Poland, Hungary, and other countries in the region have witnessed a revival "of the very old conservative style of politics, including the resurrection of the extreme right-wing movements and, in Poland, of religious fundamentalism."[7] Populism is on the rise in several countries. The 2008 crisis delegitimized neo-liberal economic reforms and liberalism in general. New political forces accused the political establishment to betray the people and reject Brussels as a "technocratic bubble" endangering national sovereignty.[8] George Soros notes that Orbán and Kaczynski

> seek to exploit a mix of ethnic and religious nationalism in order to perpetuate themselves in power. In a sense they are trying to reestablish the kind of sham democracy that prevailed in the period between the First and Second world Wars in Admiral Horthy's Hungary and Marshall Pilsudski's Poland.[9]

The right-wing populist Viktor Orbán has unveiled a program to establish a different constitutional order than that of the liberal West: an "*illiberal-democracy.*" He denounced the "decadent and money-based West" and embraced "a work based society ... of a non-liberal nature."[10] Some authors have pointed to an alarming similarity between these new forms of "democracy" and Putin's "managed" democracy in Russia: "Like Moscow, the governments of these countries are careful to maintain their democratic facades by holding regular elections. But their leaders have tried to systematically dismantle institutional checks and balances, making real turnovers in power increasingly difficult."[11] A startling decline in democratic norms is more than apparent in Hungary, Poland and Slovenia, three former success stories of transformation and stability. But, as Abby Innes argues, the problem of state "capture" (state dominance over the society) is pervasive in the entire region.[12] Crisis situations have automatically led some to revert back to old habits.

Following the 2008 economic crisis, Viktor Orbán's nationalist-populist FIDESz Party attained power in the 2010 national elections in Hungary. After its first term, it won reelection handily in 2014. During its first five years, it initiated the "systematic destruction [of Hungarian democracy] .... In actual practice the executive and legislative branches are no longer separate, as they are both controlled by the energetic and heavy hand of the political leader."[13] A penetrating analysis of the situation has been provided by Princeton law professor Kim Lane Scheppele and the Ljubljana law professor Bojan Bugarič.[14] Maintaining a façade of democracy, the Orbán government has successfully imposed virtual authoritarian rule two ways.

One was to change the law according to their needs. Recklessly exploiting its parliamentary majority's rubber stamp between 2010 and 2014, FIDESz passed 88 bills within a week – enacting 13 new laws in one or two days. When its electoral base began to shrink, it modified election laws seven times to assure future victory, and it amended the constitution on several occasions.

Viktor Orbán and his party "cemented themselves in" with cronyism, by appointing friends and followers to key positions. They dismissed a majority of those belonging to other parties from the state and legal apparatus and from the media. A good example of Orbán's practices was his changing the law to subordinate the independent National Bank to his government. On that occasion, however, the European Union quite uniquely intervened, as Orbán had clearly violated EU law. Forced to formally restore the National Bank's independence, Orbán proceeded to dismiss the bank's president and replace him with a loyal follower, thus assuring the same outcome. At the same time, Orbán has begun to renationalize private property and expand the state sector. The government nationalized private pension funds and (in an indirect way) savings and loan cooperatives. Expanding the state sector has significantly strengthened the government's authority and buttressed its clientelist character. While pocketing the EU's generous aid packages, Hungary's government emphatically avows that it is not subject to the "dictates of Brussels" and has allied itself with Putin's Russia and made advances toward China. An OECD report on Hungary in May 2015 has brought to light Orbán's real social policy:

> Income inequalities and material deprivation have increased sharply in Hungary …. The Gini coefficient has markedly increased since 2010 [from 24.1 in 2007 to 30.5 in 2013], and is above the CEEC average (26.0) …. The poverty rate … (percentage of people who live with less than 50 percent of the median national income level) has risen from 6 percent in 2007 to more than 10 percent in 2013 …. The number of people who report not having enough money to buy food has also increased in Hungary, rising from 17 percent before the crisis to 31 percent in 2012, which is more than twice the share in OECD countries (14 percent).[15]

The regime's "official historians" in a newly established Institute of History, *Veritas,* started whitewashing the authoritarian Horthy regime, including its anti-Jewish legislations.

Poland has begun to follow a similar path to Hungary, with the election of Jaroslaw Kaczynski's Law and Justice Party in the fall of 2015 – caused to a great degree by the flood of Middle Eastern, African, and Asian migrants into Europe. Prior to this, Poland was seen as the "*Wunderkind*" of the region and, in some ways, of the entire European Union, for it was the only country in Europe to escape the 2008 economic crisis. Its GDP has nearly doubled since it joined the EU in 2004. True, it was the main beneficiary of the European Union's cohesion policy, and it received – from 2004 to the end of the EU's budget period by 2020 – more than twice as much aid from the EU in today's terms than did all the sixteen recipient countries of the postwar legendary Marshall Plan combined. Quite understandably, then, its leaders have been strongly pro-European, and one of its Prime Ministers, Donald Tusk, was quite uniquely elected President of the European Council. Although Poland's government at first joined forces with other Central European countries to oppose the EU's mandatory quota system of taking in immigrants, it ultimately agreed to toe the EU line. This enabled Jaroslaw Kaczynski's Law and Justice Party to return to power with a landslide electoral victory in the fall of 2015. The new government immediately adopted authoritarian policies. It began removing political opponents from the state administration and replacing them with their "own" people. With new laws successfully paralyzed, the Constitutional Court that became virtually unable to declare a new law unconstitutional.[16] An ardent admirer of Viktor Orbán, Kaczynski has adopted the Putin-Orbán model of illiberal democracy hook, line, and sinker. His government has combined illiberal foreign and cultural policies with statist economic schemes and unaffordable populist measures, such as a drastic *lowering* of the retirement age in a rapidly aging country and the providing of free healthcare for citizens over 75. Budget deficits may hit 4 percent in 2016. The government is planning to build new coal-based power plants, even though 85 percent of its electric energy is produced by coal. Kaczynski has resurrected an anti-German and anti-EU approach. The so-called Visegrad Group, established by Poland, the Czech Republic, Slovakia and Hungary in the early 1990s, "lacks the votes to block [European] Commission decisions, but if it becomes an illiberal bulwark, Europe's east-west divide will become a chasm."[17] The Hungarian and Polish examples are frightening and reminders of the political fragility of the entire region.

Dependent dual-economies at their halfway point of transformation

In terms of economic transformation, the region remains fragile and dependent. Here, too, path dependence is an important factor. Throughout the modern era, the region was not part of the West and exhibited typical peripheral characteristics. It remained agricultural until the mid-twentieth century. Its income levels have consistently varied between 40 to 50 percent of those of the West ever since the early nineteenth century. The successor states of the former Soviet Union mostly still do not have democratic market systems. Belarus is one of the most extreme examples. The share of the private sector of the economy is still less than 30 percent and state enterprises are working on Soviet-type mandatory state plans. According to the Economic Freedom Index the country is listed as 153rd among 178 countries of the world.[18] In 1995, the region's income level was still below 40 percent of the West's.[19] Some 20–30 percent of the region's populace sunk into poverty after 1990, and the region saw a sharp rise of income differentiation from 0.22–0.24 to 0.31–0.35 on the scale of the Gini index.[20] Income differences have become quite stark in Romania, Hungary, and the Baltic countries. A corrupt, kleptocratic oligarchy closely tied to government is now ubiquitous. This social phenomenon first became a reality during the privatization campaigns throughout Eastern

Europe, when privileged groups, close to power, gobbled up state resources with abandon. Corruption and tax evasion, that old malaise of the region remains a staple of the political establishment, including its highest echelons. According to the 2015 corruption perception index, the countries of the region ranked at non-European levels of corruption. Some of them such as Hungary, Romania, and Bulgaria are 50th, 58th, and even 61st, respectively, among 168 countries of the world.[21] Former Soviet republics, now independent states exhibit even much worse corruption level: Belarus is placed 119th on the list, but Azerbaijan, Kazakhstan, Kirgizstan, Russia, Ukraine, Tajikistan, Uzbekistan, and Turkmenistan are all at an even lower level.[22]

And yet, despite these drawbacks, the region has undergone rapid development. In most cases this was largely due to the huge inflow of foreign direct investment (FDI) into the region. The economic transformation was mostly financed by a newly established financial sector that was not native but Western-owned. On average, 87 percent of the region's banking assets were in the hands of European multinational banks, with the highest numbers in countries that had virtually lacked a banking sector at all: 88 percent of Romania's, 96 of Slovakia's, and 99 percent of Estonia's banking assets were foreign-owned in 2005–8.[23] The same is true for insurance. Since the mid-1990s, Western bank holdings, between $5 billion and $15 billion annually, made up roughly half of all corporate funding.[24] At around the turn of the century, 26 percent of capital inflow consisted of loans, and 19 percent of portfolio investments. The largest part of inflowing capital, 55 percent during the transformation period, was made up of foreign direct investment. Up to the 2008 crisis, capital inflow into the region amounted to more than $200 billion. More than 13,000 foreign-owned companies are doing business in Hungary, as are 5,000 in Poland. Multinational companies hold the key positions in the region's industries. Since the mid-1990s, $15–30 billion of Western capital has been invested in the region annually. These investments are equal to 10–15 percent of the Czech Republic's, Estonia's, and Hungary's GDP, and to 2.6 percent of the region's average GDP. It is not particularly surprising, therefore, that foreign multinational companies have dominated the economies of several of these countries during the early twenty-first century. Nearly half the people employed in industry now work for foreign companies. In Hungary, for example, foreign companies have carried out 82 per cent of investments, 73 per cent of sales, and 89 per cent of industrial exports. One-third of Hungarian industrial exports are in the hands of four Western multinational companies. In Poland and the Czech Republic, foreign-owned companies conduct some 60 per cent of all industrial exports.[25] The major Western retail chains (e.g., the German Metro, the British Tesco, and the French Carrefour) have taken over a huge chunk of the region's markets; in the Czech Republic, sales by Western retail chains total nearly half the country's retail sales. In the early twenty-first century, capital inflow to the Balkans increased dramatically – rising by 374 percent, from $15 billion to $57 billion, between 2000 and 2005.

Multinational car manufacturers have also permeated the region. Even before the collapse of communism, General Motors had set up a plant in Szentgothárd,

Hungary, and Volkswagen opened an engine factory in the west-Hungarian city of Győr. VW went on to purchase the Czech Škoda factory in 1991, and to establish factories in Slovakia, Poland, Ukraine, and Bosnia. KIA and Peugeot have also built factories in Slovakia, which has become the world's number one car manufacturer on a per capita basis, producing 800,000 cars per year by 2006.[26] The world's ten leading car manufacturers were responsible for 82 per cent of Central and Eastern European car production in 2000, with Volkswagen conducting 22 percent and Fiat 10 percent. The multinational car parts industry (including Visteon and Delphi) have also invested heavily in the region. Thousands of multinational corporations have built up a giant subsidiary network in Eastern Europe, among them Philips, Siemens, and Nokia. Asea Brown Boveri (of Switzerland) has opened thirteen subsidiaries in Poland, and IBM has established a worldwide center for notebook hard-disk production in Székesfehérvár, Hungary. Sony began by subcontracting in Hungary, Poland, and Slovakia, and then established its own production plants. As Sony's chief executive observed, these operations "point to a coming of age for Central Europe as a manufacturing base." [27] Several multinational companies established Research & Development centers and service bases in the region. The Ameritech-Deutsche Bundespost consortium, the Royal Dutch Telecom, Swisscom, and the Ameritech-France Telecom have begun buying up the region's telephone systems. The Swedish company Telia and the Finnish Sonera have taken over the telecom systems of the Baltic countries.[28]

The processing industries of the region, especially engineering, car, and electric industries, are parts of the value chains of the West European countries. The share of exports in the production of these industries is extremely high, in each of the Czech Republic, Slovakia, and Hungary reaching about 80 percent. Exports, mostly to the European Union, are representing more than 80 percent of the GDP in these three countries because their productions are parts of West European countries' value chains and deliver their products to the Western mother company.[29]

Development in Central Eastern Europe was not only the result of private foreign investments but also of massive amounts of aid from the European Union. Poland was the main recipient, getting 25 percent of the funds that the EU earmarked for the Community's backward regions. A country with a GDP of $518 billion in 2013, Poland would receive a total of $318 billion of EU aid in the period between 2008 and 2020.[30] As already noted, this is more than twice the modern-day value of the amount allotted by the Marshall Plan. While the Marshall Plan accorded an average of $2.5 billion to each recipient country annually over a four-year period, Poland received $26.5 billion per year between 2014 and 2020. Over the last decade, the EU gave its backward regions, including Central and Eastern Europe, fourteen times more aid than what the Marshall Plan had granted sixteen countries over four years. This generous assistance provides an additional 5–7 per cent to these countries' GDP per year. Hungary, with an annual GDP of $125 billion, will receive nearly $40 billion of aid in 2014–20.

In other words, the region's economic growth for the most part has had little to do with domestic research and development. It is therefore more appropriate to speak of the rise of a dual-economy with advanced, foreign-owned export sectors and a less developed, local sector with a domestic market orientation. As Andreas Nölke, Arjan Vliegenhart, and Lawrence King argue, the Central and Eastern European economies represent a distinct, dependent market economy type of capitalism because of their dependence on Western capital, knowledge, and technology.[31]

When the 2008 financial crisis hit Europe, the transformation and continued development of Central and Eastern Europe was put at risk. It was clear that the region, with its backward-peripheral past and its dependent present, with its relatively weak market institutions, and in the midst of a historic transformation, was more than vulnerable. Most importantly, the region lacked the experience of running a market economy, and was quick to revert to old cultural habits and behavioral patterns. Furthermore, nearly half the 12 years of prosperity in the transition countries between 1996 and 2007 were credit-boom years, especially after 2002 when a credit boom became the norm in that region. How was it to manage without it?

The former Soviet Bloc countries could easily have been the weakest links in Europe, and were presumably more exposed to an economic crisis than were Western countries with established market systems. In reality, however, this was not the case for the region as a whole. In a very surprising way, the transforming countries were less homogenous than were the former Southern European peripheries. The Mediterranean countries sunk into a deep crisis almost simultaneously. In contrast, the Central and Eastern European countries were highly dissimilar in how they were affected by the crisis. Some of them, namely Hungary, Latvia, Estonia, Lithuania, Bulgaria, and Romania (and, outside the EU, Serbia, Ukraine, and Russia), were especially hard hit. In 2009, two new member countries in the region experienced a double-digit decline: Lithuania (17.4 percent) and Estonia (14.3 percent). Slovenia (8.1 percent) was not far behind. The region's average decline, however, was 6 percent – not much different from that of the West. In 2010, only Croatia and Romania had negative growth, while all the others had begun to recover. Among the transition countries, only Hungary, Latvia, Bulgaria, and Romania had to be bailed out to avoid collapse through the end of 2011. Surprisingly enough, a great proportion of the former Soviet Bloc countries were not among the worse off in the European Union. How and why did this happen?

Slovakia, Slovenia, and the Czech Republic were able to restore relative financial order and had strong economic recoveries after the early 1990s. These countries came close to balancing their budgets with direct investment. Most of the transition countries were anxious to join the euro-zone, and, unlike those that were already members, they took the Maastricht requirements seriously – requirements that mandated countries to keep budget deficits below 3 percent of GDP, and indebtedness below 60 per cent. Most put their finances in good order. Slovenia, Slovakia, the Czech Republic, and Poland fulfilled the EU requirements between 2002 and 2007, just in time before the crisis hit. This was probably their most important weapon during the financial crisis, or, at the very least, it put them in an advantageous position to cope with the crisis and to recover relatively quickly.

The transforming countries in Central and Eastern Europe, however, were in a unique situation. Their strong dependence on the West turned out to be an advantage. As already noted, their banking system – 87 percent of bank assets – was in the hands of big Western banks, and there was at least a temporary danger, and some initial signs, that the mother institutions would stop financing the region. However, after the first shocks of financial panic that paralyzed the banking system, the foreign-ownership of the banks turned out to be a great advantage. In Estonia, for example, the Swedish-owned banks soon continued issuing credit, as the Swedish banks had remained solvent. Estonia did not have to recapitalize its banking industry by increasing government debt, as did Ireland and the Mediterranean countries, which consequently went bankrupt. The foreign-owned banks in the Baltic countries assured that they would return to impressive growth within two years.

The European Union also took great pains to defend its new member countries. In March 2009, the EU, the IMF, the World Bank, the European Bank for Reconstruction and Development, and some 40 private banks involved in cross-border operations in the East reached an agreement in Vienna to keep the region crediting and afloat – and did so again in 2012. These two so-called Vienna Initiatives saved the region's banking system from collapse, as had occurred in most of the other peripheral countries.

The big surprise was that, as noted, one of the transforming countries, Poland, became the *only* country in Europe to avoid any crisis at all. Foreign capital inflow had never really stopped in Poland. In 2011, the country ranked fourth in the amount of capital raised; 38 new companies were listed on the Warsaw Stock Exchange, and Poland ranked only behind China on the number of initial public offerings during the third quarter of that year. The relatively large domestic market of 38 million people assured strong domestic demand – retail sales went up by 7 percent in 2009 – and the country did not have to overly rely on exports, which accounted for only 40 percent of its GDP, half that of the Czech Republic or Slovakia. As mentioned, large amounts of European Union funds were earmarked for Poland: "It is reported that the transfer from the Union made it possible for the Polish government to minimize effects of the crisis of 2008–10."[32] Altogether, during the worse crisis years between 2007 and 2012, when the euro-zone had zero percent growth, Poland's economy grew 3.4 percent annually. Its per capita income level increased further by 7 percent between 2012 and 2014, although with somewhat slower growth.[33]

After the first shock of the crisis, Slovakia remained so fiscally sound that it was able even to join the euro-zone, as had Estonia and Latvia. Slovakia, a small country of 5.5 million inhabitants is virtually attached to the German economy. Journalists often call it "Volkswagen Land" or "Detroit in the East," because German companies (along with others, including Asian firms) massively invested and built huge subsidiary networks there, creating the largest and most advanced car industry in the region. Slovakia manufactured 630,000 cars in 2010, thus becoming the world leader in car production per inhabitant. Its close connections to the strongest and most solid European economy stabilized Slovakia's economic situation as well. The country's economy grew by 1.9 percent per annum between 2007 and 2012, and by 2.3 percent in 2014.

The Baltic countries, dubbed the "Baltic Tigers" because they commanded two-digit economic growth before the crisis, sustained a hard landing in 2008 and suffered the sharpest decline in Europe. Latvia's GDP dropped by 3.3 percent in 2008, and a dramatic 18 percent in 2009. Its decline slowed down to 0.3 percent in 2010, but unemployment in the country rose to nearly 20 percent of the workforce – more than twice the euro-zone average of 9.1 percent. Despite their 15–18 percent decline in 2009, and their 0.5–2.5 percent decline between 2007 and 2012, the Baltic countries resumed their rapid growth. Estonia and Lithuania enjoyed 3.2 percent, and Latvia 4.4 percent, growth in 2014. They were able to achieve this because of their close ties to Scandinavia and Finland.

The principal advantage that the majority of the transition countries had was their low level of indebtedness related to their GDP. The average debt level of 12 transition countries was 30.2 percent of GDP, half the level that the European Union required.[34] As Poland and the Baltic countries demonstrated more than anywhere else, low wages and a well-educated labor force in proximity to abundant markets can lead to continued growth.

On the other hand, three transition countries (Hungary, Bulgaria, and Romania) fell into a deep crisis. Indebtedness in Hungary and Bulgaria exceeded the amount of their GDP; in the case of Hungary, it rose to 78.7 percent of its GDP by 2009. Not surprisingly, the three countries had to be bailed out. As the *IMF Survey Magazine* reported on October 28, 2008, "[t]he IMF, the European Union, and the World Bank announced a joint financing package for Hungary, totaling \$26.1 billion …"[35] Austerity measures were immediately introduced in December 2008 that reduced wages in the public sector by 20 percent and increased the value added tax by 3–21 percent, aiming for 7 percent of GDP. In June 2009, a second austerity package cut a further 4 percent of GDP with a second 20-percent wage cut and a slimming of the public administration by 20 percent. Pensions were slashed by 10 percent, and funding of the healthcare and educational systems was cut dramatically. The healthcare budget was reduced by 30 percent, 24 of 49 hospitals were shut down, and teachers' salaries were cut by one-third. These harsh measures halted the decline and seemingly stabilized the economy by 2011. All three countries resumed growth. Hungary enjoyed 1.7 percent, Bulgaria 2.2 percent, and Romania 3.3 percent growth rates in 2014 – in stark contrast to their 1 percent annual decline between 2007 and 2012. Unlike Greece, none of the East European transforming countries needed a second bailout. Interestingly enough, the ways that the northeastern Baltic countries and Poland differed from the more southeastern countries of Hungary, Romania and Bulgaria were pretty much the same as those between the northwestern and southwestern EU countries.

A catching-up process had clearly started around the turn of the millennium. The 4 percent growth that the Central European countries experienced was about twice as fast as the growth in the advanced West European countries. Compared to where they were in 1989, when they lingered at about 40 percent of West European levels, their progress was indeed impressive. Their integration into the European Union led to a very positive outcome. In 2005, the five highest performing Central European countries reached already about 63 percent of the advanced EU level, while the Balkan countries managed only 30 percent. The catching-up process slowed down significantly after the 2008 crisis; by 2014, the income levels of the five highest performing Central European countries' plateaued at 62 percent of Western and Southern Europe's. The Balkan countries made somewhat better progress, reaching 41 percent of the Western level, but they remained very much behind. Altogether, the average per capita GDP of the ten Central and Eastern European countries, including the Baltic and Balkan countries, was $21,876 in 2014, 57 percent of the EU-12 average of $38,583.

Hence, the region definitely began catching up during the first 25 years of its transformation, but its progress has been much slower than that seen in the Mediterranean countries and particularly Ireland. The transformation of Central and Eastern Europe is still only half done, and the region has a long way to go. Far more important than per capita GDP figures would be the region's emergence from its dependent economic status and its transcending its dual economic character that conditions its economic development on capital inflow and foreign multinational activity. It must turn instead to an intensive development, based more on domestic accumulation and innovation within the advantageous framework of the European Union. This process may take several additional decades, but it might very well lead to outcomes that are far different from today's failures and semi-success stories.

Notes

1 The term "Washington Consensus" usually refers to a set of policies advocating economic liberalization, privatization, and fiscal austerity, which were initially designed in the late 1980s by the IMF, the World Bank, and the US Treasury to respond to the economic crisis in Latin America. These policies were applied to former communist countries after 1989. The term was coined by John Williamson in 1989; see John Williamson, "What Washington Means by Policy Reform," in John Williamson (ed.), *Latin American Readjustment: How Much Has Happened* (Washington, DC: Institute for International Economics, 1989).
2 *The European Council, 1993. Conclusion of the Presidency, 1992–1994*, European Council in Copenhagen, 21–23 June (Brussels: European Commission).
3 See: Ivan T. Berend, "What is Central and Eastern Europe?" *European Journal of Social Theory,* Vol. 8, No. 4, 2005, 401–416.
4 In the following paragraphs I used our study, Ivan T. Berend and Bojan Bugaric, "Unfinished Europe: Transition from Communism to Democracy in Central and Eastern Europe," *Journal of Contemporary History*, Vol. 50, No. 4, 2015, 768–785.
5 *Freedom House, Nations In Transit 2014 Report; Eurasia's Rupture with Democracy* (https://freedomhouse.org/sites/default/files/NIT2014%20booklet_WEBSITE.pdf).
6 *Archive of European Integration,* Swedish Institute for European Policy Studies, European Policy Analysis, Issue January 2016, Christoph Hillron, "Overseeing the Rule of Law in the EU. Legal Mandate and Means." See also: *Archive of European Integration,* Communication from the Commission to the Council and the European Parliament, A new EU framework to strengthen the rule of law, COM (2014) 158 final.
7 Irena Grudzinska-Gros, "The Backsliding," in *East European Politics and Society and Culture,* Vol. 28, No. 4, November 2014, 664.

8 *Archive of European Integration,* Foundation Robert Schuman. European Issues No. 378, December 15, 2015, Thierry Chopin, "Euroscepticism and Europhobia: The Threat of Populism."
9 Georg Soros, "The European Union is on the Verge of Collapse," *New York Review of Books,* February 11, 2016.
10 Kester Edy, "EU Urged to Monitor Hungary as Orbán Hits at Liberal Democracy," *Financial Times*, July 30, 2014.
11 Jan-Werner Müller, "Eastern Europe Goes South, Disappearing Democracy in the EU's Newest Members," *Foreign Affairs,* March/April, 2014, 15.
12 Abby Innes, "The Political Economy of State Capture in Central Europe," *Journal of Common Market Studies*, Vol. 52, No. 1, 2014, 88.
13 János Kornai, "Hungary's U-Turn," *Capitalism and Society,* Vol. 10, Issue 2, Article 1, 2015.
14 See Kim Lane Scheppele, "The Unconstitutional Constitution," 2012, posted to Paul Krugman's blog The Conscience of a Liberal for *The New York Times,* accessed October 31, 2014, http://krugman.blogs.nytimes.com/2012/01/02/the-unconstitutional-constitution/#more-27941; Kim Lane Scheppele, "Hungary, The Public Relations Offensive," 2013, posted to Paul Krugman's blog The Conscience of a Liberal for *The New York Times,* accessed October 31, 2014, http://krugman.blogs.nytimes.com/2013/04/08/guest-post-hungary-the-publicrelations-offensive/?_r=0#more-34278; see also Bojan Bugaric, *Protecting Democracy and the Rule of Law in the European Union: The Hungarian Challenge* (London School of Economics, 2014), "Europe in Question" Discussion Paper Series, LEQS, Paper No. 79/2014, accessed January 28, 2015; European Parliament (2013), "Report on the Situation of Fundamental Rights: Standards and Practices in Hungary (Pursuant to the European Parliament resolution of 16 February 2012)," A7-0229/2013, 25 June 2013, Committee on Civil Liberties, Justice and Home Affairs, rapporteur: Rui Tavares, accessed October 31, 2014.
15 *OECD Report on Hungary,* May 2015, accessible at www.oecd.org/governance/government-at-a-glance-how-hungary-compares-9789264233720-en.htm
16 The new law introduced the need of two-thirds majority for any Court decision, eliminated the right of the Court to select cases according to their importance, and has to rule on cases due to their arrival to the Court; the Minister of Justice got the right to run disciplinary procedures against the judges of the Court. In addition, the government increased the number of judges at the Court and appointed several new judges. *Archive of European Integration,* EPIN Commentary, No. 31/22, January 2016, Adam Lazowski, "Is There a Way Out of the Polish Pickle?"
17 *The Economist,* December 5, 2015, "Europe's New Headache" and "Poland, the Return of the Awkward Squad."
18 *Archive of European Integration,* Bruegel Policy contribution, Issue 2016/02, January 2016, Marek Dabrowski, "Belarus at a Crossroads."
19 See: I. Teodorović, Ž. Lovrinčević, D. Mikulić, M. Nušinović, and S. Zdunić (eds), *The Croatian Economic Development: Transition Towards the Market Economy* (Zagreb: Institute of Economics, 2005), 326; Angus Maddison, *Monitoring the World Economy* (Paris: OECD, 1995), 228; Stephen Broadberry and Kevin O'Rourke (eds), *The Cambridge Economic History of Modern Europe*, Vol. 2 (Cambridge: Cambridge University Press, 2010), 299, 302. The latter, although having somewhat different calculations, except the 2005 figure (35 percent), in most time periods did not differ significantly from the others.
20 The Gini coefficient measures income diversity from 0 to 1 (when 0 means that everybody has the same income, and 1 means that only one person received all the income of the country) elevated.
21 Corruption Perception Index, 2015. *Transparency International*, March 18, 2016 (www.transparency.org/cpi2015).

22 *Archive of European Integration,* Bruegel Policy contribution, Issue 2016/02 January 2016, Marek Dabrowski, "Belarus at a Crossroads."
23 European Bank for Reconstruction and Development, *Transition Report 2009. Transition in Crisis?* (London: EBRD, 2009), 13.
24 European Bank of Reconstruction and Development, *Transition Report 2000* (London: EBRD, 2000), 84–86.
25 *Revue Elargissement,* April 12, 2003.
26 *Automotive News Europe,* Vol. 9, No. 10, May 17, 2004.
27 *Wall Street Journal,* April 5, 1996.
28 *Wall Street Journal,* June 2, 1995; March 30, 1998; Ian Jeffries, *The Countries of the Former Soviet Union at the Turn of the Twenty-First Century* (London: Routledge, 2004), 171, 211, 246.
29 See Sóos Károly Attila, "Földrajzi és ágazati koncentráció a cseh, a magyar és a szlovák exportban," in *Külgazdaság,* Vol. LX, No. 1–2, 2016, 86–117.
30 *New York Times,* October 5, 2014.
31 Andreas Nölke and Arjan Vliegenhart, "Enlarging the Varieties of Capitalism: The Emergence of Dependent Market Economies in East-Central Europe," *World Politics,* Vol. 61, No. 4, 2009, 672. Similarly, Lawrence King described Central and East European countries as examples of "liberal dependent post-communist capitalism." See L. King, "Central European Capitalism in Comparative Perspective," in Bob Hancke, Martin Rhodes, and Mark Thatcher (eds), *Beyond Varieties of Capitalism: Conflict, Contradictions, and Complementarities in European Economy* (Oxford: Oxford University Press, 2007), 309.
32 Ivan T. Berend, *Europe in Crisis: Bolt from the Blue?* (London: Routledge, 2013), 145.
33 The Economist, *Pocket World in Figures,* 2015 edition (London: Profile Books, 2015), 198; The Economist, *The World in 2014* (London: The Economist, 2014), 103.
34 European Bank for Reconstruction and Development, *Transition Report 2011. Crisis and Transition: The People's Perspective* (London: EBRD, 2011), 30.
35 *IMF Survey Magazine,* October 28, 2008 (www.imf.org/external/pubs/ft/survey/ so/ 2008/car102808b.htm).

Part II

International factors
and outside challenges

7   Malaise of modern capitalism

Speculative crises, unemployment, and inequality

Capitalism and the more modern industrial capitalism were both born in Europe, and were both challenged in Europe by alternative ideologies after World War I. Those alternatives all failed, but, partly because of the challenges, capitalism itself went through a major transformation. Europe produced a new version of "social market" or welfare capitalism, at times mockingly referred to as "capitalism with human face."[1] The old malaise of the system, however, is still with us, and was painfully so during the decade of crisis in the 2010s.

Early criticisms

Soon after the birth of modern industrial capitalism, almost simultaneous to the publishing of its theoretical foundation by the famous trio of British political economists (Adam Smith, David Ricardo, and John Stuart Mill), a whole series of critical analyses brought to light on a deeply rooted malaise in the capitalist system. These critiques were mostly combined with utopian ideals of a just and egalitarian society. The utopians often emulated the millennial dreams of Plato, Thomas More, and Jean-Jacque Rousseau. In his monumental *The Republic*, Plato describes five social-political regimes beginning with an ideal "aristocratic" one ruled by enlightened philosophy, justice, and equality. This regime, however, degenerated into a less perfect but still mostly fair "timocracy." A further deterioration led to the rise of the "oligarchic" regime, the characterization of which Plato provides the world's first prophetic criticism of capitalism before capitalism was even born. In the oligarchic regime, one sees the

> government resting on a valuation of property, in which the rich have power and the poor man is deprived of it …. The accumulation of gold in the treasury of private individuals is the ruin of timocracy …. One seeing another grow rich, seeks to rival him, and thus the great mass of the citizens become lovers of money …. And so they grow richer and richer, and the more they think of making fortune the less they think of virtue … men became lovers of trade and money; they honor and look up to the rich man, and make a ruler of him, and dishonor the poor man …. The inevitable division: such a State is not one, but two States, the one of poor, the other of rich men …

[The oligarchs'] fondness for money makes them unwilling to pay taxes ...
[In this society emerges] a criminal class, as they are termed .... The existence of such persons is to be attributed to want of education, ill-training, and
an evil constitution of the State.[2]

Marx about the original sin of capitalism

Leaving aside the similar views of several modern nineteenth-century utopians
such as Henri de Saint-Simon, Charles Fourier, and the more practical Robert
Owen, let me turn to the first scholarly critic of the mid-nineteenth century, Karl
Marx. In his towering three-volume *Das Kapital. Kritik der politischen Ökonomie*
(1867), Marx offers the first scholarly critical analysis of modern industrial capitalism, based on the world's first embodiment of this regime in Britain. At that
time capitalism had actually not yet become a dominant world system. Marx sees
capitalism as a stage of human development and notes that the present reality in
Britain's most developed capitalism "only shows to the less developed the image
of its own *future*."

His main point of departure is the theory of surplus value, a critical application
of David Ricardo's theory that value is produced by labor.[3] Marx maintained that
wage laborers produced the equivalent value of their work (including the reproduction of their labor force and the laboring class, i.e. the worker's family) during
a part of the work day, and then, in the remaining part of the day, went on to produce surplus value that is expropriated by the owner of the means of production,
the capitalist. The essence of capitalism, therefore, is exploitation. In a capitalist
mode of production (Marx did not use the term capitalism), labor becomes a com-
modity that is bought and sold on the market, and capitalist ownership, including
property rights, is protected by the entire legal system. While it massively mobi-
lized productive forces, developed technology, and attained an economic output
that had never been seen before, capitalism also led to an accumulation of wealth
in the hands of capitalists while impoverishing the proletarian segment of society.
This invariably led to class struggle.

Marx's critique of capitalism was part of his philosophical mega-theory of
historical materialism. In this theoretical concept, he predicted a sharpening class
struggle that would lead to an "expropriation of the expropriators," and thus to
the destruction of exploitative capitalism and the introduction of socialism in the
most advanced parts of the world. Not unlike Plato, Marx envisioned the existence of five social-economic-political regimes that would invariably emerge in
history following an ancient primitive communism of shared property. The first
class society was the slave society, followed by feudalism and capitalism, and
then naturally followed by socialism and its higher stage, communism – all based
on a higher level of economic development.

Marx's situating communism within the framework of the historical development of the modes of productions was a materialist "translation" of the idealistic
Hegelian philosophy of history, in which when the state develops in a dialectical
way and reaches the highest end-stage of development in an objectified Absolute

Spirit or Idea. Marx described this future development as a logical outcome of solving the contradictions of capitalism and following the natural course of historical development. Communism, the highest stage of human development, creates an abundant and free society where humans do what they wish because they are free from need. Separation of private and community interests disappears as does the state, replaced by an association of free men. Marx painted this portrait of an ideal, egalitarian, and just society based on the highest level of material development. His realistic critique of capitalism culminated in a utopian fantasy of communism.

Improving social conditions and social democratic revisionism

Rosa Luxemburg, Marx follower, in her *Die Akkumulation des Kapitals. Ein Beitrag zur ökonomischen Erklärung des Imperialismus* (1913), corrected Marx's reproduction scheme. Instead of Marx's bipolar society of capitalists and proletarians, Luxemburg describes a world in which non-capitalist and non-proletarian "third persons" also play an important role. (Marx neglected this issue and maintained that this layer would gradually disappear as it appeared to be doing in Britain.) Capitalism, Luxemburg suggested, actually cannot exist without the exploitation of that "third person," which was the peasantry in industrial societies and the entire population in the colonies and non-capitalist, less developed areas later dubbed the "Third World." Luxemburg's analysis of capitalism paved the way for later "development theories" that would prevail along with globalized capitalism in the later twentieth century.[4]

Another disciple of Marx, Rudolf Hilferding, also developed and modified Marx's analysis of capitalism in his 1910 book *Das Finanzkapital*. Based on Germany's development at around the turn of the century, Hilferding depicts a more advanced, twentieth-century financial capitalism in which a high concentration of capital and a dominant role of the banks created "consciously regulated social relations."[5] A few years later, influenced by the experience of the German war economy, he went even further:

> We arrive at a capitalist organization of the economy, where the road leads from an economy determined by the free play of forces to an organized economy .... In reality, organized capitalism means that the capitalist principle of laissez-faire is replaced by the socialist principle of planned production.[6]

Since the end of the nineteenth century, Germany's social democrats concluded that a proletarian revolution was not necessary, and that reforms would suffice in bringing out about a socialist distribution in advanced capitalism. The apogee of this revision of Marx was a series of articles in 1899 by Eduard Bernstein.[7] The leader of the German Socialist Party argued that Marx's description of an accumulation of wealth on the one side and poverty and misery on the other no longer applied in a more advanced capitalist society; thus a proletarian revolution need no longer be on the agenda, for a politically organized workers' party could achieve its goals through parliamentary reform.

Indeed, as has happened many times throughout history, Marx came up with his theory based on past events at precisely the moment that the historical reality had started changing. The same thing occurred with Thomas Malthus' theory on demographic development in the late eighteenth century (see Chapter 4). When Marx worked on *Das Capital* in the mid-nineteenth century, income differentiation in Britain had indeed increased dramatically. The French economist Thomas Piketty stated that from the first to the sixth decade of the nineteenth century, workers' wages stagnated at very low levels – close or even inferior to the levels of the eighteenth and previous centuries, and that accumulation of capitalist wealth and proletarian poverty dominated life.[8] This was graphically portrayed by Charles Dickens (1838), Friedrich Engels (1844), and even by Pope Leo XIII, whose encyclical *Rerum Novarum* (1891) described the proletariat in terms strikingly similar to those of Marx:

> some opportune remedy must be found quickly for the misery and wretchedness pressing so unjustly on the majority of the working class …. A small number of very rich men have been able to lay upon the teeming masses of the laboring poor a yoke little better than that of slavery itself.[9]

During the 1960s and 70s, a harsh and highly political debate raged between "optimist" and "pessimist" historians regarding living standards during the age of industrial revolution in Britain.[10] Today this controversy has been settled with an historical consensus that, indeed, wealth had increased tremendously during that period, but workers' wages and living standards did so only in a very limited way until the last third of the nineteenth century. Three generations of British and West European workers had experienced human degradation and extreme need, but their wages began to increase and their living standards significantly improved during the last third of the century – just when *Das Kapital* had been published.

Legislation restricted child labor and limited work days from what was often more than 12 hours to 9 or 10; housing conditions improved, public health institutions were established, and real wages rose. Between 1890 and 1910, calorie intake surpassed that of the first half of the nineteenth century by 50 percent. The average calorie intake varied between 1,800 and 2,500 calories per day between the late eighteenth century and the mid-nineteenth century; by 1910, however, it rose to 3,100–3,560 calories per day. The share of animal products, meat, eggs, milk and milk products grew from 16 to 35 percent of consumed calories, replacing the one-sided bread and potato diet that had previously composed 69 percent of calorie intake. The nominal share of wealth for the bottom 40 percent of the population rose from 9 percent in 1802 to 16 percent by 1911, while the share of the top 5 percent of the population dropped from 35 to 20 percent.[11] The first welfare institutions offering pension relief and health care were established in Bismarck's Germany at the end of the nineteenth century, and served to take the wind out from the sails of the growing socialist movement. These measures were soon seen in Scandinavia.

And yet, despite this economic development and increasing growth, inequality, that inner rule of capitalism, began increasing again after the turn of the century. To quote Thomas Piketty:

> The data we have assembled ... reveal no structural decrease in inequality prior to World War I. What we see in the period 1870–1914 is at best a stabilization of inequality at an extremely high level, and in certain respects an endless in-egalitarian spiral, marked in particular by increasing concentration of wealth.[12]

Inequality also characterized the gap among nations. The Human Development Index, which combines per capita GDP, life expectancy, and years of schooling, improved in Europe by about 20–30 percent in the half century before World War I. But the peripheries remained the "bottom of the welfare league": by the end of the period, Spain, Bulgaria, and Russia attained a level in the Human Development Index that the Western core had reached 40 years before.[13] Even the relatively fast-developing peripheries such as Ireland, Finland, and Hungary lagged more and more behind the West. Their combined GDP equaled 62 percent of the West European level in 1820, 59 percent by 1870, and 57 percent in 1913.[14] The much larger peripheral regions of the Mediterranean countries and Russia remained economically pre-modern, pre-industrial, and almost entirely agricultural, with only a few mostly foreign-owned industrial pockets. In 1820, the combined GDP of the Russian-Iberian region, including southern Italy, was 66 percent of that of Western Europe; in 1870, that number dropped to 50 percent; and by 1913, 42 percent. The Balkans, under Ottoman rule for half a millennium, failed to modernize and to industrialize. Before the Great War, agriculture still employed 72 percent of the Balkan labor force and produced 71 percent of its GDP. The Balkans' economic standing, measured by per capita GDP, was hardly more than a quarter of Western Europe's.

Capitalism and inequality

The interwar years were the gloomiest chapter in the history of European capitalism. Appalling poverty and high (often hyper-) inflation characterized the early 1920s, followed at the end of the decade by the worst economic depression in world history, with an unprecedented decline in production and living standards and massive unemployment. Free market capitalism was transformed into a regulated market system. Laissez-faire and supply-side economic theories were replaced by Keynesian demand-creating state interventionism in the 1930s. This was the time when alternative economic models proliferated, such the fascist regimes in Italy and Germany, duplicated in Spain and several other peripheral countries on the continent, and the world's first non-market system, the Bolshevik type of state-owned, centrally planned economy in Russia. The United States, the world's leading capitalist country, introduced the New Deal, a strongly state-interventionist policy. Throughout the 1930s, the advanced capitalist countries turned their focus to war preparations and then a war economy. This was a major transformation of the system.

One of the leading economists of the age, the Austrian-born Harvard economist Joseph Schumpeter, diagnosed this radical transformation of capitalism and went so far as to state that it was only a matter of taste on how to name it, for it was probably some form of socialism. "Can capitalism survive?" he rhetorically asked in his 1944 book, *Capitalism, Socialism, and Democracy*. His answer could not have been clearer:

> No. I do not think it can … its very success undermines the social institutions which protect it, and "inevitably' creates conditions in which it will not be able to live and which strongly point to socialism as the heir apparent.[15]

Nearly seven decades later, with the postwar experience of social markets, the welfare state, and lessening income inequality behind her, the leading American historian Joyce Appleby developed a rather different view. In *The Relentless Revolution,* she interpreted the history of capitalism as a system able to renew and rejuvenate itself by adjusting to new situations and requirements:

> Schumpeter raised the possibility that capitalism was doomed because of its tendency to destroy the institutions that protect it …. But Schumpeter failed to take into account the different experiences market participants drew upon when making decisions …. There is no reason to think that societies won't continue to modify and monitor their economies.[16]

The system's transformation led to a turning point in Europe after World War II. This was the culmination of a long process between the 1930s and 1950s. The travails of depression, war, and reconstruction created a new spirit of solidarity. Nothing characterized this new approach better than Sweden's newly elected Social Democratic government's resolve to establish the world's first comprehensive welfare state in 1932. A number of groundbreaking programs were enacted during and after the Great Depression, including Franklin D. Roosevelt's social security program of 1935. The French Popular Front introduced a forty-hour workweek, paid vacation, and collective bargaining in 1936. Winston Churchill's war government appointed an Interdepartmental Social Insurance Committee in 1941 which led to the first comprehensive social welfare program covering all citizens, and introduced the concept of "social citizenship," in Britain. "The purpose of victory," the committee's chairman declared, "is to live in a better world than the old world … to win freedom from want."[17] Post-World War II Europe became the cradle of the welfare state.

Public expenditures increased markedly – averaging 26.3 percent of the gross national product in eight West European countries in 1950. This figure would increase to 35.8 percent by 1965, and would double to 52.8 percent by 1980.[18] Welfare expenditures were paid for with high taxation and a redistribution of income. While the welfare state certainly had a "Robin Hood function," more than half its payments went back to the taxpayer in the form of pensions, health care and free education. Hence, the system employed a "piggy bank function" more than anything else.[19]

Inequality among Europe's countries was also mitigated. The Human Development Index revealed a general improvement on the continent, though it was surprisingly better in the peripheries: while the Western core's index improved by an average of 12 percent, it rose by 26 percent in Mediterranean Europe and 27 percent in Eastern Europe. This was also true of life expectancy: it rose to 62 years in 1950 both in Mediterranean and Eastern Europe, and to 70 years (East) and 73 years (South) by 1975. Life expectancy increased from 67 to 73 years in North-Western Europe during this same period.[20]

Social and political developments during the postwar period had a strong impact on income distribution. Thomas Piketty has pointed to a longer historical trend:

> The shocks that buffeted the economy in the period 1914–1945 – World War I, the Bolshevik Revolution of 1917, the Great Depression, World War II, and the consequent advent of new regulatory and tax policies along with the controls on capital – reduced capital's share of income to historically low levels in the 1950s.[21]

Indeed, during the postwar decades Europe enjoyed a unique Gini coefficient of 0.26–0.28, which reflected rare income equality. (The Gini index quantifies income inequality on a scale between 0 and 1, with 0 meaning that every citizen earns an equal income and 1 representing the other end of the spectrum: a single person earning the sum total of the country's income.) Decreasing inequality was caused by developments outside the economy. In other words, Piketty rejected the so-called Kuznets Curve, the long-standing and widely accepted explanation of income distribution developed in the 1950s. The American economist, Simon Kuznets, theorized that capitalist income distribution looks like a bell-shaped curve. In the first stage of capitalist development, inequality increases (this is the first half of the bell shape); when, however, capitalism reaches maturity with industrialization around the turn of the twentieth century, inequality begins to decrease (this is the second half of the bell shape). In other words, decreasing inequality is a "law" of advanced capitalism. Piketty's critique of Kuznets' theory is that decreasing inequality was actually not inherent in capitalist development, but was instead the result of political shocks.

Indeed, inequality began rising again in the 1970s and reached early capitalism's levels at around the turn of the millennium. Since the last third of the twentieth century, globalization has become the norm, as has globalized neoliberal theory and policy. Deregulation of the financial sector has led to rampant speculation, resulting in several speculative bubbles world-wide at around the turn of the century. At that time, local and regional financial crises hit the world economy virtually every three years – crises like the American savings and loan crisis of the early 1990s, the Japanese banking and real-estate crisis of the mid-1990s, the Mexican financial crisis in 1994–5, and the Asian and Russian crises soon afterwards. The "hot money" invasion of several Asian countries created a credit bubble in Thailand between 1997 and 1999, the sudden bursting of which led to a major financial crisis in Asia that spread even to Eastern Europe. Speculation with high tech industries led to the so-called "dot-com bubble," characterized by skyrocketing stock prices in the late 1990s and their collapse in 1999–2001. CISCO's stock temporarily dropped by 86 percent, and Amazon shares plummeted from $107 to just $7. There were frequent stock-market crises, including the Taiwanese in 1987–89 and the Japanese in the 1980s. At that time, the fabled Japanese economic boom kicked off a wide-ranging speculative mania, which led to unrealistically inflated prices. Giant real-estate and stock-market bubbles peaked in 1989. The Japanese Nikkei stock index tripled in value between 1985 and 1989, but its stocks dropped by 60 percent when the bubble finally burst. In 2004, residential housing prices plummeted to 10 percent of the 1989 levels. Argentina suffered a severe crisis in 2001.[22]

It was no different in Europe. Housing bubbles popped up in Ireland, Spain, and Portugal. Cheap credit flooded the European Union, as the euro-zone was awarded the best bond-rates because its common currency was seen as a guarantee for repayment. Countries such as Greece engaged in irresponsible spending sprees for decades. The speculative bubbles burst when the collapse of the Lehman Brothers generated a liquidity crisis on the international financial markets, and new loans could not be found to repay the old ones. The Irish and Mediterranean governments rallied to bail out their bankrupt banks and consequently fell into a huge indebtedness crisis. Capitalism was now showing its worst face: profits in boom times were privatized, but losses were to be socialized with taxpayers' money or from IMF and EU bailouts. Several peripheral countries were hit particularly hard and were forced to introduce harsh austerity measures to balance their budgets. Ordinary people suffered the most. In hardest hit Greece, which required three bailouts, about a third of its retirees sunk into poverty.

In the 1960s and early 1970s, four leading West European countries averaged an exceptional 4.6 percent annual growth rate; between 2007 and 2012, however, those same four countries could muster an average growth of only 0.1 percent. At the same time, unemployment rose from an average of 2.2 percent in 1973 to 10.5 in 1983 and 7.13 percent in 2012. In the EU, unemployment in 2012 lingered above 11 percent, with 16.3 percent unemployment in the peripheral countries and 38.7 percent youth unemployment (under the age of 25). The hardest hit countries suffered 25 percent unemployment and a youth unemployment rate of 54 percent.[23]

With globalization, inequality began rising once again from the 1970s on. A Groeningen Institute analysis of 25 European countries concluded that their global Gini coefficient was 0.49 in 1820 and 0.66 in 2000. After the "egalitarian revolution" between 1950 and 1980, inequality rose again and reached 1820 levels. The Gini among countries in 1820 was 0.16, and had increased to 0.55 by 1950 and had remained stable. In 1820, Britain was five-times richer than the average poor countries; in 2000, the US was twenty-five-times richer.[24]

Indeed, we see a sharp rise in income disparity in almost every country in Europe during the globalized, neo-liberal era of the last third of the twentieth and early twenty-first centuries. The French economist, Thomas Piketty, has convincingly demonstrated in his monumental bestseller, *Capital in the Twenty-First Century,* that the famous "Kuznets curve-theory" is wrong. Inequality does not decrease as the economy matures. The mitigation of inequality during the first half or two-thirds of the twentieth century was politically determined by the two world wars, the Great Depression, the rise of new-found social solidarity, and political necessity. Moreover, global arms-races increased consumption, and life-style changes in the twentieth century were also highly connected to Cold War competition. The collapse of the Soviet Union and its satellites in 1989–91 took place at precisely the time that globalization took off. When the Cold War ended, so too ended the most critical political factor in post-World War II Europe in over half a century. "Since the 1970s," Piketty writes, "income inequality has increased significantly in the rich countries" and even exceeded the infamous level of early capitalism of the 1820s.[25] In 1985, Europe as an average had a 0.24 Gini index; but in 2000, it had risen to 0.33. Still, while Sweden and Germany had preserved income equality and their Gini index had changed only slightly (from 0.21 to 0.25 and from 0.25 to 0.28, respectively), Russia's index jumped from 0.25 to 0.46.[26] Between 1987 and 2013, the wealth of the top richest 1 percent in the world increased by 6.8 percent per annum, while the average wealth of adults increased only by 2.1 percent. The income of high management 10–17 times that of a manufactory worker in 1992, jumped to 13–25 times by 2000. The European country that most closely resembled the US in this regard was Britain, where management earned 25 times more than workers, in contrast to the socially more sensitive Germany and Sweden, where management earned only 11 and 13 times more.[27] In 2015, when the Volkswagen Group admitted to manipulating emissions in 11 million diesel-cars and its CEO, Martin Winterkorn, was forced to resign, he left with a pension and severance package of $67 million. "The boss-class awards itself by huge pay packets regardless of success or failure."[28]

Critiques of capitalism are again gaining ground. Several critics maintain that the free market is a myth, and that increasingly unpopular corporations have become monopolies. "Big Business came second to bottom ... with only 21% expressing confidence in them according to a Gallup poll even in the United States."[29] The above-quoted French economist, Thomas Piketty, echoed Marx's *Das Capital* when he chose the title of his popular book *Capital in the Twenty-first Century,* on income inequality. Social democratic parties may have shifted to the center during the last third of the twentieth century, but the British Labour Party elected Jeremy Corbin, an old-timer left-winger, as its leader in 2015. Left-wing parties are on the rise in Greece and Spain, while Pope Francis harshly criticizes the "tyranny of the market" system and calls for a more human and just economic system. Also a sign of the times, Bernie Sanders, a self-avowed socialist, was running for presidency and attracting huge crowds in the United States. In various countries in Europe left- or right-wing populism is gaining ground.

In the globalized world system of the early twenty-first century, enormous income inequality still characterizes the various regions of the world: the average per capita income in the world, including China, was between €600 and €800 in the early 2010s; in the United States, Japan and Western Europe, it totaled €2,500–3,000; but in India and Sub-Saharan Africa, it did not exceed €150–250.[30]

Still, while this does reflect major differences among countries, the picture overall is one of decreasing income differentials among countries. The most important factors in this development are the rising living standards and decreasing poverty in China and some other Asian countries. *The Economist* noted when reviewing new statistics on income inequality: "Globalization contributed to higher income inequality within countries, while at the same time leading to a decline of income inequality between countries."[31]

A catching-up process has characterized Europe as a whole. Five former peripheral countries of the North and South have achieved higher growth between 1973 and 2012 than has Western Europe. These countries attained only 61 percent of West European levels in 1950, 72 percent by 1973, but more than 86 percent in 2012. Though not quite as dramatic, a similar catching-up can be seen in Eastern Europe as well. The same can today be said of life expectancy: Western Europe's 80.55 years are not much higher than Mediterranean Europe's 79.49 or Eastern Europe's 74.08 (calculated on the average of 4–6 countries from each of the regions).[32]

Despite changes during the globalization era, European capitalism has still preserved its welfare system and social market orientation. Scandinavia has managed to score the best economic performance while retaining its more egalitarian character. With a system often dubbed "Scandinavian democratic socialism," it remains the only place in the world that has proven Schumpeter's prophecy true that capitalism has been transformed into something that can be even called socialism. Is this the future of the entire European Union? Will the peripheral countries be able to follow in its footsteps after they recover from crisis and austerity? Only time will tell, but it will strongly depend on continued European integration and homogenization.

Notes

1 This term emerged by paraphrasing of the slogan of the so-called Prague Spring, "socialism with human face," a revolt against Soviet-type socialism in 1968.
2 Plato, *The Republic* (New York: Vintage Classics, 1991), 301–304.
3 Before Smithian political economy, according to dominant "Mercantilist" concept, exports that surpassed imports thus led to the accumulation of gold is the source of value and wealth.
4 Rosa Luxemburg, *Gesammelte Werke,* Band 5 (Berlin: Herausgegeben vom Institut für Marxismus-Leninismus beim ZK der SED, 1975).
5 Rudolf Hilferding, *Das Finanzkapital. Eine Studie über die jüngste Entwicklung des Kapitalismus* (Vienna: Wiener Volksbuchhandlung, 1910).
6 Hilferding speech at the Social Democratic Party Congress, 1927: *Protokoll, Sozaldemokratischer Parteitag, 1927, Kiel* (Glashütten im Taunus: Auvermann, 1927).
7 Eduard Bernstein, *Die Voraussetzungen des Sozialismus und die Aufgabe der Sozialdemokratie* (Stuttgart: Dietz, 1899).
8 Thomas Piketty, *Capital in the Twenty-first Century* (Cambridge, MA: Harvard University Press, 2014).

9 Rerum Novarum, 1891, available at w2.vatican.va/content/leo-xiii/es/encyclicals/documents/hf_l-xiii_enc_15051891_rerum-novarum.html

10 See: Eric Hobsbawm, *Laboring Men. Studies in the History of Labour* (London: Weidenfeld and Nicholson, 1964); Max R. Hartwell, *The Industrial Revolution and Economic Growth* (London: Methuen, 1971); Peter H. Lindert and Jeffrey G. Williamson, "English Workers' Living Standard During the Industrial Revolution. A New Look," *Economic History Review,* Vol. 36, No. 1, 1983.

11 See: Mats Essemyr, "Nutrition Needs and Social Estee: Two Aspects in Diet in Sweden During the 18th and 19th Centuries," in Hans J. Teuteberg (ed.), *European Food History Review* (Leicester University Press, 1992); Şevket Pamuk, and Jan Luiten van Zanden, "Standard of Living," in Stephen Broadberry and Kevin H. O'Rourke (eds), *The Cambridge Economic History of Modern Europe,* Vol. I: *1700 to 1870* (Cambridge University Press, 2010); C. H. Feinstein, *National Income, Expenditure and Output of the United Kingdom, 1885–1965* (Cambridge University Press, 1972); Arora Suchit, "Health, Human Productivity, and Long-Term Economic Growth," in *Journal of Economic History,* Vol. 61, No. 3, 2001; Adel P. den Hartog, "Modern Nutritional Problems and Historical Nutrition Research, with Special Reference the Netherlands," in Hans J. Teuteberg (ed.), *European Food History. A Research Review* (Leicester University Press, 1992); Philip P. Hoffman, David Jacks, Patricia A. Levin and Peter H. Lindert, "Real Inequality in Europe Since 1500," in *Journal of Economic History,* Vol. 62, No. 2, 2002.

12 Piketty, op. cit., 2014, 7–8.

13 Carol Leonard and Jonas Ljungberg, 2010, "Population and Living Standard, 1870–1914," in Stephen Broadberry and Kevin O'Rourke, (eds) *The Cambridge Economic History of Modern Europe,* Vol. 2, *1870 to the Present* (Cambridge University Press, 2010), 111–113, 122–125.

14 Angus Maddison, *Monitoring the World Economy 1820–1992* (Paris: OECD, 1995), 194, 198, 200.

15 Joseph Schumpeter, *Capitalism, Socialism, and Democracy* (London: Allen and Unwin, [1944] 1976), 62.

16 Joyce Appleby, *The Relentless Revolution. A History of Capitalism* (New York: W.W. Norton, 2010), 435–436.

17 Sir William Beveridge, *Social Insurance and Allied Services* (London: His Majesty's Stationery Office, 1942).

18 Jürgen Kohl, *Staatsausgaben in Westeuropa. Analysen zur langfristigen Entwicklung der öffentlichen Finanzen* (Frankfurt: Campus, 1984), 315.

19 See Nicolas Barr, *The Welfare State as Piggy Bank. Information, Risk, Uncertainty, and the Role of the State* (Oxford: Oxford University Press, 2001).

20 Dudley Barnes, Neil Commins and Max-Stephan Schulze, "Population and Living Standard, 1945–2005," in S. Broadbarry & K.H. O'Rurke, (eds), *The Cambridge Economic History of Modern Europe,* Vol. 2, *1870 to the Present* (Cambridge: Cambridge University Press, 2010), 400, 406.

21 Piketty, op. cit., 2014, 41.

22 Robert Brenner, *The Boom and the Bubble: the US in the World Economy* (London: Verso, 2002); *The Economics of Global Turbulence* (London: Verso, 2006).

23 Angus Maddison, *Two Crises: Latin America and Asia 1929–38 and 1973–83* (Paris: OECD, 1985); *Explaining the Economic Performance of Nations. Essays in Time and Space* (Aldershot: Edward Elgar, 1995), 361, 370; The Economist, *Pocket World in Figures,* 2015 edition (London: Profile Books, 2014).

24 *The Economist*, October 4, 2014.

25 Piketty, op. cit., 2014, 13–15.

26 Stephen Broadberry and Kevin H. O'Rourke, op. cit., Vol. 1: *1770–1870;* Vol. 2: *1870 to the Present* (Cambridge: Cambridge University Press, 2010), 398.

27 *Archive of European Integration,* "Reform of Corporate Governance in the EU." CEPS Policy Brief, No. 38, October, by Karel Lannoo and Arman Khachaturyan, 2003.
28 *The Economist,* October 3, 2015, "Capitalism and its Discontents."
29 Ibid.
30 Piketty, op. cit., 2014, 435, 64.
31 *The Economist*, October 4, 2014.
32 Broadbarry & O'Rurke, op. cit., 2010, 408.

8 The Russian challenge

The EU's security and energy independence

The Cold War essentially ended during the Gorbachev era in the second half of the 1980s, and was finalized with the collapse of the Soviet Union in 1991. The painful chapter of the division of Europe was seemingly closed. After two decades of stagnation, the European integration process was invigorated by this momentous turning point: in the 1990s, an expanded European Union (EU-15) became the predominant power in a safe Europe.

A quarter of a century later, however, the security of Europe and the predominance of the European Union are both being questioned. Russia has launched a military intervention in the Ukrainian civil war, annexed the Crimean Peninsula, and dominated eastern Ukraine by assisting the ethnic Russian minority's fight for independence – prompting the United States and its western allies to impose economic sanctions against it. Ruled by the authoritarian Putin regime, Russia is becoming militarily increasingly stronger and is flexing its military muscles. Forming its own alliances with Iran and the Assad regime in Syria, Moscow intervened in the Syrian civil war with impressive authority, demonstrating the power of its rebuilt armed forces. It has used its enormous energy resources as a political weapon, and has not shrunk from blackmailing countries dependent on its oil, going so far as to stop deliveries on noncompliant importers. Moreover, the Russian navy and air force regularly violate the national airspace and territorial waters of various Baltic and Scandinavian countries. Such violations led to a dangerous incident when Turkey shot down a Russian fighter jet.

In the *Russkiy Mir* (Russian world), there are 25 million ethnic Russians or "Russian-speaking people' as Putin described them, living in the former Soviet republics, now independent states, bordering Russia, becoming a Fifth-Column in its new expansionist policies. In various speeches and interviews, President Vladimir Putin enunciated the "Putin Doctrine," a clear-cut plan on reconstructing Russia's great power status. He has proclaimed that Russia would defend the interests of all Russian-speaking people "using political, diplomatic and legal means." He has pointedly added, however, that Moscow would recognize the sovereignty and territorial integrity of post-Soviet states only if they pursued a policy "of good neighborly relations" with Russia. In a press conference in March 2014, Putin also declared that Russia reserved the right to use military force to defend Russian-speaking people if they were in danger or they asked for help.

As he unambiguously asserted in his Valdai Club speech, Putin considers the "Russian nation" to consist of "three parts ... with common Church, common spiritual source and a common destiny." Russia and Ukraine constitute the core of the Russian world,[1] which is actually larger than the area populated by ethnic Russians: "When I speak of Russians and Russian speaking citizens," Putin explained at a meeting with Russian ambassadors in Moscow in the summer of 2014, "I am referring to those people who consider themselves part of the broad Russian community, [who] may not necessarily be ethnic Russian, but [who] consider themselves [to be] Russian People." [2]

In an article on the Russian national question in the *Nezvavivisimaya Gazeta* in January 2012, Putin – that time prime minister running for presidency again – building his political ideology actually reinvented important elements of the old Slavophile ideology. He has spoken about the failure of the European ethnic state compared to the traditional Russian, "inherited historical state" which has "an inherent ability to integrate various ethnicities and faiths." He promised to "strengthen the historical state that we inherited from our ancestors."[3] The nineteenth century Slavophile view well-serves Putin's political ideology by its rejection of Europe and Europeanization of Russia, by presenting Russia as a special cultural-historical type of civilization, superior to the European one. He stressed that Europe has an "irreconcilable hostility toward Russia" and Westernization would be a disease and tragic for the Slavic people... The aspiration to transplant foreign institutions onto Russian soil... are wrong and Russia's national organism (*narodnye organizy*) cannot be converted. "Does Russia belong to Europe?" was the question famously asked by Nikolai I. Danilevskii, the prophet of Slavophilism in his 1869 book, *Russia and Europe. The Slavic World's Political and Cultural Relations with the Germanic-Roman West*, which became the bible of the ideology. His answer was a definite "thankfully it does not." Europe is only a peninsula of Asia and the "exalted word Europe is a word without significance." He considered Russia a country where "the whole people freely recognized authority and formed a great family, a patriarchal state." The Russian development is "purely internal," coming from the soul of the people (*narodnyi dukh*). This is the source of the "spiritual and political health" of the Russian people and state. The anti-modernization populist Slavophiles were also pan-Slavist, dreaming about a federal all-Slavic state.[4] It is not accidental that Danilevskii's book was not republished for more than a century; since 1991 it has sold more than 100,000 copies in eight new editions. Putin made an effort to rebuild the inherited old Russian state by a union of as many as possible former Soviet Republics. He stressed that together with those republics "we were victorious in the most terrible wars." Putin also sent a message: "To those who want and try to divide us, I say – in your dreams."[5]

Through Putin's words and actions, including military interference, Russia has indeed challenged and successfully countered NATO's and the European Union's influence and expansion plans in Georgia, Ukraine, Armenia, and Moldova. Russia has clearly emerged as a serious challenge to the European Union in the early twenty-first century.

Russia's "Versailles shock"

History sometimes repeats itself. Nearly a century ago, the Versailles Treaty punished the losers of World War I. Germany, the most ambitious economic and military powerhouse, but a latecomer in the great power competition of attaining a "fair share" of the world, had sought to rearrange the world order and secure its own allotment of colonies. In defeat, however, Germany was eviscerated and humiliated, its military was strictly limited, and its economy burdened with unbearable reparation requirements. It sank into devastating hyper-inflation and mass poverty. In his prophetic book,[6] John Maynard Keynes harshly criticized the Versailles arrangement as a counterproductive and dangerous historical failure in 1920 (!). Counterproductive it most definitely was. It led to a revival of nationalism and revisionism, and to a deep desire for revenge. It led to Hitler and World War II.[7]

This situation was, *mutatis mutandis,* repeated with Russia during the 1990s. The Soviet Union had lost the Cold War and its "outer Empire," the Central and Eastern European satellite states of the so-called Soviet Bloc. This military super-power was marginalized and pushed to the periphery of world politics, and it disintegrated into 15 successor states.[8] Aside from the Baltic States, most of the Caucasus, and several other areas, Russia lost Ukraine, where the first Russian state, the *Kievskaya Rus* (Kievan Rus), had been born in the ninth century. Russia's borders were pushed back 600 kilometers in the northwest, and 1,300 kilometers in the southwest of Europe. Its new frontiers were roughly the same as they had been in the sixteenth century. The country lost parts of its heartland, and it saw its maritime power diminished when it lost the Baltic and Black Seas. These territorial changes were more than painful for Russians. Not only Putin called them "the greatest geopolitical catastrophe of the twentieth century," but even Mikhail Gorbachev declared that they were unacceptable. In 1993, already out of power, he maintained that the loss of Ukraine and Belarus went "against geography and Russian history and would not last."[9]

The disintegration of the Soviet Union was followed by the collapse of Russia. The country's GDP declined by nearly 15 percent in 1992, by nearly 9 percent in 1993, and by almost 13 percent in 1994. Between 1991 and 2001, its annual growth rate was negative, at –3.3 percent per year. Russia's per capita income level dropped by 45 percent and its industrial output by 43 percent at the end of the 1990s. Hyper-inflation devastated the country. Consumer prices rose by an astounding 2,506 percent in 1992 and then continued to rise over the next three years, at 840, 204 and 129 percent, respectively. Inflation persisted until the end of the decade at annual rates ranging between 10 and 85 percent. Companies were often unable to pay wages for several months. Even in 1993–94, 60 percent of the workforce was not paid fully on time, and 32 percent of the population fell below the poverty level. Quite uniquely in Europe, some three-quarters of the Russian population lived at or below the poverty level. A profound human crisis, unmatched in other transforming countries, decreased life expectancy by 10 years to 58.6 years. Russia lost 3 million people between 1989 and 2005. In contrast, privatization led to the rise of a super-rich oligarchy, those with close links to power who robbed the state by privatizing its assets for themselves. Living standards plummeted and income inequality dramatically increased. The Gini coefficient, which was 0.33 in 1991, jumped to more than 0.48 by 1996. Russia became as unequal as the notorious banana republics in Latin America or the autarkies in Africa. Unemployment was 15–16 percent even at the end of the century. Russia was characterized by the collapse of the state and the rise of a criminalized, kleptocratic, and highly corrupt regime.[10]

All this was deeply humiliating for Russians and led to negative political developments in the country. Since the turn of the millennium, Vladimir Putin and his former KGB network have ruled the country with an iron hand. He has strictly controlled the media and eroded all vestiges of democracy: members of the opposition and courageous journalists who wrote about the reality of the regime were often imprisoned or even murdered.

In his *Globalization and its Discontents,* Joseph Stiglitz rightly excoriated Western advisers and the IMF, "who marched in so quickly to preach the gospel of the market economy" and its immediate introduction with "shock therapy." But he was quick to add that "those in Russia must bear much of the blame for what happened."[11]

Nevertheless, Putin's authoritarian regime won significant popularity, partly because he exploited nationalist tendencies and popular yearnings for restored Russian greatness and partly because of the steep rise in oil and gas prices after 2000. One of the world's most important exporters of these energy sources, Russia doubled its GDP between 2000 and 2008 and began to normalize its standard of living and economic standing. In the first years of the twenty-first century, Russia's per capita GDP had dropped to 20–23 percent that of the United States during the 1990s but by 2012, it shot back up to 46 percent.

The West takes advantage of Russia's weakness

At a symposium on the twenty-fifth anniversary of the fall of the Berlin Wall, Mikhail Gorbachev declared:

> Euphoria and triumphalism went to the heads of the western leaders. Taking advantage of Russia's weakening and the lack of counterweight, they claimed monopoly leadership and domination of the world .... To put it metaphorically, a blister has now turned into a bloody, festering wound.[12]

Indeed, the United States and Europe, under the rubric of NATO and the European Union, rushed into the region and incorporated the Baltic States and the East-Central European former Soviet Bloc countries almost immediately after the collapse of the Soviet Union in 1991. They then sought to expand NATO and the EU further with other former Soviet republics: Ukraine, Moldova, Georgia, and Armenia.

In various speeches and statements in the 2010s, the European Commissioner for Enlargement and European Neighborhood Policy, Štefan Füle, called for full

European Union membership for Ukraine, Georgia, and Moldova. Comparing the three countries to the Western Balkans, Füle suggested that they had already decided to join Europe ten years previously, and that each of them already constituted a "potential member state, or a candidate country. Now in the case of Ukraine, Moldova and Georgia, we are at the beginning of this road, we are trying to build more of the EU in those countries.[13] Speaking in Kiev on May 30, 2014, he proclaimed: "If we seriously want transformation in Eastern Europe countries, we should use for the transformation a serious and powerful tool that we have, namely, enlargement," He also informed the German daily *Die Welt* "that the Association Agreement with Ukraine, Moldova and Georgia will not be the ultimate goal of cooperation between these countries and the EU, and that countries move towards full integration"[14] (see Chapter 5).

History teaches us that defeated and humiliated great powers are often dangerous. They are incapable of accepting their reduced status, they seek to recover their lost strength, and they at times yearn for revenge. Germany after World War I is an outstanding example. Versailles led to Hitler. A weakened Russia was not just humiliated by the disintegration of its historic empire; it considered itself surrounded and endangered by a Western invasion of its traditional zone of interest. The veteran American foreign policy expert, former Secretary of State Henry Kissinger, clearly recognized and understood Russia's position during the 2014 Ukrainian crisis, and harshly criticized the US's Russian policy. "Breaking Russia has become an objective [for US officials]," he declared. Instead, "the long-range purpose should be to integrate it." The West misunderstands Russia's relationship with Ukraine, Kissinger emphasized.

> "The relationship between Ukraine and Russia will always have a special character in the Russian mind. It can never be limited to a relationship of two traditional sovereign states, not from the Russian point of view, maybe not even from Ukraine's. So, what happens in Ukraine cannot be put into a simple formula of applying principles that worked in Western Europe .... The European Union [also] did not understand the implications of some of their own conditions [to Ukrainian associate membership of the EU regarding its domestic politics] ... or for Russia to view them as purely economic .... We should explore the possibilities of a status of nonmilitary grouping on the territory between Russia and the existing frontiers of NATO.[15]

Another American veteran foreign policy expert, former national security adviser Zbigniew Brzezinski, concurred and called for the "finlandization" or neutralization of Ukraine.[16]

A European Union Security Policy Brief document in 2014 also assessed the causes of the rising conflict with Russia. It determined that the "Revolution of Roses" in Georgia in 2003, the "Orange Revolution" in Ukraine in 2004, and the "Tulip Revolution" in Kyrgyzstan in 2005 were dangerous developments for Russia. The suggestions at NATO's Bucharest summit of including Ukraine and Georgia in the alliance (nipped in the bud because of German and French opposition), and the continued buildup of Western missile defenses around Russia, created a sense among Russians of a growing Western threat to the country. Putin articulated those apprehensions at the Munich security conference in 2007, when he expressed frustration over NATO enlargement.

In a major speech in Berlin in August 2008, Russia's then President Dmitry Medvedev criticized "a bloc politics approach that continues by inertia." He proposed convening a summit of European governments to draft a new legally binding European treaty that would establish equal and indivisible security throughout the continent. Although NATO and other European security institutions would have a role, Medvedev specified that "all European countries should take part in this summit … as individual countries [and not as blocks or other groups]."[17] Russia's sense of endangerment was further intensified when the West rejected Medvedev's proposal. "By the end of Putin's second term," the EU document concluded, "Russia had given up all hope of joining the West or even being associated with it … Russia began looking for an alternative project where it could be a regional hegemon in the post-Soviet space."[18]

Russian over-reaction: the Eurasian Economic Union and opening toward the East

The alternative quickly became an over-reaction, an aggressive move to anchor former Soviet republics to Russia. The idea of forming a regional trading block with the participation of former Soviet republics had first been broached by Nursultan Nazarbayev, the President of the Republic of Kazakhstan, at a speech in Moscow in 1994. The project, however, took off only in the 2010s, when President Putin began hammering out his response to the European Union. On January 1, 2010, he launched a Customs Union, formed by Russia, Belarus, and Kazakhstan. In an article in the journal *Izvestia*, Putin spoke of "a new integration project for Eurasia, the future in the making."[19] He then created a single market with the Eurasian Economic Space in January 2012. Based on these initiatives, a more ambitious Eurasian Economic Union of Russia, Belarus, and Kazakhstan was established on January 1, 2014– joined by Armenia and Kyrgyzstan in October and December. The five countries, spanning a territory of 7.8 million square miles, have more than 183 million inhabitants. The alliance, however, is totally dependent on Russia, which produces 86 percent of the Eurasian Union's GDP, with Kazakhstan contributing by 10 percent, Belarus by 3.5 percent, and Armenia and Kyrgyzstan together by 1 percent. Emulating the European Union, Putin established his own supranational institutions such as the Eurasian Economic Commission, the Court of the Eurasian Union, an Inter-parliamentary Assembly, and a Eurasian Development Bank. He partly succeeded in enlarging the Eurasian Economic Union by blackmailing neighboring countries (the former Soviet republics of Armenia, Ukraine, Moldova, and others) with a halt of imports and gas deliveries. He secured the participation of Armenia, which had originally turned to the European Union, and intimidated Ukrainian president Yanukovich to change his policy and apply for Eurasian membership. Tajikistan was also invited to do so, as were the break-away regions of Transnistria (from Moldova), Donetsk-Lugans (from Ukraine), and South Ossetia and Abkhazia (from Georgia). In June 2014, Nazarbayev invited Turkey to join.

The member countries established a common market, assuring the free movement of goods, capital, services, and people, with joint external tariffs and plans to create a common electric, oil, and gas market, a shared airspace, and (within 5–10 years) a common currency. Still, in 2012 and 2013, only 12 percent of the member states' total trades were with each other. The future plans, however, are very ambitious and clearly political. Russia and Belarus have already signed a political union agreement, and all the member states belong to an intergovernmental mutual defense alliance. As a Ukrainian journal put it, the "Soviet Union [will] be restored in the form of new customs union." This is certainly the political aim of Putin's Russia, to the extent that it is possible.[20] Via the creation of the Eurasian Union, Russia has multiple targets. "The Eurasian Union is an instrument in a geopolitical game, which is intended to prevent states were formerly part of the Soviet Union from integrating with Western structures." Meanwhile it may also serve to strengthen Russia's international position as well demanding the West and China to recognize his Union as an equal partner in talks on Ukraine and other issues.[21] Putin stated in his already-quoted Valdai Club speech: "The Eurasian Union is a project to preserve the identity of the peoples of the historical Eurasian space … as an independent centre of global development and not just the periphery of Europe or Asia."[22]

Russia has also used the Russian minority in Eastern Ukraine to destabilize Ukraine and reverse its western orientation. The outbreak of civil war provided an opportunity for Russian military intervention and the annexation of Crimea. Although Putin, in any rational consideration, does not pose a real danger to the Baltic countries, which are members of the EU and NATO, he is keen to destabilize these countries as well. Using various means of subversion to create political unrest, Russia has launched cyber-attacks and engaged in provocations by violating the countries' air space and territorial waters. Russia announced that its judiciary would reinstate criminal charges for Lithuanians who had deserted the Soviet army after 1990 when Lithuania regained independence. Among the methods Russia has employed against the Baltic States are the abduction of an Estonian intelligence officer from Estonian territory to Russia and his being charged with espionage.[23] Nevertheless, the roughly one-quarter of Russian minorities in Estonia and Latvia are a potential danger for Russian intervention in those countries. A NATO analysis went so far to state that it would be mistaken not to count with some Russian attempt to challenge the West in the Baltics:

> Russia may not be so much interested in the Baltic states themselves, but might use them as a convenient place to try to demonstrate the uselessness of NATO. Humiliating the United States … is generally seen as a major strategic aim for the Kremlin. Therefore it would be reasonable to assume that Russia would look for opportunities to test NATO and its Article 5 commitments.[24]

There are, indeed, frightening signs. The Russian 76th Guards Air Assault Division was moved to Pskov, 100 kilometers from Estonia. Large-scale military exercises, "Zapad 2009 and 2013," were organized near to the Baltic borders with massive deployment of forces.

Creating a formidable Russian-led regional power is a central pillar of Putin's agenda, combined with an opening to the East. Russia began building closer ties with the rising Asian superpower, China. Putin announced his policy change and the need to turn to the East in 2000,[25] and stepped up the policy in 2010. Russian and Chinese leaders met five times in 2013, and, quite exceptionally, Chinese President Xi visited the Command Center of the Russian Armed Forces. More than 30 meetings were arranged on ministerial levels. Military cooperation was also established, with the countries conducting ten joint military and maritime exercises between 2003 and 2013. This cooperation was anchored with a 30-year $400 billion contract between China with Russia's Gasprom in 2014.[26]

Toward a new EU strategy of security and energy independence

The EU's ambitious Eastern Partnership program failed because of Russia's successful counter measures. Mutual mistakes and misunderstandings led to the Ukrainian crisis, which had clearly demonstrated Russia's readiness for aggressive action. "Russian adventurism means … a real threat to peace in Europe."[27] The European Union was forced to reinvent its policy toward Russia, strengthening its military security and ending its energy dependence on Russia.

Certainly any major military provocation on the part of the European Union is out of the question. Still, the Baltic States with their significant Russian minorities and even Poland continue to feel exposed and vulnerable. NATO's presence in these areas and the revitalization of Europe's plans to build its own unified military force within NATO definitely suffice to guarantee European security. But the Russian challenge pushes the EU toward further integration.

The security crisis of the 2010s led to harsh criticism of the EU's inaction. "The EU is an ostrich [with its] head in the sand while the world around it is in deep trouble."[28] This situation brought back to the fore the need for creating a joint European army. This was an old idea from the postwar years that had gone nowhere. It is quite ironic that Europe does not have a respectable military force, even though the EU-28 countries' combined military spending is $212 (€192.5) billion, second largest in the world after the United States' $577 billion, and much more than China's $145 billion. Europe's military expenditures are roughly three-and-half times larger than Russia's $60.4 billion. The total number of the member countries' troops is more than 1,551,000. These are from 28 independent armies, however, and only the British and French represent real international strength. Britain's exit from the EU further weakened the military strength of the Union. True, 22 of the EU-28 member countries, including Britain, are members of NATO, a military alliance with the US, Canada, and a few more non-EU member states. NATO has about 100 nuclear warheads in Belgium, Italy, the Netherlands, and Germany; added together with Britain's and France's nuclear weapons,

Europe can claim 525 nuclear warheads, the world's third largest nuclear arsenal after the US and Russia.

The idea of creating a European Union army resurfaced and gained new impetus during the Kosovo crisis in 1999, when Europe was unable to act and had to ask the United States to do so. The EU Council decided that "[t]he Union must have the capacity for autonomous action, backed by credible military forces." This led to the so-called Helsinki Headline Goal process to establish a 60,000-strong mobile European army. Nevertheless, virtually nothing has happened to carry out this plan except the formation of a small and inconsequential Eurocorp.

With the new crises in the 2010s, and with instability and wars surrounding the EU, its inertia is probably evaporating:

> On the day the plane [Malaysian Airline flight MH17] went down, the structures of post-war European security, crashed too. For many across Europe, MH17 showed that the war in Ukraine was more than an incomprehensible bloodbath somewhere far to the east – that the breakdown of a stable security order would have consequences for them as well.[29]

American policy has also changed regarding Europe's military power. After NATO's founding, the United States opposed an independent European military force. During the first decades of the twenty-first century, however, American interests shifted to the Middle East and to the danger of ISIS, and will ultimately focus on the new competitor, China. "The more capable Europe is, the more safely the US can focus on Asia."[30] Europe got the green light and also recognized that "we must be more powerful in light of the Ukraine crisis."

The need to create a strong and unified EU army has become particularly important because the American military presence has significantly weakened in Europe. During the Cold War peak years, 300,000 well-equipped American forces were stationed in Western Europe. Because of the end of the Cold War, the number of American forces was reduced to 213,000 in 1990 and to 63,000 troops in 2000. In the early twenty-first century, sharp cuts in spending have led to further reductions: the number of American troops in Europe was only 40,000 in 2012 and no more than 26,000 in 2015. Moreover, at a NATO military exercise, the commander of troops, Lt. General Ben Hodges, asked for weapons from Fort Stewart for nine months of temporary use. "I don't have bridges," he added. "I don't have the trucks that can carry tanks, we don't have enough helicopters to do what we need to do .... Practicing with British helicopters ... using British and German bridges, using Hungarian air defense" are needed for the exercise.[31]

True, in early 2016, NATO decided to increase its multinational forces in Europe including Eastern Europe. The military organization made

> one of the most aggressive moves ... in the region since the fall of the Soviet Union ... [to] send a message to President Vladimir V. Putin of Russia that his aggression in the region will no longer be tolerated.

The United States increased its military expenditure from \$789 million in 2016 to \$3.4 billion in 2017 to contribute the defense of Eastern Europe.[32]

Nevertheless, the EU has to respond to its security problems. In December 2013, the EU Council resolved to develop its military capability, improving its capacity to carry out military operations, develop air transport by creating A-400 strategic airlift units, and improve its rapid response capabilities.[33] Security is now a priority. The EU Council discussed security issues at its Brussels meeting in June 2015, and the Heads of States and Governments met to discuss these issues in Warsaw in July 2016. As an EU document put it: "Economic crisis, foreign dangers, immigration invasion together are too much to deal with, but the revitalization of common defense and security policy is before the door and requires solution."[34]

The new president of the European Commission, Jean-Claude Juncker, told the German weekly *Welt am Sonntag* that a joint EU army would

> convey to Russia that we are serious about defending the values of the European Union …. EU's joint army would react credibly to any external threat and defend the bloc's values. An army like this would help us to better coordinate our foreign and defense policies, and to collectively take on Europe's responsibilities in the world.

Germany's defense minister Ursula von der Leyen welcomed the proposal: "Our future as Europeans will at some point be with a European army." She called the project to be the "main goal and the future of the bloc."[35] Other leading German politicians have similar views. The chairman of the Bundestag's Committee on Foreign Affairs, Norbert Rottgen, concurred that

> a joint army is a European vision whose time has come …. The European countries spend enormous sums on the military, many times more in total when compared to Russia. Yet our military capabilities remain unsatisfactory from a security standpoint …. And they will for as long as we're talking about national mini-armies, which are often doing and purchasing the same things in their minor formats.

According to Hans-Peter Bartels, the chairman of the Defense Committee of the Bundestag, "the past 10 years have added little to Europe's defense …. It is important that we now swiftly implement concrete measures. We should not wait for an overall concept of all 28 EU members, but start with agreements between the nation states." The former EU commissioner and NATO Secretary General, Javier Solana, chaired a task force that presented a report entitled "More Union in European Defence." It calls for new defense cooperation under EU protection, which would have "a political and military ability to autonomously conduct intervention operations beyond the EU's borders." The report proposes policies to develop the EU's strategic and institutional capabilities, and to pool its resources for defense. Ultimately, in the view of the task force's experts, additional integration should culminate in a European Defense Union with military headquarters in Brussels.[36] The crisis of the 2010s has pushed the European Union toward further integration in military affairs, the possibility of a populist takeover in the United States even more so. Donald Trump's potential presidency foreshadows a major change in American policy toward NATO. He made clear several times during his campaign in 2016 that he wants a change in policy towards NATO. He is "questioning NATO's relevance and arguing its members aren't paying their fair share .... Either they pay up, including for past deficiencies or they have to get out. And if it breaks up NATO, it breaks up NATO," as he said in an interview with the *Washington Post*.[37] As is well known, only five countries from the 28 members of the NATO meet the 2 percent standard of military expenditure from the country's GDP. Bernie Sanders, the former Democratic runner for presidency, who in many ways sharply differs from Trump, had the same view about NATO and also maintains that the "United States should not be the world's policeman and that America's allies should not get their defense on the cheap from American taxpayers .... Their views represent a large and growing part of the United States electorate."[38] It is only a question of time before the European Union will have to reconsider its defense policy.

From the security perspective, energy dependence from Russia is highly problematic. President Putin has already used his energy resources to blackmail Ukraine and Moldova to keep them from turning to the EU and to incorporate them into his Eurasian Union. The unpredictability of Russia pushes Europe toward energy independence. The EU-28 countries are highly dependent on Russian oil and gas, and also need Russia for nuclear power generation. In 2013, 34 percent of the EU-28 countries' crude oil came from Russia, as did 39 percent of its natural gas and 28 percent of its coal. As a whole, the EU imports 53 percent of its energy resources from Russia. A number of countries, such as Austria, Bulgaria, Hungary, Lithuania, and Poland, import more than 75 percent of their oil and gas from Russia. The Baltic States, Hungary, Slovakia, Bulgaria, the Czech Republic, and Finland are dependent on nuclear fuel deliveries from Russia.[39] Since 2006, energy independence has been recognized as a major security issue. According to the analysis of the European Commission, Europe needs to invest €200 billion per year in the next decade to attain energy independence. Donald Tusk, Poland's Prime Minister between 2007 and 2014 and then president of the European Council, proposed the creation of a European Energy Union. In October 2014, the European Council resolved that it must have energy security, and agreed to a plan to achieve this by 2030.[40] It has become clear that the "Europeanization" of energy policy is unavoidable. "The main challenges are deeply interconnected and can no longer be treated separately and without a large role of the European Union."[41] The Union's energy plan has five dimensions: securing energy supplies; completing an internal energy market; reducing demand; decarbonizing the energy mix; and promoting research.

One element in this project is to guarantee energy supply from countries other than Russia. Lithuania, for example, signed an agreement with Norway in the fall of 2014. The EU contracted to import liquefied natural gas from Algeria, Qatar, and Nigeria, gas from Norway, and shale gas from the United States. The Union has called for a common purchasing agreement and a fully integrated energy market in the place of separate contracts and markets of single member countries. In 2009, the EU adopted the 20–20–20 energy target: decreasing energy consumption by 20 percent, using 20 percent renewable energy, and reducing emissions by 20 percent, compared to 1990. "The European Union" already in 2014 "is largely on track to meet [the targets]."[42] In 2005–11, the EU's energy consumption dropped by 7 percent, its share of renewable energy rose by 4.5 percent, and its greenhouse emissions decreased by 13 percent. The European Commission's new proposal in 2014 called for the reduction of emissions by 40 percent, its share of renewable energy to rise to 27 percent, and a decrease of consumption by 30 percent. Instead of the 20–20–20 plan, the new target was 40–30–27.[43] Europe soon will be the leader in renewable energy production and consumption.

The Russian challenge and the deeply troubled neighborhood around the European Union have led it to enhance its military capability and energy security by shifting toward military cooperation and unification and a European Energy Union. These further steps of integration became especially urgent after the Brexit that highly served Russian foreign policy interest. These initiatives will certainly not lead to speedy results, but both are on the horizon.

Notes

1 *Archive of European Integration,* OSW Commentary, No. 131, 28/03/2014, Marek Menkiszak, "The Putin Doctrine: The Formation of a Conceptual Framework for Russian Dominance in the Post-Soviet Area." Putin's Valdai Club speech in September 2013 (http://eng.Kremlin.ru/news/6007): Interview (http://eng.Kremlin.ru/transcripts/5747); Press conference on March 4, 2014 (http://eng.Kremlin.ru/news/6763).
2 *Archive of European Integration,* Egmont, Security Brief, No.58, November 2014, Patrick Nopens, "Beyond Russia's Versailles Syndrome."
3 *Nezvavivisimaya Gazeta*, January 30, 2012, Official English translation: Prime Minister Vladimir Putin's article for Nezavisimaya Gazeta, "Russia: The National Question" (archive.premier. gov.ru/eng/events/news/17831/).
4 Nikolai Iakovlevich Danilevskii, *Russia and Europe. The Slavic World's Political and Cultural Relations with the Germanic-Roman West,* Translated by Stephen M. Woodburn (Bloomington, IN: Slavica Publishers, 2013), 47–48, 225, 365.
5 *Nezvavivisimaya Gazeta*, January 30, 2012, Official English translation: Prime Minister Vladimir Putin's article for *Nezavisimaya Gazeta*, "Russia: The Ethnicity Issue" (archive.premier.gov.ru/eng/events/news/17831/).
6 John Maynard Keynes, *The Economic Consequences of the Peace* (New York: Harcourt, Brace and Howe, 1920).
7 Germany was not alone with its Versailles shock. Italy started the war on Germany's side but changed side and belonged to the victors, did not get what it wanted, and the disappointment in Versailles led to Mussolini's Fascism. Hungary, drastically mutilated by the Trianon Treaty, losing 60 percent of its territory and pushing 3 million Hungarians into minority status in neighboring countries, became the closest ally of Mussolini and then Hitler, heated by revenge and territorial revision, and joined Hitler's war.
8 Revolts started in the three Baltic republics and continued in the Caucasus. In September 1989, Azerbaijan declared independence, in March 1990, Georgia, Lithuania, and Estonia, in May Latvia, in June Russia and Uzbekistan, in July Ukraine, in August

Turkmenistan, Tajikistan, and Armenia, in September Moldova, in October Kazakhstan, and in December Kirgizia. On December 25, 1991, the Russian flag replaced the Soviet flag on the Kremlin. In January 1992, the Commonwealth of Independent Republics was announced.

9　www.zei.uni-bonn.de/dateien/discussion-paper/DP_C226_Ruehl.pdf
10　*Transition Report 2000, Employment, Skills and Transition* (London: European Bank for Reconstruction and Development, 2000), 204–5; *Economic Survey of Europe*, 2000 No. 2/3, United Nations, Economic Commission for Europe (New York: United Nations, 2000), 125; Angus Maddison, *The World Economy. A Millennial Perspective* (Paris: OECD, 2001); The Economist, *Pocket World in Figures* (London: The Economist and Profile Books, 2004 and 2015 editions).
11　Joseph Stiglitz, *Globalization and its Discontents* (London: W.W. Norton, 2002), 133–134.
12　Reuters, Berlin, November 8, 2014, "Gorbachev Says World is on Brink of a New Cold War" (www.reuters.com/article/ukraine-crisis-gorbachev-idUSL6N0SY0P520141108)
13　www.rt.com/shows/worlds-apart-oksana-boyko/170128-fule-ing-enlargement-eu/
14　*Die Welt*, May 30, 2014, "Ukraine, Moldova und Georgia sollen in die EU"; gbtimes.com/world/georgia-moldova-and-ukraine-must-become-eu-members
15　www.rt.com/usa/312964-kissinger-breaking-russia-ukraine
16　www.bloomberg.com/news/articles/2014-04-11/brzezinski-sees-finlandization-of-ukraine-as-deal-maker
17　archive.kremlin.ru/eng/speeches/2008/06/05/2203_type82912type82914type 84779_202153.shtml.
18　*Archive of European Integration*, Egmont, Security Brief, No. 58, November 2014, Patrick Nopens, "Beyond Russia's Versailles Syndrome."
19　*Izvestia*, October 3, 2011.
20　See: *Archive of European Integration*, OSW Commentary No.157, January 20, 2015, "The Eurasian Economic Union – More Political, Less Economic"; *Russia Today*, July 7, 2014, "Russia, Belarus, Kazakhstan Sign 'Epoch' Eurasia Economic Union"; *Financial Times*, October 6, 2011, Neil Buckley, "Putin's Eurasian Push Challenges West"; *Kyiv Post*, December 18, 2009, "Soviet Union to be Restored in the Form of New Customs Union"; *Washington Post*, May 29, 2014, "Russia, Kazakhstan, Belarus, form Eurasian Economic Union."
21　*Archive of European Integration*, OSW Commentary No. 195, January 27, 2016, Jan Strzelecki, "The Eurasian Economic Union: A Time of Crisis."
22　Putin's Valdai Club speech: http://www.rg.ru/2013/o9/19/stenogramma.site.html
23　*Archive of European Integration*, Egmont Policy Brief, No. 64, June 2015, Biscop Svens, "Hybrid Hysteria"; *Think Tank Review,* Issue 22, March 22, 2015; OSW Commentary, January 23, 2015, "The Baltic States on the Conflict in Ukraine."
24　*Archive of European Integration*, Research Division of NATO's Defense College, Rome, No. 124, December 2015, Henrik Praks, "Hybrid or Not: Deterring and Defeating Russia's Ways of Warfare in the Baltics – The Case of Estonia."
25　*Nesavisimaya Gazeta*, November 14, 2000, "Rossiya novyie vostochnyie perspektivy."
26　*Archive of European Integration*, OSW, Witold Rodkiewicz, "The Turn to the East. The Flowed Diversification of Russian Foreign Policy."
27　*Archive of European Integration*, EPC Challenge Europe, No. 22, September 2014, Janis A. Emmanouilidis and Paul Ivan, "State of the Union and Key challenges for European Future."
28　*Archive of European Integration*, CEPS Commentary, July 21, 2014, Karol Lannoo, "Europe Wake Up!"
29　*The Economist*, October 17, 2015, "Crash Course. An Airliner Shot Down by a Missile Was a Wake-up Call for Europeans Unprepared for War."
30　*Archive of European Integration*, Egmont Paper 67, Sven Biscop, "Game of Zones. The Quest for Influence in Europe's Neighborhood," June 2014.

31 *The New York Times,* October 19, 2015, "Despite Cuts, Army is Alert for Threats in Europe."
32 *The New York Times,* February 11, 2016, "NATO will Expand its Military Presence in Europe."
33 *Archive of European Integration,* Security Policy Brief, No. 62, April 2015, Laurent Donnet, "Time to Think About a European Union Operated Airlift Capability?"
34 *Archive of European Integration,* Egmont Paper 79. David Fiott (ed.), "The Common Security and Defence Policy: National Perspectives."
35 Andy Eckardt, "European Union Army Plan Aims to Protect Continent from Russia, ISIS," NBC News, www.nbcnews.com/news/world/could-joint-european-army-protect-nato-russia-isis-n322841
36 Quotes from Rottgen, Bartels, and Solana from www.rt.com/news/238797-eu-joint-army-threat/; see also report "More Union in European Defence" (www.ceps.eu/publications/more-union-european-defence).
37 thehill.com/policy/defense/275290-trumps-nato-criticism-wins-positive-reviews
38 www.huffingtonpost.com/sarwar-kashmeri/trump-and-sanders-natos-p_b_9394366.html
39 *Archive of European Integration,* European Policy Center, Policy Brief, March 3, 2015, Annika Hedberg, "EU's Quest for Energy Security. What Role for the Energy Union?"
40 Ibid.
41 *Archive of European Integration,* European Policy Center Commentary, March 18, 2015, Marco Gioli, "The Energy Union: What is in a Name?"
42 www.eea.europa.eu.publications/european-union-greenhouse-gas-inventory-2014
43 *Archive of European Integration,* Bruegel Policy Brief, 02, Issue 2014/05, September 2014, Georg Zachman, "Elements of Europe's Energy Union."

9   The immigration crisis and its explosive consequences

History: the continent of emigration

One of the most startling and dangerous crises that has struck Europe in the 2010s was mass migration to Europe from the Middle-East, North- and Sub-Sahara Africa, and as far away as Pakistan, Afghanistan, and even Haiti. This was an essentially unprecedented event in the millennial history of the continent. The Great Migration or "barbarian invasion" of Europe between the third and seventh centuries was estimated to have comprised a few hundred thousand tribal Germans, Franks, Vandals, Goths, Huns, and others. It more or less continued, but with much fewer numbers, until the tenth century, and in the process transformed the European continent. Settled, stable states were established, and new mass migration did not rock Europe for another millennium.

Moreover, during modern times, especially in the nineteenth century, Europe became a continent of mass emigration. During a demographic revolution in the late eighteenth and nineteenth century when the continent's population nearly quadrupled, Europe was unable to provide land, work, and food to its suddenly expanded population. Inspired by the "push effects" of landlessness, poverty, and religious discrimination, and the "pull effect" of the allure and promise of America (free land, jobs and equality), some 50–60 million people left Europe and established the so-called white colonies in America, as they did in Australia, New Zealand, South Africa, and parts of Latin America. Emigration started off in Britain (including Ireland) and Germany, and culminated around the mid-nineteenth century. In 1880, more than half of Europe's emigrants were still from these two countries. This ended in the last decades of the nineteenth century, but it was followed by a new migration of landless Italians, Scandinavians, East Europeans, as well as Russian Jews fleeing from pogroms. Emigration from the poor European peripheries increased from less than half in 1880 to 80 percent of the total in the early twentieth century. It declined sharply after World War I because of strict immigration restrictions in the United States, but it nonetheless continued – albeit slowly – especially during the 1930s.

Postwar migration crises and the first arrival of non-Europeans

After World War II, however, migration from Europe radically changed. The continent stopped sending huge numbers of emigrants abroad. During the 1950s and

1960s, migration was fundamentally within Europe, mostly from Mediterranean countries and Eastern Europe to the West. Roughly 12–13 million ethnic Germans returned to Germany from the East, where most of their families had lived for two-three centuries. Some had escaped with the withdrawing German army; others were expelled, especially from Poland and Czechoslovakia. Another 2–3 million uprooted people, including half of the Holocaust survivors and escapees from communism in the East, looked for new countries in which to settle.

Since the 1950s–60s, European migration has consisted of destitute people from the Mediterranean region, Spain, Portugal, and Yugoslavia moving to affluent Western countries to work. Italy, Spain, Portugal, Ireland, Norway, and Finland continued to be countries of emigration until the 1980s. There were periods when refugees engulfed other countries, such as the mass migration of 1.2 million Serbs, Bosnians, and others during the Yugoslav civil war in the first half of the 1990s. The former communist countries, after the collapse of their regimes in 1989, and especially after their acceptance into the EU in 2004–7, continued to send emigrants to the West. The younger generations in several of these countries do not see a future for themselves in their homelands. Some one million Poles left for the West in the 1990s, and some 500,000 Hungarians did so during the 2000s and especially in the 2010s – a shockingly high number, given that it was three times higher than those who left Hungary after the crushing of the 1956 revolution. A large part of the several-million strong Roma population has fled poverty and discrimination, especially in Bulgaria and Romania, for generous welfare benefits in mostly Scandinavian countries. The free movement of people, including the right to work in other EU member countries, has already led to opposition and resistance in certain countries. As a result, Britain wanted to stop providing welfare assistance for migrants from other EU countries. Migration became one of the main issues for Britain to decide in the summer of 2016 to leave the EU.

From the 1960s on, Europe also became the destination of immigrants from a number of non-European regions. This new trend had started with the *collapse of the colonial empires*. Millions moved back to their homelands from Asia and Africa. A million French Algerians returned to France in 1962, and 4 million "*retornado*" moved back to Portugal after its 1974 revolution and the collapse of the last remnants of its colonial empire. Millions of Brits, French, Dutch, and Belgians came back from Asia and Africa during the 1960s, with no fewer than 10 million settling in Europe by the end of the decade. Many British and French citizens in the colonies were native Asians and Africans, and many of them also moved to Europe. This trend slowly continued. Around the turn of the millennium, 16 percent of immigrants (600,000 people) were still returnees to their home countries from former colonies. However, the migration of European citizens from former colonies became increasingly insignificant in European immigration.

Instead, the most important new factor has been the influx of *guest laborers* into Europe since the 1950s on. Unprecedented economic growth and a flourishing economy in postwar Europe required millions of new laborers, first to do the dirty and physically demanding jobs that had been spurned by local inhabitants. Europe created a new class of *gastarbeiter*, first in Germany, Switzerland,

and Luxembourg. No less than a quarter of Switzerland's and a third of Luxembourg's population were guest workers at around the turn of the millennium. Between 1955 and 1964, Germany signed guest worker agreements with several Mediterranean countries, Italy, Spain, Portugal, Greece, and also Turkey (1961). Only 0.7 million foreigners lived in Germany in 1960; that number jumped to 5 million at the end of the 1980s and 8 million– about 9 percent of the country's population– in 2010. Turkish Muslims constituted a significant minority in Germany, with Berlin becoming the second largest Turkish city after Istanbul. Some 220,000 guest workers came to Europe each year during the 1960s and 1970s, rising to 500,000 in the late 1980s. By that time, France, Italy, and Britain could each claim some 4 million immigrants. In 1985, net immigration had a positive balance for the first time; that is, the number of immigrants in Europe exceeded the number of emigrants. By then, 8–10 million immigrants were already living permanently in Europe. Immigration would only increase over the next quarter of a century: 300,000–400,000 people have applied for asylum in the EU-15 countries every year since the turn of the millennium, and 20–30 percent of them have been accepted.[1]

Mass immigration in the 2000s

Since the first decades of the twenty-first century, immigration to Europe has accelerated. Nevertheless, until 2014 the inflow of people was stable and not over-whelming. In 2014, the largest group of immigrants arrived from Ukraine. Poland issued 355,000 first-residence permits, mostly for Ukrainians. The second and third largest groups were Chinese (200,000) and Indian (135,000). Only 82,000 permits were issued for Syrians, virtually equal with permits for Belarussians. More importantly, 680,000 first-residence permits were issued for family unifica-tion, 477,000 for educational purposes, and 572,000 for employment.[2]

Immigration in 2014 and especially 2015, however, created a severe crisis. Millions of migrants "invaded" Europe in a chaotic way from around the world. To understand this new phenomenon, one has to consider the radical global changes that have taken place. Millions have been displaced in a number of troubled countries, tormented by civil wars, violent tribal, ethnic, and religious conflicts, ruthless dictatorships, and untold suffering. This includes half of the population of civil-war-ridden Syria, large numbers of Iraqis, Afghans, Libyans, Palestinians from Gaza, Arab Christians, North- and Sub-Saharan Africans, and refugees from Eritrea and the Democratic Republic of Congo. In the mid-2010s, some 65 million people were displaced throughout the world and many were on the move. David Miliband, president of the International Rescue Committee, observed that thanks to nearly 30 civil wars in weak countries unable to handle the situation, "one in every 122 people on the planet today is fleeing conflict." Europe had fundamen-tally nothing to do with this crisis, which was triggered by American interventions in Iraq and Afghanistan and the meltdown of several countries; nevertheless, mass migration became "a real arrow pointed at the heart of the European Union."[3]

Aside from these tragedies, millions are living in profound poverty in mismanaged countries without any hope of making a sufficient living. Consequently, economic migrants have fled Bangladesh, Pakistan, Senegal, Haiti, and several other regions. Together with man-made calamities, we find climate change, unprecedented natural disasters, rising sea levels, and desertification of land that eliminate sources of livelihood, all of which, some analysts suggest, may drive 500 million out of their homelands over the next five years or so. In the midst of the biggest migration crisis in 2015, when one million refugees besieged Europe, Joschka Fisher, the former German foreign minister, ruefully warned: "This is only the beginning of the crisis, because the conditions inciting the people to flee their homelands will only worsen."[4]

Indeed, a Gallup Poll of 93 percent of the world's adult population in more than 150 countries between 2009 and 2011 reveals that 40 percent of the 174 million Nigerians would emigrate to the West if they could; 33 percent of Sub-Saharan Africans would cross the Sahara Desert by foot to reach Europe; and altogether 630 million adults wish to move to another country, out of whom 48 million intend to do so "next year." Of these, 19 million have already made preparations to leave. The polls have indicated that 145 million of these potential migrants aspire to go the United States, and 142 million would go to the European Union.[5]

The European Union's well-established, and in some countries, very generous welfare system, and the high wage levels particularly in its Western half (specifically Germany and Sweden), made it extremely attractive for migrants from around the world. Although only relatively few potential migrants make it to their destinations, the numbers are frightening. During the first decade of the twenty-first century, Spain, Italy, Britain, France, and Germany each had 100,000 net increases of migrants per year. Belgium, Sweden, Ireland, Austria, Portugal, the Netherlands, Greece, Finland, Denmark, Cyprus, Malta, and a few former communist countries such as the Czech Republic, Hungary, Slovenia, and Croatia, each netted roughly 50,000 migrants per year. During that decade, only a few East European EU member countries, such as Bulgaria, Lithuania, Latvia, Poland, Slovakia, and Estonia, could still claim a negative migration balance of at least 1,000 people per year. Romania had the most: 161,000 net emigrants.[6]

Nevertheless, the Gallup Poll cited above revealed that an additional 36 million Europeans are considering moving mostly from the peripheries to the Western half of the continent. By January 2014, the number of immigrants born outside the EU totaled 33.5 million, while immigrants from other EU member countries numbered nearly 18 million in the EU-28. More than three-quarters of immigrants from outside the EU settled in five countries: Germany (7 million), the United Kingdom (5 million), Italy (5 million), Spain (4.7 million) and France (4.2 million).[7]

In addition to legal immigrants, however, millions of illegal immigrants entered Europe as well – estimated at between 3 and 10 million as early as 2008.[8] In Spain, 47 percent of immigrants originated from Latin America; in France, 40 percent came from Africa; in Portugal, 47 percent were from Africa and 21 percent from Latin America; and in Britain, 29 percent arrived from Asia. In 2008, immigrants constituted more than 12 percent of Europe's population, and 15–16 percent in some EU-15 countries: 16 percent in Ireland and Austria, 15 percent in Germany and Sweden, 13 percent in Spain, 12 percent in Belgium, and 11 percent in France, the Netherlands and Britain. Nearly one-quarters of these immigrants are Africans. An increasing number of second generation immigrants (children of immigrants) were born and educated in Europe.[9]

Foreign workers play an important role in Europe's labor force. In the early twenty-first century, they constituted a quarter of the labor force in Switzerland, 15 percent in Germany and Austria, and 10–13 percent in Spain, Sweden, the Netherlands, France, Britain, and Ireland. Because of rapid aging and a lack of demographic reproduction in the EU (see Chapter 4), "Europe needs migrants. It has too few workers to pay for its citizens' retirement and to provide the services they want."[10] According to some estimates, the number of immigrant laborers needed in Europe might be 40 million by the late 2020s.

Some of European countries have allowed immigrants only a transitory guest worker status, and have blocked any path toward citizenship. Switzerland, for instance, issues only guest worker visas for three years and regularly exchanges its foreign population. This was actually the case in several countries during the early period of immigration. Germany, one of the largest immigrant destinations, had a special citizenship law requiring a blood connection (*jus sanguinis*) as a prerequisite for citizenship.[11] In 2000, however, it modified its citizenship law and permitted immigrants to acquire citizenship. In the 1980s, only 2 out of 1,000 foreigners who had lived in the country for more than ten years became citizens; during the first decade of the twenty-first century, however, one-and-half million foreigners acquired citizenship in Germany. In France and Britain, the territorial principle (*jus soli*) predominated and citizenship was automatically granted to anyone born in the country. Altogether, more than 7 million immigrants acquired citizenship in the EU-27 countries during the first decade of the new century. These numbers are rapidly accelerating. According to Eurostat data, nearly 1 million immigrants became EU citizens in 2013 alone, 871,000 of whom were immigrants from non-EU countries.

The mass movement and even migration of people within an integrating Europe began to be commonplace in the second half of the twentieth century, especially after the Schengen Agreement on a borderless European Union. A million Brits retired and bought homes in Spain; large numbers of Mediterranean and East European peoples became guest workers, and a good part of them settled in the North West. The governments of several countries adopted integration policies that facilitated the immigrants' integration into the host societies. The EU maintained a consistent immigration policy since 1980 that worked toward integrating immigrants and provided them equal rights and working conditions. One of the European Commission's first proclamations on the topic in March 1979 affirmed the goal of "equal treatment as regards living and working conditions, social security provisions, vocational training, adult education and especially the education of migrant workers' children concerning health and accommodation."[12] A second report on the topic in 1990 included a paragraph entitled "Integration or what else?" that flatly declared integration to be "inescapable." The immigrants have to "be one of us socially, economically and, at least in a rudimentary sense, politically."[13] In 2000, the European Commission again affirmed that civil and political rights must be given to immigrants, and it stressed the importance of family unification in the integration process (EU Family Reunification Directive).[14]

Despite considerable opposition among its citizens, the target countries of migrants in Western Europe have also sought to integrate immigrants into their societies– either through assimilation, as in France, or under the banner of multiculturalism, as in Britain, Germany, and the Netherlands. Every immigrant to Sweden receives an "integration plan" that provides assistance in finding employment and housing as well as free language studies. In the Netherlands, immigrants receive free and compulsory language and history courses. A number of countries and even individual cities maintain their own integration policy programs.

Immigration crisis of the 2010s

Immigration to Europe is the result of the sheer desperation of millions of migrants in the mid-2010s. Mass migration quickly became chaotic and mostly took place outside the legal framework of the various European countries. Millions of illegal immigrants turned up in Greece, Italy, Spain, France, the Netherlands, and Britain – totaling between 5,000 and 10,000 a day in the summer and fall of 2015. An enormous number engulfed the southern, central, and east European countries, often from neighboring areas, but also from as far away as China, Pakistan, Sub-Sahara Africa, and Afghanistan. The numbers slowed down somewhat when winter came early that year, but it still remained alarmingly high. Only 23,000 people had arrived in Europe in October, 2014; the following October, the number was 220,000.

During the 2010s, when conditions in Africa and the Near East deteriorated dramatically, an unprecedented flood of emigrants destabilized Europe. Syrians, Iraqis, Tunisians, Eritreans, Nigerians, Sudanese, and Chadians fled wars, massacres, hunger, and hopelessness. The peoples of the Middle-East and North Africa began moving to Europe *en masse,* with their numbers multiplying from year to year. Center stage in the migration crisis was civil-war-torn Syria, where 12 million people, half the population, were displaced. Nearly half of them had fled and were temporarily settled in neighboring countries. Turkey took in more than 2 million, Lebanon about 1.1 million (a quarter of its population), and Jordan 1.4 million (20 percent of its population). More than a million migrants embarked for Europe in 2014 and 2015. A part of them, mostly from Syria, can definitely be categorized as refugees, defined by the United Nations in 1951 as those "unable or unwilling to return to their country of origin owing to a well-founded fear of being persecuted for reasons of race, religion, nationality, membership of a particular social group, or political opinion."[15] As the year of its enactment suggests, the UN's refugee policy reflected Cold War politics and sought to weaken the Soviet Bloc, as US immigration policy toward Cuba had done a few years later. Such political motivations disappeared after 1989, but the moral imperatives of the refugee policy remained. Still, a number of immigrants in the 2010s, mostly from Africa, but even from Pakistan and Afghanistan, do not belong to the refugee category, but are rather economic migrants. They are trying to escape from economic hopelessness, looking for jobs and a better life.

In 2014 and 2015, a genuine migration catastrophe hit Europe. An incessant flood of migrants, a new Great Migration, put unbearable pressure on several European countries. From January to June 2015, some 300,000–400,000 emigrants engulfed Europe. Many crossed via Turkey to Greece, Montenegro, and Serbia to Hungary, a way-station of sorts for entering other EU countries. Hordes of people – crossing borders, traversing countries, spanning the entire Balkans by foot – arrived in Hungary: 20,000 in 2013, 40,000 in 2014, and then hundreds of thousands in 2015. Proportionately, this was the equivalent of 6–7 million illegal immigrants entering the United States in a six-month period. After a chaotic summer, Hungary began to fortify its borders and halted additional immigration. Immigrants inundated Italy and Spain as well. Most tried to enter Spain between 2005 and 2007, prompting the government to strengthen its border and sea controls and to curb immigration. 75,000 were reportedly caught trying to enter the EU via Spain in 2012, and 107,000 in 2013. It was much the same story in Italy: 150,000 migrants entered the country; many through the small island of Lampedusa, south from Sicily, and an additional 100,000 arrived in the first half of 2015. That year Germany declared a readiness to receive migrants "with open arms," took in more than a million of them, and became a target country for most of those entering Europe.

The various crises in the Middle East and North Africa provided a great business opportunity for human traffickers, who charged $1,000 to $4,000 per person to smuggle migrants, through Turkey and across the Mediterranean Sea, into southern Europe. The smugglers put thousands at risk by recklessly using small fishing boats ill-equipped to cross the Mediterranean, and outraged the world when 500 perished at sea in October 2013. Another 500 migrants drowned in September 2014, and 1,600 in the first half of 2015. Since 2000, some 23,000 people have died at sea trying to escape from Africa and the Middle East.[16] Dramatic photos of the corpses of small children washed up on beaches became emblematic symbols of an unparalleled human tragedy. Human traffickers have caused the deaths of migrants inside the territory of the European Union as well.[17] In August 2015 came the shocking news of more than 70 decomposing bodies being found in a sealed truck with Hungarian license plates parked on the Austrian side of the Hungarian border. As a quite symbolic coincidence, the bodies were found only kilometers away from the palace where European leaders had discussed plans "to devise new ways to cope with the migration crisis." Angela Merkel, one of the participants of that EU meeting, angrily declared: "We are all shaken by this terrible news that … people have lost their lives because they got into a situation where smugglers did not care about their lives." The German chancellor used this occasion to call for the "need for Europe to pull together and ease the migration crisis …. But the meeting ended on a discordant note with no apparent consensus on how to proceed."[18]

Europe's leaders began seeking solutions to the crisis already in the early 2010s, partly because of the repeated spectacles of dead migrants at sea and on the ground, and partly because of the chaos across Europe that the hordes of migrants had generated. "EU member states adopted security measures, which led to an increasingly restrictive interpretation of the right to access the asylum system and state territory of the European Union."[19] Border control, especially the surveillance of the Mediterranean Sea, became crucially important. Calls for resolving the crisis were magnified after a particularly odious incident in 2011, when a boat packed with refugees was given no assistance nor allowed to land anywhere after 14 days at sea, and ultimately returned from the straits of Sicily to Africa with 11 survivors out of the original 72 on board. The EU proclaimed that this had been a clear breach of human rights, but it was quick to add that such irresponsible human trafficking must be stopped. Italy unilaterally launched Operation Mare Nostrum rescuing more than 142,000 people between January and October 2014, and costing €9 million a month. The Union established the *European Agency for the Management of Operational Cooperation at the External Borders* (or Frontex) in 2004 to prevent illegal immigration, and allotted the agency a budget of €94 billion in 2013. In May 2014, the Union accepted the External Sea Border Surveillance Regulation[20] and the Protected Entry Procedure for asylum seekers outside Europe. The European Commission also came up with a common European migration and asylum policy. In April 2015, the European Council published an agenda of cooperation in handling the migrants with a jointly accepted relocation system. Experience showed that 70 percent of the immigrants had intended to go to, and ultimately entered, five Western countries of the Community. The EU sought to establish a system by which all admitted immigrants are to be distributed by a compulsory quota system among the member states based on their population (40 percent), GDP (40 percent), unemployment rate (10 percent) and the number of immigrants in the country (10 percent). The EU was planning to resettle 20,000 migrants per year.[21] In June 2015, in the middle of the new migration crisis, the EU launched a common military campaign to "identify, capture and dispose of vessels as well as enabling assets used or suspected ... by migrant smugglers or traffickers."[22]

While pursuing a humanitarian policy to assist and rescue migrants at sea, the EU at the same time planned to build up better border controls and adopt a community-wide common policy on migration. The EU issued eight directives regarding migration and the rights of migrants. The Blue Card Directive of 2009 dealt with labor migration policy. The Single Permit Directive introduced a single residence and work permit together with a single application process. The minimum wage, working hours, and health regulations for seasonal workers were jointly regulated. The Commission proposed a directive on students and researchers to attract educated immigrants. If accepted, it would allow students from foreign countries to apply for jobs or start business after completing their studies. There are plans to unify the asylum system as well. The Long-term Residence Directive regulates the rights of immigrants residing in EU countries for at least five years.[23]

Nevertheless, very little has actually resulted from these attempts to regulate and control immigration. Most of the measures have not gotten off the ground. The EU's plans to distribute migrants among the member states were met with the strong opposition of several countries, who refused to take in or settle any migrants.

Originally Britain and Denmark opted out, and five Central-Eastern European countries declared that they would accept only Christian immigrants. Hungary's Prime Minister Viktor Orbán firmly declared that immigration was not a Hungarian or a European problem, but rather a German one, for the simple reason that Germany's acceptance of migrants was inspiring others to migrate to Europe. Finally, the EU summit in September 2015 overruled four dissenting former communist countries and adopted a plan to distribute 120,000 migrants among the member countries. But even that agreement was annulled by a few countries two months later. By the end of the year, only some 20,000 refugees had been "distributed."

The crisis, therefore, was far from over at the end of 2015 and early 2016 – partly because immigration has continued unabated, with more than a million migrants coming to Europe in 2015, and with two to three million more expected over the coming years. Aside from the daunting numbers of new arrivals, there is also Europe's less than stellar record of integrating earlier immigrants in various host countries. A large number of immigrants have no desire to integrate into their host societies, and the native populations are often far from inclusive and are resistant to accepting immigrants with different social and cultural backgrounds. As some European leaders have openly acknowledged, multiculturalism, a political ideology to integrate newcomers with different cultural backgrounds, has failed. Moreover, Europe's attempt to maintain border security and stop the continuing flood of migrants, as well as confront and arrest human traffickers, has also failed. Consequently, more than anything else, the migration crisis has begun to undermine the EU. Overt discord and disobedience of member states have become the rule. All this has created huge cracks in the Union.

Moreover, after 2001, the migration issue eventually merged with security concerns. Some of the immigrants, even among the second generation born in Europe, have become radicalized, and so-called home grown terrorism has become an enormous problem. Several thousand EU citizens who had immigrated to Europe, or had been born on the continent to immigrant parents, have traveled to Syria and Iraq and joined the Islamic State (ISIS) terrorist organization. Several others have committed terror attacks at home. This development has seriously undermined liberal democracy in Europe. The situation naturally fed suspicions, and created a real danger, that ISIS might infiltrate migrant groups and send terrorists to Europe. According to a well-based intelligence report, Salah Abdeslam, one of the Paris attackers in November 2015, had travelled to Hungary in September of that year to recruit terrorists from a desperate crowd at the Keleti (East) train station in Budapest. Probably as many as four people connected to the Paris terror attack had entered Europe posing as refugees with Syrian passports. Mr. Abdeslam was believed to have found two recruits in Budapest, and had taken them to Paris. In Finland, two Iraqi refugees were arrested in December 2015 on suspicion (actually proven on video) of participating in ISIS massacres in Tikrit, Iraq in 2014.[24] During a routine search of a house in a suburb of Malmo, Swedish police found a video showing two Muslim Swedish nationals taking part in beheadings in Syria in 2013. Nine Belgian citizens with immigrant backgrounds have been arrested for having connections with the Paris terrorists.[25] In early 2016, ISIS terrorists posing as immigrants murdered a dozen German tourists in Istanbul with suicide attacks. Hidden terrorists may mask themselves as refugees who escape from terror. The case of Haisam Omar Sakhans in Sweden offered another example. He was a Syrian rebel who participated in the execution of prisoners of war in 2012, a major war crime, and asked and gained asylum in Sweden in June 2013.[26]

Even if ISIS infiltration of the escapees is marginal, it is still reasonable to fear that some of the immigrants may later grow dissatisfied with their new lives and become radicalized. It is also reasonable to be concerned about teenagers of immigrant backgrounds seeking outlets for rebellion. Most of the Paris terrorists were European citizens, and one of the San Bernardino attackers had been born in the United States. The analysis of the participants of the Belgian terrorist attack offers an interesting and frightening lesson. Some of the so-called home-grown terrorists already had some criminal background. They joined kinship and friendship gangs and were involved in trafficking, rioting, and other violent juvenile actions. They were not fundamental religious Muslims at all. Joining the Islamic State terrorists for them was merely a shift to another form of deviant behavior, but in a "thrilling, larger-than-life dimension to their way of life." Another group of home-grown terrorists who joined ISIS was also not religious Islamist, but adolescent people with personal difficulties. They felt exclusion, isolation, and inequality in the society they lived, had been frequently at odds with their families, and did not see a future. "The accumulation of such estrangements resulted in anger." Both above-mentioned groups of young people in immigrant Muslim families had a "nothing-to-lose" desperation.[27]

Mass immigration to Europe, called the "European migration crisis," is not actually a European issue, but an international one. Unfortunately, the United Nations and the entire advanced world have shown a total inability to solve the problem, even to provide sufficient funds for refugee camps in countries bordering Syria. Some have alleged that Turkey also bears responsibility for the crisis, as it sought to empty its refugee camps by "supplying [the migrants] with the necessary means for … the long journey toward the dream of Europe." In addition, the Turkish government has turned a blind eye to "the activities of organized gangs of smugglers" to move thousands of migrants by sea to the Greek islands of Lesbos, Kos, and Samos, from where they can move on to other countries of Europe.[28]

The wealthy Arab and non-European Western countries have also kept their distance and have accepted immigrants only in an extremely limited way. Europe did not cause this mass exodus, and should not be expected to deal with it alone. The first inkling of international recognition of global responsibility came with the Obama administration's call for the US to accept refugees, but it was soundly rejected by Congress and several Republican governors in November 2015.[29]

Negative consequences and political backlash

The European Union has conflicting interests regarding immigration. On the one hand, Europe needs a new labor force to counterbalance its otherwise shrinking and aging population (see Chapter 4). In early 2015, the European Commission clearly articulated this: "There is a growing recognition that, in the new economic and demographic context, the existing 'zero' immigration policy which has dominated thinking over the past thirty years is no longer appropriate."[30]

On the other hand, the EU and its member countries' governments cannot ignore the harsh social-political backlash to open immigration. Europe's population has traditionally lived in states with clearly defined borders. Throughout the nineteenth and twentieth centuries, they lived in national communities and were socialized to be prepared to kill and die for their nations. The two world wars in the twentieth century strengthened their national self-identification exponentially. Of course, minorities had always existed, but, except for some countries and regions with mixed populations, they were not overly numerous. That did not prevent, however, their being regularly discriminated against and even massacred, as they had been especially in the twentieth century – in genocides in Ottoman Turkey, Nazi Germany, authoritarian Central and Eastern Europe, and Bosnia-Herzegovina, and in violent anti-Roma incidents in post-1989 Eastern Europe.

At a certain point, especially in the early twenty-first century, anti-immigration sentiment merged with anti-Muslim hostility, which dramatically increased after a number of radical Islamist terror attacks in the West. This was clearly expressed by Geert Wilders, one of the leading anti-immigration politicians in the Netherlands. During a visit to the United States, he warned:

> The Islamic immigration to our free western societies has proven to be a Trojan horse. The jihadists are among us today. And of course not all Muslims are terrorists; it would be ridiculous even to suggest that, but almost all terrorists seem to be Muslims today .... Trust me: go to Europe and see with your own eyes, Islam and freedom, Islam and liberty are incompatible. Go to any country, any Arab or Islamic country where Islam is dominant, that Islam and freedom are incompatible, and we should be warned that what is happening there, the Trojan horse of mass immigration from Islamic countries to our societies, will also happen here, and I don't want that to happen .... Over its 1400-year history of carnage, Islam has become expert in the use of warfare, terror, intimidation and politics to conquer large swaths of territory.[31]

In an op-ed piece in the *New York Times* in November 2015, he added that the majority of the population in the Netherlands affirmed to pollsters in 2008, long before the migration crisis, that "the importation of a huge number of immigrants [would] be the biggest mistake in their country's postwar history." Angela Merkel's policy of welcoming immigrants, he insisted, "was foolish, because millions now want to come to Western Europe .... Other European countries should not be the victims of Ms. Merkel's policies." He thus drew the obvious conclusions to his anti-EU stance: "There is a perfectly good alternative to the European Union – it is called the European Free Trade Association, founded in 1960 .... Leaving the European Union would ... be beneficial for the Netherlands."[32]

As Geert Wilders clearly demonstrated, anti-immigration sentiment is invariably connected to dangerous anti-European integration policies. Right-wing nationalist forces have entered the European political realm. Politicians and political movements have begun to use the term "clash of civilizations," a concept that gained renown after it had been coined by Samuel P. Huntington in a famous 1992 lecture and book (in 1996), *The Clash of Civilizations and the Remaking of World Order*.[33] As the title reflects, Huntington predicts the rise of a new world disorder after a short-lived euphoria and hope of a harmonious new world at the end of the Cold War – naively suggested by President George H.W. Bush in 1991.[34] Instead of a harmonious world order, Huntington points to the rise of a new global conflict among civilizations. A decade later, this idea was transformed as a clash of civilizations *within* the Western world, including Europe.

Meanwhile, the number of immigrants, and thus the "mixing of civilizations" within Europe, is permanently on the rise. Official policy in Europe embraced the concept of multiculturalism, affirming that naturalized immigrants had become part of each European nation. "Islam is part of Germany," Angela Merkel declared. "I am the Chancellor of all Germans. And that includes everyone who lives here permanently, whatever their background or origin."[35] This idea confronted the 200-year old tradition of European self-identification head-on. It contradicted the fervent belief of large numbers of ordinary, less educated Europeans (represented by rapidly rising political forces) that mixing cultures in harmonious cohabitation is a pipe dream.

Two dark prophesies regarding Europe's future serve to illustrate this pessimistic position. Both were expressed in 2007, long before the real migration crisis. The well-known German-born American historian, Walter Laqueur, speaks of a Europe with a dramatically decreasing population that by 2050 would require 700 million immigrants just to keep going. He also bemoans its dried-up "immune system" or self-defense reflex. Burdened with the shame of its colonial past, Europe, Laqueur suggests, has "surrendered" to multiculturalism. A "clash of civilizations" within Europe, he grimly concludes, is thus unavoidable.[36] Sharing this pessimism was another American, Bruce Thornton, who speaks of Europe's "slow motion suicide" and of a future "Islamized Europe" governed by Sharia Law.[37]

Such despairing predictions had come to the fore in response to the 9/11 terror attacks in the United States in 2001, which were duplicated in Europe soon afterward. The rise of the Islamic State and its gruesome beheadings of captured European and American journalists and aid workers added fuel to the fire. Moreover, home-grown Islamist terror attacks followed in Europe, especially in Britain, Spain, France, and Belgium. The vast majority of terrorist attacks that have taken place in the Western world in recent decades were carried out by native extremist groups or separatist movements, as in Northern Ireland, Spain, and especially the United States. Nevertheless, terror attacks in the West by ISIS and other Islamist groups have had a long-lasting impact.

Such terrorism includes the massacre of nearly 200 commuter train passengers in Spain in 2004, the London underground and bus bombings killing 37 in

2005, and the murderous attack against the satirical journal *Charlie Hebdo* in Paris in 2015. What is more frightening, terror attacks are becoming an almost daily phenomenon. In August 2015, a Moroccan citizen with a Spanish residency card, 25-year-old Ayoub El Khazzani, traveled to Amsterdam and boarded an express train to Paris with the goal of killing as many passengers as possible. The slaughter was prevented by three American servicemen who happened to be traveling on the same train.[38] As part of the typical reaction to such events, on January 7, the day of the *Charlie Hebdo* attack, a provocative Islamophobic novel by Michel Houllebeck, *Submission,* envisioning a Muslim-run France in 2022, was published.[39] In November of 2015, a coordinated and well-organized attack on five different locations in Paris killed and wounded hundreds of people at a concert hall and restaurants. Another major attack followed in March 2016 in Brussels, killing more than 30 people. The terrorists were home-grown Muslim radicals probably joined by some new immigrants. The unstoppable series continued when a truck driver, after a carefully planned preparation, deliberately ran into a crowd in Nice who were celebrating Bastille Day and then two refugees slit the throat of an elderly priest in a Catholic church in the suburb of Rouen, symbolically initiating a religious war. As Markus Söder, leader of the Bavarian Christian Social Union and government put it: "Paris changed everything."[40] The Paris attack has indeed changed the atmosphere: it has replaced compassion with anxiety and has reinforced the dire need for security. Many wholeheartedly agreed with President François Holland and others that Europe is at war. This belief only intensified when a Muslim couple killed and wounded dozens of people in San Bernardino, California. Similar attacks are occurring almost daily throughout the world, including Egypt, Turkey, and Indonesia. Suspicions against refugees and even settled immigrants strongly increased after those terrorist attacks. All in all, extreme anti-immigrant sentiment permeated Europe in the 2010s. Increasing parts of the population have become skeptical about absorbing and integrating any more immigrants. Even tolerant Scandinavia has introduced border controls, and violence against immigrants in liberal Germany has become more and more frequent. Sweden has seen several arson attacks on mosques, the burning of the Eskilstuna Islamic Dawa Center, severe clashes and grenade attacks in Malmo (with 25 attacks taking place in 2014, and 18 in the first half of 2015 alone), and significant violence in the suburbs of Stockholm. Arson attacks on the housing units of asylum seekers in Germany jumped from 58 in 2013 to 175 in 2014, and to 173 in the first half of 2015 alone. Extensive violence was seen in Treglitz and Dresden. Three times more attacks took place in Germany in 2015 than had occurred a year earlier and six times more than in 2012. Ms. Merkel's coalition partners have openly demanded that she "acknowledge that the opening of the borders for an unlimited period of time was a mistake."[41] Hans-Peter Friedrich, Germany's interior minister, castigated his country's immigration policy already in 2013 as being "totally irresponsible."[42] Millions of Europeans feel uneasy "when they see crowds of unassimilated, jobless immigrants, as in part of Paris or Malmo …. Not all who express such fears are bigots."[43] Europe began to experience immigration-fatigue at the end of 2015. "Europe's Nordic countries, which have long set the world standard for welcoming refugees ... are rapidly scaling back their generosity, slashing benefits and issuing ever more restrictive asylum policy."[44] Indeed, Denmark and Norway have cut benefits by 50 and 20 percent, respectively. In Finland, asylum seekers have to report to the authorities every six months. All the Nordic countries have made family reunification for immigrants more difficult. A major factor contributing to the crisis has been Europe's inability to defend its borders and prevent human traffickers from smuggling African, Asian, and Middle Eastern migrants into Europe. The required response did not materialize. EU resolutions regarding immigrants were met with wild resistance on the part of several member countries. Hungary's brutal and inhumane actions against arriving immigrants became routine news stories in the late summer of 2015, with pictures of atrocities and hastily erected fences along borders splashed across the pages of newspapers worldwide. Since then, several borders have been closed, at least temporarily, including Sweden's, Austria's, and Germany's, and similar fences have been built in Croatia, Slovenia, Serbia, Bulgaria, and elsewhere. This was in sharp contrast with Germany's policy of *Willcommenskulture* that opened its borders and welcomed immigrants. However, the "only" difference that distinguished Hungary from Germany and Sweden was the fact that those burning mosques and attacking dormitories in Germany and Sweden were in the opposition, while xenophobe nationalists in Hungary were in power.

Immigration has become a burning political issue throughout the European Union. Opposition to immigration has gradually merged with anti-European-integrationist, or anti-euro political sentiment. New opposition parties have appeared on the scene in several countries in recent decades, some openly espousing neo-fascist ideology, such as Greece's *Laïkós Sýndesmos – Chrysí Avgí* (Golden Dawn), Hungary's *Jobbik,* which came in second in the 2014 elections, and Germany's *Nationaldemokratische Partei Deutschland* (German National Democratic Party).

Most of these parties are made up of extreme nationalists and foreigner-hating xenophobes. Many have gradually turned against European integration in general. With increased immigration and the EU's enlargement, these movements and parties have begun to mushroom. Viktor Orbán's *FIDESz* party in Hungary is one anti-European party, and is enjoying its third term in government. In late 2015, the "Orbanization" of Poland became a reality, with the electoral victory of the populist-nationalist Law and Justice Party of Jaroslaw Kaczynski. He immediately set off on his illiberal course, purged public officials and journalists, and pursued an Orbanist-Putinist political agenda combined with an anti-immigration and anti-EU policy.

One of the oldest and strongest parties of this stripe is the French *Front National* of Marine Le Pen, which won a quarter of the votes at the last European Parliamentary elections in 2014. In regional elections in December 2015, the Front scored an overwhelming victory in two of France's thirteen regions, and won leading positions in four of them. Marie Le Pen triumphantly declared that her party was "regaining" lost territory, among them the suburbs of the big cities. Geert Wilders' *Dutch Partij voor de Vrijheid* (Party of Freedom), which was founded only in 2005, came in third in the 2014 EU parliamentary elections and promptly proceeded to forge an alliance with the French National Front. Among the strong right-wing nationalist anti-European parties on the rise today are Italy's recently established *Movimento Cinque Stelle* (Five Star Movement) led by Beppe Grillo, which won 25 percent of the vote in the 2013 national elections and one of its member was elected mayor of Rome. Spain's *Podemos (We Can) anti-integration party became the second largest in the country*. Britain's *UK Independence Party* also captured 27 percent of the vote in 2014 and at last became triumphant at the referendum decision to step out from the EU. Austria's *Freiheitliche Partei Österreichs* (Freedom Party) could claim a longer history, but won only 11 percent of the vote in national elections in 2006. Ten years later the party's candidate almost became the president of Austria. Less influential examples of this political genre include Finland's *Perussuomalaiset* (True Finns Party), Germany's *Alternative für Deutschland* (Alternative for Germany Party), Belgium's *Vlaams Belang (*Flemish Interest Party), and small opposition groupings in Denmark, Croatia, and elsewhere. The Neo-Nazi *Sverigedemokraterna* (Sweden Democrats) party has suddenly jumped to the top of the polls in traditionally tolerant Sweden. Founded in 1988, it won 5.7 percent of the vote in 2010 (reaching the 4 percent parliamentary threshold), and then captured 13 percent in 2014. These parties are able to mobilize mass resistance especially against immigration, but also against the "dictate of Brussels."

These parties gained significant ground in the 2014 EU parliamentary elections, and no fewer than 30 percent of the members of the EU Parliament paradoxically hold anti-integrationist and even anti-EU positions. Some attempts have been made to unite these representatives into one bloc, but political differences and tactical considerations have so far precluded this. The EU's enlargement with Europe's peripheries and mass immigration has both undermined the Union's reputation among a great part of the European population, especially during the economic crisis of the 2010s. As early as 2012, only 30 percent of Europeans told Eurobarometer pollsters that they believe the EU is good for them.[45] "Trust in the European Union is at its lowest level since records had begun in 1997, with less than one in three EU citizens expressing trust in the EU in 2013."[46] In mid-2015, for the first time in the more than four decades of Eurobarometer polling, Europeans listed immigration as their number one concern. The prospects of the European Union would be seriously threatened if some of these anti-EU parties, especially France's Front National, were to win the upcoming national elections. Marine Le Pen has effectively posed as the savior of the "little French men, the forgotten ones," and as an ardent opponent of immigration. To quote an oft-repeated National Front slogan: "Two million unemployed is two million immigrants too many!" She is adept at manipulating the mounting fear in French society, and has skillfully positioned her party as a reasonable alternative. She readily purged her father Jean-Marie Le Pen, the party's founder, to remove his tactless, openly racist, and anti-Semitic remarks as an issue that can be used against her, and she has successfully concealed the real character of her party. Polls conducted in the early fall of 2015 reveal the Front's growing popularity, now in second place in the upcoming national elections.[47] It emerged as a mainstream party in the local elections in December 2015, the clear favorite of the less educated: it was the choice of 36 percent of those without a high-school education, but only of 14 percent of those with at least three years of post-high-school education.[48] A Le Pen victory may very well lead France to leave the Union, or at least reduce the EU to being a loose free trade zone.

Germany's admirably humanitarian policy on immigration proved to be counterproductive already in the second half of 2015, when even Chancellor Merkel's coalition partners turned against immigration. Dozens from her own party signed an open letter against her immigration policy. The head of the Bavarian wing of Merkel's Christian Democratic Union brashly invited Hungarian Prime Minister Viktor Orbán to Munich to speak against the chancellor's migration policy. Germany's President Joachim Gauk, an absolute moral authority in the country, raised his own objections to the unlimited entry of refugees at the annual World Economic Forum in Davos in early 2016:

> A limitation strategy may even be morally and politically necessary in order to preserve the state's ability to function .... Limiting numbers is not itself unethical; it helps maintain acceptance in society .... If democrats refuse to talk about limits, they leave the field to populists and xenophobes.[49]

Mass immigration has thus become one of Europe's most pressing challenges, as it poses a fundamental threat to the future of Europe, the unity of EU member countries, and European integration as a whole. Donald Tusk, the President of the European Council, acknowledged the danger when he declared: "We have no more than two months to get things under control. [Otherwise the European Union would] fail as a political project."[50]

The peril has become quite palpable. Both the mounting crisis of 2015 and the growing opposition within Europe to the unrestricted acceptance of immigrants have led the EU's leaders, including those from the most liberal countries, to look for some kind of solution. After several failed attempts, they came to a consensus of sorts at a meeting in October 2015, which "signaled a shift from the policy of open armed welcome conveyed over the summer by Chancellor Angela Merkel of Germany toward what critics describe as a 'fortress Europe' approach."[51] The latter position was strengthened further at an EU summit in late December, but Merkel refused to set fixed limits for refugees.

The complex measures that the EU has agreed to include reaching an agreement with, and offering financial compensation to, Turkey to enable it to keep the millions of refugees there in camps; to register refugees in Turkey, thus enabling European countries to select refugees there; and to prevent illegal migrants from crossing the EU's borders. In November 2015, the EU's leaders met with the head of African states in the Maltese capital of Valletta and offered $2 billion in development assistance and scholarship grants, a "tailor-made package of support" for those African countries that are willing to cooperate with Europe to keep people in their countries and even to take back those who had failed to obtain asylum.

These potential agreements, particularly the one with Turkey, may contribute to a kind of solution. Around the end of 2015, Turkey finally started controlling its borders with Syria. Building concrete walls, trenches and barbed wire fences, and lighting large areas, might insulate the porous Turkish border. Turkey has also begun to patrol its waters. The European Union offered paying Turkey €3 billion to keep migrants in the country, and, together with the United States, is pushing for results. Smugglers who had easily crossed the Turkish border bringing jihadists to Syria and refugees to Turkey are now complaining about their difficulties to do so, and how Turkish border guards "who once fired warning shots … now shoot to kill. Whoever approaches the border is shot."[52] Nevertheless, Turkey's authoritarian President Recep Tayyip Erdogan is driving a hard bargain, insisting that, in addition to an increased amount of money, Turkey must get in return an early entrance to the EU and the abolition of visa requirements for Turkish citizens traveling to Europe. An agreement between the EU and Turkey was reached in March 2016. One cannot exclude the possibility that the agreement would only lead to further problems for Europe down the road and not contribute to a solution of the refugee crisis.[53] The potential for failure is even greater with the African countries that are dependent on the money their expatriates send back home to their families ($33 billion in 2015). "For Africa, the exodus of young ambitious men is potentially a political relief valve and an economic lift. It not only brings in cash, but also provides an exit rout for frustrated young men."[54]

Because of the mass dissatisfaction with Europe's German-led immigration policy, the EU also began making serious efforts at the end of 2015 to stop the incessant flood of migrants. It will now strengthen its border defenses by arming and reinforcing Frontex, the border control arm of the EU,

> which currently has no guards, vehicles, boats or aircraft of its own. The leaders also agreed on tougher measures to ensure the swift deportation of migrants who do not qualify for refugee status, including the use of detention as a legitimate measure of last resort.[55]

European armies have been authorized to patrol the Mediterranean Sea and, if necessary, to seize the boats of human traffickers. Frontex seemingly has become a real force, with its own troops, ships, helicopters and weaponry, to defend the EU's borders, which national governments such as Greece have been unable to do. Moreover, Frontex can act independently of the national governments. Nevertheless, Frontex is still not a European border-guard but consists of a standing corps of a minimum 1,500 national border guards make available by member states, deploying 2–3 percent of their national border guards to Frontex.[56]

The EU's humane and moral approach, and its maintaining international norms regarding asylum seekers, is admirable. In promoting this policy, Germany's government has demonstrated that it has learned the lessons of the Nazi past. Admirable though it may be, the German policy nonetheless has proven to be counterproductive even in Germany. The turning point was the mass atrocities in Cologne on New Year's Eve (2015–16), when hundreds, probably even a thousand

"Arab and North-African looking people" attacked, robbed, and sexually molested hundreds of women at the city's railway station and main square. News of the attacks, which was kept secret for four days, caused a firestorm. A few dozens of the attackers, who were identified in the first weeks of January, were indeed young men who had recently immigrated and were seeking asylum. The attack had finally undermined Angela Merkel's open-arms policy. It was not just bigoted xenophobes who were turning against it. After the Cologne incident, only 29 percent of Germans agreed with open-arms policy, and more than 60 percent maintained that too many immigrants were already in the country. If Cologne was a symbolic turning point, the summer of 2016 made terrorist attacks everyday phenomena in Germany as well. Attacks, mostly by radicalized refugees and asylum seekers in Nuremberg, Ausbach, and Reutlingen, and a knife and axe attack on a train dramatically changed the political atmosphere in Germany and strongly challenged Chancellor Merkel's hardnosed defense of her immigration policy. Realists recognized that Germany has to give up "the fond illusion that Germany's past sins can be absolved with a reckless humanitarianism in the present."[57] Merkel's belief that 82 million Germans "can do it," that is, assimilate a million immigrants, is mathematically wrong. The one million immigrants have to be compared to the fewer than 10 million Germans in their twenties or younger, some of whom are themselves immigrants. If we consider that 73 percent of the 1.2 million asylum seekers in 2015 were men, and that 40 percent of them were young males between the ages of 18 and 34, who in the future may bring brides and families from their original home countries, we would have to conclude that the entire demography of Germany would be transformed. Half of the future cohorts of young people under 40 might belong to Middle Eastern and North African immigrant families.[58]

Such a major transformation of the pro-immigration countries in Europe is certainly more than not acceptable for the majority of their population. At the very least, the humanitarian approach has to be combined with a strong, and if need be, militarized, defense of the borders of the European Union. Asylum seekers should be registered and selected in refugee camps outside Europe, in the Middle East and North Africa. Those who are not granted asylum, the hundreds of thousands of economic migrants, should not be allowed to illegally enter Europe because sending them back has proven to be almost impossible. At the end of 2015 and the beginning of 2016, there is definite, albeit incremental movement toward a solution. Chancellor Merkel has to recognize that her policy has failed.

Without a working solution, one of the European Union's most important and most popular achievements, the free movement of people within the so-called Schengen area, cannot survive. As the President of the European Council, Donald Tusk, unambiguously affirmed: "The recent developments in Germany, in Sweden, in Slovenia and in other countries all show with utmost clarity …. I have no doubt without effective control of our external borders, the Schengen rules will not survive."[59] The EU has rejected the Dutch proposal to create a "small Schengen" with the Western core countries of the Union.

Compassionate voices supporting immigration to Europe are heard less and less. A number of politicians are quick to emphasize the fact that the Muslim immigrants are not the same as the terrorists, but are just the opposite; they are precisely the ones who are fleeing from Islamist terror. Jean-Claud Juncker, the President of the European Commission, has described the immigrants as "well-managed resources rather than the problem." The Commission has estimated that employment might increase by 1 percent, and that the economy might grow by 0.2–0.4 percent, at least in some countries.[60] Nevertheless, very few continue to share the sanguine view of the Hungarian writer Péter Zilahy: "Barbarians," he reminds us, had often attacked and even occupied Europe, or parts of it. But "all those once feared enemies turned into Europeans … Europe has always conquered her conquerors … and [has been] regularly reborn at the hands of the Barbarians."[61]

Nevertheless, everything depends on an effective European response to the migration crisis. It would be a mockery of history if Chancellor Angela Merkel's most humanitarian and moral immigration policy ended up helping right-wing nationalist-populist parties attain power and destroy European integration. As did some of her predecessors (Chancellors Adenauer and Kohl), Ms. Merkel master-fully combined the German national interest with that of Europe as a whole. This time the unintentional consequences of her policies might prove disastrous. The other unpredictable factor, the EU's decision-making apparatus, is also decisive. As in several other crisis situations, this apparatus is working extremely slowly. This is unavoidable given that there are 28 member countries in a non-federal alliance. The EU's snail pace decision-making procedures already caused serious difficulties at the time of the euro-crisis and the Greek debt crisis. The time factor in 2016, however, might prove to be more critical.

The endgame in spring 2016?

The lack of common action led to various countries to close their borders in early 2016. Some did it for a transitional period, other permanently. By March 2016, already nine countries built walls and fences and closed their borders tight. Other countries follow. Instead of common action, various groups of countries – based on old, historical ties – tried to agree in a common regional policy. The former four so-called post-communist Visegrad countries jointly rejected the EU deci-sion on the distribution of immigrants by a quota system. Two of them, Hungary and Slovakia, had filed a lawsuit against the EU's quota system decision at the European Court of Justice.

Austria decided not to accept more than 37,500 refugees in 2016 and closed its borders. Because Greece is unable to defend its borders, countries with a com-mon border with Greece such as Bulgaria and Macedonia built fences to stop the flow of immigrants. Austria invited eight Balkan countries, partly members of the Union, such as Croatia, Slovenia, and Bulgaria, and partly non-members, such as Macedonia, Montenegro, Serbia, Kosovo, and Albania to sign an agreement with them in Vienna in late February 2016 to restrict migrant flow. They fortified their borders and did not allow people to cross who are not refugees but economic immigrants. The Greek government was outraged and withdrew its ambassador from Austria. But, as the Austrian foreign minister Sebastian Kurz stated, "There is no willingness from the Greek side to reduce the influx." To exclude Greece from this agreement, the Austrian minister of interior Ms. Mikl-Leitner said, was "a question of survival for the European Union."

Instead of the dysfunctional Greek government, the Union asked NATO to defend Europe's borders on the Mediterranean Sea.[62] NATO however, offers only information to Frontex and the countries concerned, and does not stop boats on the sea. The winter months in early 2016 signaled an increasing flow of migrants. In January 2016, despite the stormy and dangerous winter sea and devastating rain, 68,000 migrants arrived to Greece, 38-times more than the record year of the same month in 2015. In the first two months of the year already altogether 140,000 people entered the EU. Donald Tusk, President of the European Council traveled to the Balkan countries and addressed to potential economic immigrants in Greece:

> 'Do not come to Europe,' ... 'Do not believe the smugglers. Do not risk your lives and money. It is all for nothing. Greece or any other European countries will no longer be a transit country.' ... effectively signaling [commented the *New York Times*] Europe's determined turn away from Chancellor Angela Merkel's more open approach to welcoming migrants.[63]

In reality, Merkel's Germany is also changing policy though the Chancellor never openly recognizes the change. In the early March 2016 elections in three German states, the far-right Alternative for Germany Party had big gains and attracted about a quarter of the voters. Although the Merkel government is not in an immediate danger, a lot of Germans do not believe any longer in integration of immigrants. In practice, at last, Germany and the EU want to stop illegal inflow and accept only registered refugees from Turkey. A series of meetings of the European leaders and long, repeated talks with Ahmet Davutoglu, Prime Minister of Turkey in Brussels targeted an agreement with Turkey not only to keep the emigrants in its camps, but also accept illegally arrived migrants back from Europe. As compensation, after each accepted returned migrant by Turkey, the EU will accept one legally qualified migrant from Turkey. In this way, the EU wants to send back all the illegally arrived migrants from Greece. Chancellor Merkel declared this as a breakthrough if implemented.

The authoritarian Turkish government, knowing its key position in the solution of the European migration problems, has tried blackmailing the EU. They demanded twice as much money, €6 billion, as originally offered by Europe. Moreover, as Prime Minister Davutoglu stated: "Turkey is ready to work with the EU. Turkey is ready to be a member of the EU as well. I hope this summit ... [will also focus] on the Turkish accession process to the EU... [that] will be a turning point in our relations."[64] The European leaders closed their eyes and remained silent about the drastic authoritarian actions of the Turkish government to attack and seize the country's largest independent journals, critical of the government, exactly in the days of talk. President Erdogan is muting critiques. In the last one-and-half years, 2,000 cases were opened against people who criticized the president, which is a crime in the country. This "breakthrough" with the unreliable Turkish government might have a very high price and its outcome, an exaggerated process of Turkish acceptance by the EU hides an even greater danger for the EU than the inflow of migrants. Nevertheless, in the first days after the agreement, Turkey accepted back a few hundred emigrants who arrived illegally to Greece and did not get asylum as refugees. If continued, this will probably discourage economic migrants illegally entering Europe, but at the moment, a new wave of African economic migrants is flowing to Italy. The problem is not solved at all.

The real solution would be to defend the borders of the Union, and stop the smugglers whose activities increased by offering new routes via Albania, Italy, and even Russia for $4,000–5,000 for hopeless migrants. The media reported on April 3, 2016 that a group of African economic migrants had already arrived in Kandalaksha, the border town of Russia, and tried entering Finland. The Finnish border-guards confiscated several Soviet era rust-bucket vehicles as soon as they crossed the frontier.[65] The real solution still does not work and does not even stand in the center of the efforts of the EU. Is the European Union able to solve the crises and save the Schengen agreement on open borders? Would the democratic forces of integration win and defeat the anti-EU political attack? All these are depending on energetic actions of self-defense and the internationalization of the migration crisis that was not created by Europe and belongs to the international community. Is Europe responsible for accepting more than a million migrants when Saudi Arabia and the Arab Emirates did not accept a single one and the United States allowed hardly more than 2,000 of them to enter?

Notes

1 *Archive of European Integration,* CEPS Paper in Liberty and Security, No. 77, January 2015, Elspeth Guild, Cathryn Castello, Madeline Garlich, Violeta Moreno-Lax and Minos Monzourakis, "New Approaches, Alternative Avenues and Means of Access to Asylum procedures for Persons Seeking International Protection."
2 *Archive of European Integration,* CEPS Essay, No. 23, January 22, 2016, Elspeth Guill, "Rethinking Migration Distribution in the EU: Shall We Start with the Facts?
3 *The New York Times,* January 27, 2016, Thomas L. Friedman, "Friends and Refugees in Need."
4 *The New York Times,* November 1, 2015, "Millions May be Poised to Follow Migrant Tide."
5 *Gallup World Poll: The Many Faces of Global Migration,* No. 43 (Geneva: Gallup, 2011).
6 *Archive of European Integration,* ISMU Foundation, Milan, "Integration Governance. Evidence on Migrants' Integration in Europe, ed. by Guia Gilardoni, Maria D'Odorico, and Daniela Carrillo, February 2015.
7 *Eurostat 2015,* accessible at: ec.europa.eu/eurostat/statistics-explained/index.php/ Migration_and_migrant_population_statistics
8 *Eurostat Yearbook 2011. Europe in Figures* (Luxembourg: European Union, 2011).
9 Christian Dustmann and Tommaso Frattini, *Immigration: The European Experience,* Discussion Paper Series, No. 6261 (Bonn: IZA, 2011).
10 *The Economist,* September 12, 2015, "Exodus."
11 Rogers Brubaker, *Citizenship and Nationhood in France and Germany* (Cambridge, MA: Harvard University Press, 1992), 172.
12 *Archive of European Integration,* Commission's Communication to Council on Consultation on Migration Policy, COM (79) 115 final, March 1979.

13 *Archive of European Integration,* European Commission, Policies on immigration and the social integration of immigrants in the European Community, SEC (90) 1813 final.
14 *Archive of European Integration,* Commission's communication on a Community Integration Policy, COM (2000) 757 final.
15 Protocol, United Nations Convention Relating to the Status of Refugees, Geneva, 1951; an additional Protocol was accepted in 1967 that made a universal coverage for the refugee status (www.unhcr.org/uk/1951-refugee-convention.html).
16 *Spiegel,* October 9, 2014; *The Economist,* August 16, 2014; *The New York Times,* April 23, 2015; *The Washington Post,* March 8, 2015.
17 *The New York Times,* August 28, 2015, "Migrant Crisis Growth in Europe with Grisly Find."
18 Ibid.
19 *Archive of European Integration,* Background Brief, No. 13, 2015, Julia Gour, "EU Policies on Mixed Migration. Flow in the Mediterranean."
20 www.consilium.europa.eu/uedocs/cms_data/docs/pressdata/en/jha/142569.pdf
21 *Archive of European Integration,* Dublin System Regulation, No. 604, July 26, 2013; *Archive of European Integration,* EPC Commentary, May 19, 2015, António Vitorino and Yves Pascouan, "The EU's Migrant Strategy."
22 *Archive of European Integration,* CEPS Commentary, June 26, 2015, Giovanni Faleg and Steven Blockmans, "EU Naval Force EUNAVFOR MED Sets Sail in Troubled Waters."
23 *Archive of European Integration,* EPC, Challenges, Issue 22. September 2014, Cecilia Malmström, Challenges and New Beginnings: Priorities for the EU's New Leadership."
24 *The New York Times,* December 19, 2015, "Hungarian Link to Paris Attacks Roils Country's Debate Over Migrants."
25 *The New York Times,* December 25, 2015, "Finnish Arrest of Iraqi Brothers in ISIS Related Case Poses Prosecution Challenges"; "Belgian Arrested as Paris Terror Inquiry Widens."
26 *The New York Times*, March 15, 2016, "Sweden Charges Syrian Tied to Killings."
27 *Archive of European Integration,* Egmont Papers No. 81, Mrch 2016, Rik Coolseat, "Facing the Fourth Foreign Fighters Wave. What Drives Europeans to Syria and to Islamic State?"
28 Kurt Nimmo, "Turkey Responsible for Flood of Illegal Immigrants in Europe," infowars.com, September 22, 2015.
29 *The New York Times,* September 21, 2015.
30 *Archive of European Integration,* Commission communication to the Council and the European Parliament on the Community Immigration Policy, COM (2000) 757 final, 6.
31 www.limitstogrowth.org/articles/2015/05/01/press-conference-geert-wilders-warns-america-against-islamic-immigration/
32 *The New York Times,* November 20, 2015, "Let My People Vote."
33 Samuel P. Huntington, *The Clash of Civilizations and the Remaking of World Order* (London: Simon and Schuster, 1996).
34 President Bush phrased it in 1991:

> Twice this century, out of the horrors of war hope emerged for enduring peace. Twice before, those hopes proved to be a distant dream beyond the grasp of man …. Now we can see a new world coming into view. A world in which there is the real prospect of a new world order.

> In this new world, instead of confrontation a new order of partnership, cooperation and collective action will dominate a shared responsibility for freedom and justice. See: George H.W. Bush Presidential Library and Museum, 1991. "Address Before the Joint Session of the Congress" (Bushlibrary.tamu.edu/research/public_papers. php, 1991=03-06); Ian Clark, *The Post-Cold War Order: The Spoils of Peace* (Oxford: Oxford University Press, 2001), 181.

35 *The Telegraph*, August 27, 2015, "Angela Merkel Joins Muslim Rally Against German Anti-Islamisation Protests."

36 Walter Laqueur, *Last Days of Europe: Epitaph for an Old Continent* (New York: Thomas Dunne Books, 2007).

37 Bruce Thornton, *Decline and Fall: Europe's Slow Motion Suicide* (New York: Encounter Books, 2007).

38 *The New York Times,* August 28, 2015, "Scrutiny Falls on a Spanish Mosque After Foiled train Attack."

39 *The New York Times,* October 13, 2015, "The Casual Provocateur. Novelist Envisions a Muslim-Run France in Submission."

40 *The New York Times,* November 16, 2015, "Attacks Change Europe's Migrant Focus from Compassion to Security."

41 Ibid.

42 *The New York Times,* October 22, 2015, "As Migrants Settle in, Fears May Be Displaced."

43 *The Economist,* August 29, 2015, "Migration to Europe. Let Them in and Let Them Earn."

44 *The New York Times,* January 3, 2016, "Nordic Countries Curtail Generosity to Migrants."

45 *Standard Eurobarometer 78,* 2012.

46 *The Telegraph,* December 7, 2015.

47 *The New York Times,* October 16, 2015, "French Far-Right Leader Finds Ready-Made Issue."

48 *The Economist,* December 19, 2015, "French Politics. Outflanking Marine."

49 *The New York Times,* January 22, 2016, "Merkel's Stance on Migrants Leaves Her Isolated at Home and in Europe."

50 Ibid.

51 Ibid., "European Leaders Agree to Strengthen Border Control Over Migrant Crisis."

52 *The New York Times,* December 23, 2015, "Turkey Moves to Clamp Down on its Borders, Long a Revolving Door."

53 See: *Archive of European Integration,* EPC Commentary, March 21, 2016, Yves Pascouau, "EU-Turkey Summit on the Refugee Crisis. Law and (Dis)order?"

54 *The New York Times,* November 12, 2015, "Europe Tries Incentives and Persuasion to Keep Migrants at Home."

55 Ibid.

56 *Archive of European Integration,* CEPS Commentary, February 24, 2016, Sergio Carrera and Leonhard den Hertog, "A European Border and Coast Guard. Fit for Purpose?"

57 *The New York Times,* January 10, 2016, Ross Douthat, "Germany on the Brink."

58 Ibid.

59 *The New York Times,* November 13, 2015, "Europe Nears Deal with Turkey on Regulating Refugee Flow."

60 *The New York Times,* November 6, 2015, "European Union Predicts Economic Gains from Migrant Influx."

61 Péter Zilahy, "How European," in Guido Snel (ed.), *Alter Ego: Twenty Confronting Views on the European Experience* (Amsterdam University Press, 2004), 131, 129–139.

62 *The New York Times*, February 25, 2016, "The Countries Agree on Action in Migrant crisis."

63 *The New York Times*, March 14, 2016, "Citing Strain on Continent, EU Leader Warns Away Economic Migrants."

64 *The New York Times*, March 8, 2016, "Turkey Places Conditions on EU for Migrant Help."

65 *The New York Times*, April 3, 2016, "For Migrants into Europe, a Road Less Traveled."

Conclusion

Further integration or disintegration?

The complex crises of the European Union

Over the past seven to eight years, the European Union has been in a deep, complex, and enduring crisis. The chapters in this volume have described and analyzed this crisis, or more accurately, a number of partly connected but cumulating crises that have challenged the European Union. The Great Recession and high unemployment were combined with a major financial-debt crisis in some member countries that rattled the common currency. The Greek crisis, which was the culmination of Europe's debt crisis, for a few months, seemed to fatally undermine European solidarity, the key ingredient of integration and the common currency itself. It has become clear that monetary unification without fiscal unification was a dangerous mistake. The euro currency also had some negative consequences on the less developed peripheral member countries; and, in at least one case, an exit from the common currency is a distinct possibility. Several peripheral countries fell into deep crisis: they were unable to repay their huge debts and had to be bailed out. Consequently, austerity was forced upon them to put their finances in order. The austerity measures led to serious social and political unrest and a clash between the affluent northwestern creditor core countries and the southern and eastern peripheral debtor countries. Certain circles in both regions began questioning whether the Union and its common currency were in their best interest.

Together with the economic crisis that gradually threatened the EU's legitimacy, a series of new crises took place that made the situation much more difficult. The European Union was surrounded by countries in the south and east, which were relatively peaceful and cooperative before the economic crisis. Europe's neighborhood policy sought to facilitate these countries' democratic transformation and economic consolidation. The EU built institutional bridges and provided financial assistance, and in some cases dangled the carrot of future Union membership. During the 2010s, however, all the neighboring countries fell into a severe crisis. The so-called Arab Spring in the Middle East and North Africa, and the elimination of secular dictatorships in the region (starting with George W. Bush's Iraq war), soon proved catastrophic. It was followed by brutal violence, civil wars, medieval beheadings, massacres, and the rise of new Islamist terror organizations, like the Islamic State, which established itself in a large swath of

Syria and Iraq, and Boko Haram, which was based in northeastern Nigeria, Chad, Niger and northern Cameroon. This made the entire Middle East and North Africa infinitely more unstable and dangerous.

In the East, a few successor states of the former Soviet Union, such as Ukraine, Moldova, Georgia, and Armenia, flirted with the idea of future EU member-ship. NATO planned to expand into this region, and the EU offered association membership, as a step toward EU enlargement. As Pierre Defraigne noted, "a division of labour was then agreed between NATO and the European Economic Community," and an "open ended process of enlargement began."[1] Miscalculations of this sort led to a harsh and adventurist Russian response: the creation of the "Putin Doctrine" defending "Russian speaking minorities" in the neighborhood, and the outbreak of fighting and even border changes through annexation. Western sanctions only served to further isolate Russia and to make it more aggressive.

Within a few years, the relatively peaceful neighborhood surrounding the European Union went up in flames, and a number of military confrontations began to endanger the EU's security. An immediate consequence of these con-flicts was the outbreak of a new crisis: the largest flow of migration in European history. Europe was transformed from being a continent of emigrants to becoming a magnet to immigrants just while it was declining demographically with reduced reproduction rates and an increasingly aging population. True, Europe had faced migration crises before – especially in the immediate postwar years, when 13–14 million people were uprooted. Much smaller waves of emigration took place after the defeat of the Hungarian revolution in 1956 and during the Yugoslav civil war in the early 1990s. These, too, were migration crises, but they had occurred *within* Europe or had compelled people to leave Europe. From the 1950s–60s on, a permanent flow of immigration began in Europe. Millions returned from for-mer colonies after the collapse of the colonial regimes and particularly with the huge inflow of guest-workers, partly from outside Europe. Nothing was compa-rable, however, to the migration crisis in the 2010s, when millions were uprooted by civil wars, ethnic-religious conflicts and economic despair, and flooded into Europe from the Middle East, North Africa, and even Asia. The majority of asylum-seekers at that time were Muslims. They arrived in the Union just as Islamist terror attacks were taking place in Spain, Britain, France, and Belgium, which sparked the rise of anti-immigration, anti-Muslim, and even anti-European inte-gration political forces within the EU. The tolerant and humanitarian reception of the refugees by some of the Western countries added fuel to the fire of political acrimony. Anti-migration attitudes, and the political parties that they gener-ated, quickly multiplied. This situation is further undermining the legitimacy of the European Union. Open conflicts broke out, with several member countries refusing to accept EU regulations on a quota to distribute immigrants across the Union. More and more people in several member countries lost faith in the EU and affirmed that it no longer served their interests. This sentiment is amply rep-resented in the European Parliament.

For the first time in thirty years of European integration and nearly fifty years of rapid enlargement, there is a plausible chance of some countries leaving the euro-zone and even the Union. The first exit is to take place in this decade. A besieged fortress Europe is in clear danger. Several experts and politicians foresee the signs of a disintegration and/or serious degradation of the EU's supranational character, and of a return to a loose alliance of a free-trade zone in the place of further integration toward a federal Europe. Hundreds of pundits and analysts have already predicted the decline and possible disintegration of the Union. For the first time in history, especially after the British decision to exit in the summer of 2016, the question arises: can the European Union survive? If so, can it preserve its *sui generis* supranational character between confederation and federal unification, or will it reverse course and again become a loose free trade zone?

Crisis solution by further integration?

Centrifugal forces are strongly at play in the European arena. Daily news stories and commentaries regularly refer to them when covering Europe. One has to recognize, however, that strong *centripetal* counter forces are also present – a fact that is rarely mentioned in the news. The complex crisis that hit Europe and each Union member state is not solvable by any one country alone. Recognition of this fact revitalized the Union in the mid-1980s, when a response to globalization with a single national framework proved impossible without integrated action. At that time it became clear that reverting to the nation state was no solution at all in today's globalized economy. Can Europe solve the financial crisis and especially the common currency crisis by eliminating the euro and returning to national currencies? As a number of studies have shown, the negative consequences of such a step would be disastrous. According to an analysis by UBS Investment Research-Global Economic Perspectives (London, September 6, 2011) the losses sustained in the first year after a return to national currencies could be €9,500–11,500 billion, about 40–50 percent of GDP, followed by €3,000–4,000 billion in the second year.[2] This was clearly understood by ordinary Greeks and the Syriza government, who had fought against the EU requirements until it became clear that their resistance would continue to be rejected and might lead to their exiting the euro-zone. Once they realized this, they immediately back-pedaled and accepted even worse and more humiliating austerity measures.

So, if it's not back to national currencies, than what? It has become clear that the only solution is to move forward by strengthening monetary unification further and by introducing some form of fiscal unification. Going toward a banking union, with euro-bonds and a "fiscal compact" of disciplined fiscal policy, could guarantee against a repetition of the crisis. Further unifying the capital markets, establishing a unified copyright policy, consolidating common industrial policy under the banner of reindustrialization, and completing the single market seemed to be the best answers to future economic challenges.

Similarly, none of the member countries is capable of facing external dangers, and the challenge of Russia and energy dependence, alone. An appropriate response to the destabilized environment around the Union requires unifying energy and defense policy, of attaining energy independence through unification and strengthening defense with a unified armed force.

Solving the demographic and migration crisis also demands the cooperation and solidarity of the entire EU. A single labor market, a joint selection of migrants to bolster the Union's labor force, and a unified migration and asylum policy are important measures that may both safeguard European values and help fight those who endanger those values from the inside, including the home-grown terrorists.

How will Europe really respond to the frightening challenges now facing the continent? Aside from hysterical proclamations, will there be real *steps* toward disintegration? Britain's exit from the Union definitely points to this direction. However, there are opposite signs as well. Today we are seeing practical initiatives and concrete steps to solve the crisis with additional integration, especially within the euro-zone. Europe has arrived at a crossroads. Will it be centrifugal or centripetal forces that prevail in the near future? Will Europe really disintegrate, or will it gradually move further with integration?

Despite the continuing debates and conflicting attitudes, actual political steps have been taken since 2010 that are consistently strengthening European integration. One analyst observed, the crisis of the 2010s and the transforming world have created a "commonality of destiny [for] Europe that [is] facing three ongoing transformations of a magnitude and of a speed never before experienced because the world has become more interdependent, more interconnected and more exposed to technological innovations."[3] All these events are pushing the European Union ahead toward further integration.

In the economic, especially financial, monetary, and fiscal arenas, the signs and practical steps to further integration are, indeed, clearly present. During the deep recession and euro-crisis since 2009, several countries (Slovakia, Estonia, Latvia, Lithuania, Cyprus, and Malta) have rushed to join the euro-zone. Having started with 10 countries, the euro-zone today comprises 19. While some countries, among them the Czech Republic and Poland, have held back on joining the zone, no one has sought to leave it. The financial crisis has led to some important new attempts to cope with pressing problems in a supranational way. Without going into details,[4] a brief summary clearly suggests this.

As early as May 2010, the Ecofin, the body made up of the Union's finance ministers, established the European Financial Stability Facility, nicknamed "European IMF," to assist troubled member countries. This institution was intended to function for a temporary three-year period with a €440 billion credit capacity. Almost at the same time, the European Council created a permanent institution, the European Financial Stability Mechanism. It's funding, budgeted at €500 billion, was to come entirely from bond sales, with the EU budget serving as collateral. Sales began in early 2011and provided €22 billion in the first year. The IMF, with the EU's agreement, guaranteed up to €250 billion more.[5] The EU has accepted in principle a recommendation of the G-20 countries that the fund be increased to $1 trillion. Loans and credit lines from the European Stabilization Mechanism have strict conditions. Every recipient country – Ireland and Portugal were among the first – must submit an adjustment program. The Stabilization Mechanism focuses generally "on prevention and will substantially reduce the probability of a crisis emerging in the future."[6] A new institutional framework was introduced to strengthen the monetary union. Among them was a Single Deposit Mechanism, formed in December 2010. The EU collectively guaranteed bank deposits up to €100,000 per person.

More importantly, the European Council introduced a new European regulatory system, the European System of Financial Supervisions, in June 2012. Then, a Single Supervisory Mechanism was established.[7] Several experts consider this action, the creation of what may be called a *banking union*, to be the most important step toward integration since the introduction of the common currency. The foundation of this institution "represent a fundamental shift in . . . financial regulation in the European Union, with authority transferring from national regulators to EU authorities."[8] The European Central Bank took control of all the major banks, which were no longer under the national governments' jurisdiction. The Single Bank Rule, the Single Supervisory Mechanism, and the Single Resolution Mechanism were established to stabilize and centrally administer the EU's banking sector. The Single Resolution Mechanism, envisioned to become fully funded in 2025, will have a €70 billion budget and a mechanism for spotting serious difficulties in any important banking institution in Europe. The Single Bank Rule consists of a set of rules with which all EU financial institutions (approximately 8,300 banks) must comply. These consist of capital requirements for banks, protection of depositors, and regulations on the management of bank failures. Based on its supervisory role, the European Commission retains the right to recommend the shutting down, shrinking, or restructuring of ailing banks. The culmination of this new policy came on June 27, 2013, when the member states' finance ministers resolved that, instead of bailout assistance, they should have a *bail-in* system in place – a system in which "losses would be suffered by bond holders and shareholders, instead of taxpayers." A group of countries led by Germany and the Netherlands pushed this resolution through.[9] As *The New York Times* reported, this new authority to supervise and close Europe's banks "is arguably the greatest transfer of sovereignty in the history of the EU and points toward a fiscal, as well as economic and monetary union."[10]

Within this new framework, several other important supranational institutions have been established. Among them is the Frankfurt-based European Systemic Risk Board, with responsibility of overseeing Europe's financial system and providing early warnings if system-wide risks emerge. Three additional supervisory institutions have also been founded: the European Bank Authority in London, the European Insurance and Occupational Pensions Authority in Frankfurt, and the European Securities and Market Authority in Paris. These EU institutions set the rules for all national establishments. They "represent the first step toward pan-European regulatory governance," and also "a new breakthrough toward more and deeper supranational integration, and even federalization."[11]

The euro-crisis made crystal clear the mistake of introducing monetary union without fiscal unity. But establishing fiscal unity means renouncing one of the most important elements of national sovereignty. Member countries still balk at the idea of giving up control of their budgets, taxes, and debt. Still, the European Union has found a way to create quasi-fiscal unification through regulatory measures. The European Parliament and the European Council introduced a *budgetary control mechanism* in 2011, including a procedure to be carried out should a member state sustain significant budgetary deficits.[12]

On March 2, 2012, the Treaty of Stability Coordination and Governance in the Economic and Monetary Union, commonly called the Fiscal Compact, was passed and went into effect in January 2013. This required member countries to legally, and even constitutionally, ban budget deficits. The European Court of Justice was awarded supervisory powers, including sanctioning those in violation of the agreement. This was probably the second most important step toward supranationalization and quasi-fiscal unification. Fiscal unity was sorely needed after the misstep of establishing monetary unification alone, and it is crucial to redesigning one of the most important elements of national sovereignty. As member countries continue to hesitate, the EU must make do for now with a unification of fiscal policy through regulatory measures.

The Fiscal Compact sought to guarantee fiscal order by making a constitutional balanced budget amendment compulsory. The Fiscal Compact made it unconstitutional for governments to incur indebtedness higher than 60 percent of GDP, budget deficits higher than 3 percent of GDP, and structural budgetary deficits no higher than an annual 0.5 percent. No fewer than 25 out of 27 member countries signed the Treaty in March 2012, and it became operative in January 2013; in reality, only five countries have so far adhered to these rules, and France and Italy, among others, have not. As an EU report concluded, "[t]he tight rules enshrined in a new Treaty and in national constitutions are being violated as soon as they become politically inconvenient."[13] These violations, however, may be only transitory bumps on a longer development road.

Further integration could also include the issuing of *Eurobonds,* in the place of national government bonds. Since the European Union would stand behind these bonds, their interest rates would be much lower than those of national government bonds in peripheral countries. However, Germany has rejected the project because it would require the mutualization of the debt burden, which would place extra financial burden on Germany. Still, Chancellor Merkel has made it clear that issuing Eurobonds would be possible if member nations put their finances in order. But Eurobonds could become a reality even before that, which would represent another important step toward full integration. In 2012, *The Economist* offered a rational proposal on bonds that could represent a reasonable compromise:

> The solution is a narrower Eurobond that mutualises a limited amount of debt for a limited amount of time. The best option is to build on an idea put forward by Germany's Council of Economic Experts, to mutualise the current debts of all euro-zone economies above 60% of their GDP. Rather than issuing new national government bonds, everybody, from Germany (debt: 81% of GDP) to Italy (120%) would issue only these joint bonds until their national debts

fell to the 60% threshold. The new mutualized bond market, worth some €2.3 trillion, would be paid off over the next 25 years. Each country would pledge a specified tax (such as a VAT surcharge) to provide the cash.[14]

The European Union's response to the financial-economic crisis, although still slow and partial, may nevertheless have real historical importance. As the economist László Csaba has noted, "[t]he management of the crisis in 2012," introducing the obligatory coordination of fiscal policy, a bank union, a permanent bailout mechanism, and the bond purchasing practice of the European Central Bank, "has brought perhaps more far reaching innovations in the actual workings of the European Union than anything since the adoption of the Maastricht Treaty in 1992."[15]

Not all the EU's efforts to push integration further have been successful, but that is largely due to the slow pace of legislating and past achievements. The need for a genuine single market had been already incorporated in the Treaty of Rome in 1957, but it took more than thirty years for it to be realized. The need for a common currency was first put on the agenda in 1970, but it became a reality only three decades later. A common *EU patent system* in the place of national patent regimes is another good example. The idea of a unitary European patent system came to the fore in the 1960s. The Strasbourg Convention on the Unification of Certain Points of Substantive Patent Law approved such a move in 1962. But the treaty did not come into effect until 1980. In 1973, the European Patent Convention in Munich established the European Patent Office to grant all-European patents, but in practice national patent offices had to approve its rules. In 2000, the London agreement decided that patents could only be issued in English, French, and German, instead of all of the official languages of the Union. This ruling became operative in 2008. In 2011, 12 member states decided to introduce unitary patents. The Italian and Spanish opposition blocked the plan, but their objections were overruled by the European Court of Justice in April 2013. However, there is a 7-year (and maximum 12-year) transition period before the all-European patent system will come into force around 2020. The practicality of unifying the system is clear, as it makes every patent valid in the EU. A unified Patent Court was also established. Besides, the cost of patenting will drop from €32,119 to €4,725.[16] Unfortunately, the long history and delayed decisions of the copyright union is typical and proceeds as major unification steps are realized. The myriad of procedural problems notwithstanding, a single market, a common currency, and a united patent system have all been created.

During the mid-2010s, the EU embarked on instituting a *common industrial policy*. Nothing of the sort had existed, but the need for it became clear during the long recession. It would certainly take time for it to be implemented. Nonetheless, the European Commission, led by Jean-Claud Juncker, began a program for a European Industrial Renaissance in January 2014, which was passed by the EU Council in March of that year. In the over-financialized economies of the advanced countries, manufacturing production is steadily declining. Globally it decreased from 30 percent of GDP in 2003 to 23 percent by 2010. Only 15 percent of the

EU's GDP comes from industry, which steadily declined from 2007 to 2014. The situation in Germany clearly indicates that manufacturing is more resilient in a recession. The EU leadership has concluded that Europe has to reindustrialize. It should be achieved with a more coordinated industrial policy and with assistance to the peripheral countries to help them catch up. Today, an average worker in Central and Eastern Europe produces only €25 an hour, while in Denmark and Ireland that worker produces €50. Capital formation has also declined in several peripheral countries – falling from 27 to 22 percent in the Czech Republic, and from 23 to 17 percent in Hungary. The EU has decided that industry's proportion of GDP must rise to 20 percent by 2020.[17] To meet this goal, the Juncker Plan is proposing a new investment policy in Europe. The Ecofin Council has accepted the plan and sent it to the Parliament. Studies show that there is an enormous investment gap: in the Union's advanced Western countries, it is roughly €260 billion less in 2014 than the average annual investments between 1970 and 2014. According to the plan, the EU will establish a European Fund for Strategic Investment with €21 billion to contribute to investment initiatives, and generate – by factor 15 acceleration – €315 billion in investments.[18]

In order to achieve an industrial stimulus plan, President Juncker called for a *Capital Market Union*. He unveiled a plan to generate capital to finance growth in a speech entitled "A new start for Europe" at the European Parliament in July 2014.[19] Indeed, Europe's capital markets are partly fragmented, partly outdated, and not nearly plentiful enough. Mario Draghi, the President of the European Central Bank, suggested this in September 2014 when he emphasized that Europe has a bank-centered lending model; in contrast, equity and bond markets, insurance companies, asset managers, venture capital, and securitization all play a huge part in more modern financial markets.[20]

The European Union immediately commenced work on the capital market project. A Capital Market Expert Group was established in December 2014. The European Parliament and the EU's Council passed a plan to eliminate all obstacles for cross-border marketing of investment funds, and to allow life insurance companies and pension funds to become long-term investors. As the commissioner pointed out in a speech in Luxembourg on September 10, 2015,

> [c]apital markets have expanded in the EU over recent decades. Total EU stock market capitalization, for example, amounted to €8.4 trillion (around 65% of GDP) by end 2013, compared to €1.3 trillion in 1992 (22% of GDP). The total value of outstanding debt securities exceeded €22.3 trillion (171% of GDP) in 2013, compared to €4.7 trillion (74% of GDP) in 1992.

Still, the EU's capital market exhibits major weaknesses compared to the US's. The value of the stock market in Europe ($13 trillion) is only half of that of the US ($25 trillion); the assets of pension funds ($8 trillion) are hardly more than a third of those of the US ($22 trillion); and venture capital, a crucial factor in financing startup companies, is less than 10 percent of the US's $30 billion. While the capital market is overwhelmingly bank-related in Europe, the European banks have barely increased their credit resources through securitization (the repacking and selling of bank loans as securities), which constitutes a paltry 10 percent of the $10 trillion of securitized loans in the US. The vast gulf between them is due to Europe's different cultural traditions and stricter bank regulation that controls and regulates securitization more seriously than does the US (a consequence of the 2008 financial crisis). The role of private pension funds in capitalization is also much smaller in Europe, where the state is much more involved in pensions. In 2010–2014, the European financial sector had €61.7 trillion assets, almost equal with the US (€43.9 trillion) and Japan (€19.0 trillion) together. However, in the EU the assets of the banking sector are 316 percent of the aggregate GDP, while in the US it is only 115 percent and in Japan 198 percent. Meanwhile the equity market share in of the EU is only the half of the American share. The European households keep nearly one-third of their financial assets in cash and 23 percent in deposits, while in the US the share of cash is only 13 percent and deposits 44 percent.[21]

Europe's capital market must be expanded across Europe if it is to help finance the economy in a more flexible way, and it must have significantly bigger assets. As the renamed "European Commissioner for Financial Stability, Financial Services and Capital Markets Union," Jonathan Hill announced that work on a gradual process is already underway. The Commission published a Green Paper on "ways of reducing fragmentation in financial markets, diversifying financing sources, strengthening cross border capital flows and improving access to finance for businesses" in February 2015. "Capital markets today," the Green Paper stated,

> remain fragmented and are typically organised on national lines .... Compared to other parts of the world European businesses remain heavily reliant on banks for funding and relatively less on capital markets. Stronger capital markets would complement banks as a source of financing.[22]

To change this situation, several existing barriers have to be eliminated. A consolidation or Europeanization of national laws is needed, especially with insolvency, taxation, security laws, and investor protection. A safe and standardized securitization law and cross-sectional risk sharing are necessary, as well as a Europe-wide collection and distribution of public information. Common informational infrastructure, common database and accounting standards, marketing rules, and insolvency proceedings all belong to an all-European capital market.[23]

> Building a Capital Markets Union is a long-term project. Work is already underway to establish a single rulebook, with a large number of key reforms in the process of being implemented. The Commission's approach will be based on an assessment of the outstanding priorities ... [The EU's goal is to create a] fully functioning Capital Market Union by 2019.[24]

New initiatives to respond to the challenges of the 2010s with further integration appeared in other economic areas as well. Some of the most promising among them were the formation of an *Energy Union*, the launching of the EU *Maritime Security Strategy*, and steps taken toward a *defense union,* such as an EU-operated airlift capability to improve joint operations and conduct missions, and a joint counter-terrorism agreement signed by the member countries' interior and justice ministers in Paris in July 2014.

Conclusion

To sum up, there are moves today, and plans for the future, to deal with the myriad challenges facing Europe by furthering integration. During the crisis years of the 2010s, the possibility that countries would leave the euro-zone or even the EU was often indicated. "Grexit" and "Brexit," the Greek or British exits, became an everyday topic of discussion. Although the Greek bailout warded off an immediate Greek exit, it is still entirely possible that it could happen in the coming years. The British exit became fact in the summer of 2016. Exits from the Union are definitely important factors of disintegration. However, in certain cases the integration of fewer countries might lead to a stronger union. If countries are unable to keep to the EU's rules (as Greece has demonstrated) or do not wish to do so (as the Brexit suggests), their exit may strengthen the remaining countries' integration. What is also clear – and is documented by the Greek crisis and all the existing calculations regarding the consequences of Brexit to Britain – is that leaving the integration framework is much more dangerous for the countries that are leaving than for those that remain.

Will the European Union head toward further integration, or will it disintegrate? At this point in time, both outcomes are still possible. True, all the practical steps the EU has made in recent years to respond to the challenges of the complex crisis lead to further integration. However, important limitations have to be acknowledged.

The first limitation is that most steps toward integration and supranationalization apply only within the euro-zone, the 19 countries that are using the common currency. To save the euro, the Union had to go further and in monetary and fiscal unification. Helmut Kohl's old metaphor perfectly characterizes the situation of the euro-zone: it is like bicycling: you must move forward or otherwise you fall.

The second limitation is that the existence of the euro-zone itself is already an institutionalized form of the endlessly debated "two-speed Europe" concept. Several intellectuals and politicians recommended for decades that a group of core EU countries might go forward and speed up their integration, and in the process set an example to be emulated by those still hesitant. The list of advocates of a two-speed Europe is a very long one. It includes Jürgen Habermas, the German philosopher and sociologist, and one of the pioneers of the idea. In 1994, when the big bang of eastward enlargement was put on the agenda, the German politicians Wolfgang Schäuble and Karl Lamers published a document about *"Kerneuropa"* or core-Europe, describing how this advanced group of founder member countries could go ahead with integration.[25] The same idea was reformulated by French

President Nicolas Sarkozy during the Great Recession in November 2011, when he proposed the formation of a federal core of at that time 17 euro-zone countries and an outer band of ten "confederate' countries.[26] It became clear quite long ago that not all the member countries wish to go ahead with integration. This recognition led to the idea that the European Union should not require joint steps and may leave out countries that are still reluctant to follow.

The steps advancing integration during the 2010s have strengthened the euro-zone as the fastest integrating core of the EU. The non-euro-zone countries point to the existence of a group of member countries in an "outer" zone of the EU that are less integrated and seek to remain so. This development preserves a "two-speed Europe" and suggests that future European integration, if happened at all, will continue in this framework. Further strengthening of the institutional framework of two-speed Europe is already on the agenda. Discussions and suggestions signal this trend: the introduction of a consistent sub-committee network for the euro-zone in the EU's committee system, a new parliamentary chamber for the euro-zone countries, and even a directly elected euro-zone parliament were recommended.[27]

The most important limitations, however, that every step forward, slow but somewhat successful as they were, served the solution of the financial-economic crisis and safeguarded the common currency. This took several years and was extremely difficult. Looking back from the summer of 2016, however, it seems to be that what happened was a relatively easy task. Much more difficult to cure is the deadly challenge of the still unsolved immigration crisis, correcting the mistaken steps Germany and the EU made about it. Much more difficult to cope with is the populist-nationalist uprising that mobilizes the population under the banner of "regaining national sovereignty." The populist, anti-establishment, anti-globalization, anti-integration reaction – partly also connected with the migration crisis – is best symbolized by Brexit. Britain's referendum itself exacerbates the crisis to breaking point. Its impact on anti-integrationist populism, especially in France and the Netherlands, is hardly possible to overestimate. Recent political events clearly showed the popularity of anti-globalization and free trade policy among certain layers of society, those who were unable to adjust to the new requirement of major structural economic changes. These layers, the voters for Brexit in Britain, the less educated relatively older population in the countryside, offer a camp of good followers of some demagogue politicians throughout Europe. How can the deepening and explosive crisis be solved when charismatic EU leadership is lacking and populist demagoguery is gaining ground? How can the obstacle, the natural over-cautious behavior, generated by the coming national elections in Germany and France in 2017 be counterbalanced? If these elections significantly strengthen populism in those countries, which is an evident possibility, disintegration becomes an imminent danger.

At the time of finalizing the writing of this book, the future of Europe strongly depends on the short-term and longer-run consequences of Brexit to Britain itself and the country's future. Equally decisive is the EU's reaction to Brexit and its agreement with Britain. In the summer of 2016 both alternatives are open for Europe, a further integration of the core of the Union by accepting and practicing the "two-speed Europe" concept and/or the beginning of a devastating disintegration process.

Notes

1 Archive of European Integration, Think Tank Review, Issue 22, March 2015.
2 http://bruxelles.blogs.liberation.fr/UBS%20fin%20de%20l'euro.pdf
3 *Archive of European Integration, Think Tank Review,* Issue 22, March 2015, Pierre Defraigne, December 2014.
4 For a detailed description and analysis see: Miklós Losoncz, *Az államadósság-válság és kezelése az Európai Unióban* (Tatabánya: Tri-Mester Kiadó, 2014).
5 The IMF recently was strongly criticized for being too closely involved in European affairs and finances, and for devoting half of its loans to Europe. One-third of the rescue packages for Greece, Portugal, and Ireland came from the IMF. "Poorer nations that contribute to the IMF's financing have grumbled about having to prop up rich Europe." On this see "Under Lagarde, the IMF Rides the Euro Zone Crisis to New Heights of Influence," *New York Times,* April, 18, 2013. On the other hand, demonstrators in Greece and other peripheral countries often accuse the IMF of neglecting their needs and call for the "end of the Troika."
6 ec.europa.eu/economy_finance/eu_borrower/efsm/
7 *Archive of European Integration,* European Commission: Proposal for Council Regulation conferring tasks on the European Central Bank concerning policies relating to the prudential supervision of credit institutions. COM (2012) 511 final.
8 Sean Tuffy, "Harmonizing EU Financial Regulation," May 1, 2011, accessible at www.ftseglobalmarkets.com/issues/issue-51-may-2011/harmonising-eu-financial-regulation.html
9 www.cnbc.com/id/100850105
10 *New York Times,* July 10, 2013, "Blank Plan Develops, but Germany Has Doubts."
11 Ivan T. Berend, *Europe in Crisis. Bolt from the Blue?* (London: Routledge, 2013), 127.
12 See the EU resolutions of 1177/2011/EU on November 8, 2011 and 1175/2011/EU on November 16, 2011.
13 *Archive of European Integration,* CEPS Commentary, November 5, 2014, Daniel Gros and Cinzia Alridi, The Case of the Disappearing Fiscal Compact."
14 "The Future of the European Union. The Choices," *The Economist,* May 26, 2012.
15 László Csaba, "On the New Economic Philosophy of Crisis Management in the European Union," *Society and Economy,* Vol. 35, No. 2, 2013, 121–22.
16 *Archive of European Integration,* Working Paper No. 21, March 2014, EU Center in Singapore, "Unified European Front: The road Towards a European Unitary Patent."
17 *Archive of European Integration,* ERC Discussion Papers, March 20, 2014, Claire Dhéret, "Sharing the Same Vision – The Cornerstone for a New Industrial Policy for Europe."
18 *Archive of European Integration,* EPC, Discussion Papers, March 20, 2015, Jan David Schneider, Growth for Europe – Is the Juncker Plan the Answer?"; *Archive of European Integration,* CEPS Commentary, March 18, 2015, Olivia Marty, "Progress on the Juncker Plan Continues – but Are Member states Behind it?"
19 ec.europa.eu/finance/index_en.htm
20 *Archive of European Integration,* Bruegel Policy Contribution, Issue 2015/05, April 2015, Nicolas Véron and Guntram B. Wolff, "Capital Market Union: Vision for the Long Term."
21 *Archive of European Integration,* Final Report of the European Capital Market Expert Group, European Capital Market institute, Brussels, February 2016, "Europe's Untapped Capital Market. Rethinking Integration After the Great Financial Crisis."

22 *Building a Capital Markets Union* (ec.europa.eu/transparency/regdoc/rep/1/2015/EN/1-2015-63-EN-F1-1.PDF).
23 Ibid.
24 Commissioner Jonathan Hill's speech (europa.eu/rapid/press-release_SPEECH-16-2529_en.htm); Commission's Green Paper, *Building a Capital Markets Union* (ec.europa.eu/transparency/regdoc/rep/1/2015/EN/1-2015-63-EN-F1-1.PDF); *The Economist*, September 12, 2015, "Animating Europe's capital markets. Vision and reality."
25 *Der Spiegel,* December 9, 1994.
26 *The Economist*, November 10, 2011, "The Future of the EU. Two Speed Europe or Two Europes?"
27 *Archive of the European Integration,* Instituto Affari Internazionali, Working Papers No. 15/48, December 2015, Giuseppe Martinico, "A Multi-speed European Union?"

Index

For Product Safety Concerns and Information please contact our EU
representative GPSR@taylorandfrancis.com
Taylor & Francis Verlag GmbH, Kaufingerstraße 24, 80331 München, Germany

www.ingramcontent.com/pod-product-compliance
Ingram Content Group UK Ltd.
Pitfield, Milton Keynes, MK11 3LW, UK
UKHW020949180425
457613UK00019B/598